Twayne's Filmmakers Series

Frank Beaver, Editor

BOTTICELLI IN HOLLYWOOD

Albert Lewin, probably late 1940s, in a photo by Man Ray.

BOTTICELLI IN HOLLYWOOD

The Films of Albert Lewin

Susan Felleman

TWAYNE PUBLISHERS
An Imprint of Simon & Schuster Macmillan
New York
PRENTICE HALL INTERNATIONAL
London • Mexico City • New Delhi • Singapore • Sydney • Toronto

Twayne's Filmmakers Series, Frank Beaver, General Editor
Botticelli in Hollywood: The Films of Albert Lewin

Copyright © 1997 by Susan Felleman
All rights reserved. No part of this book may be reproduced or transmitted in any form or by any means, electronic or mechanical, including photocopying, recording, or by any information storage and retrieval system, without permission in writing from the Publisher.

Twayne Publishers
An Imprint of Simon & Schuster Macmillan
1633 Broadway
New York, NY 10019

Library of Congress Cataloging-in-Publication Data

Felleman, Susan.
    Botticelli in Hollywood : the films of Albert Lewin / Susan Felleman.
        p. cm. — (Twayne's filmmakers series)
    Filmography: p.
    Includes bibliographical references and index.
    ISBN 0-8057-1625-4 (pbk.)
    1. Lewin, Albert, 1894–   —Criticism and interpretation.
I. Title.   II. Series.
PN1998.3.L4678F46   1997
791.43'0233'092—dc21   97-19700
                                                                                                                                   CIP

The paper used in this publication meets the minimum requirements of American National Standard for Information Sciences—Permanence of Paper for Printed Library Materials, ANSI Z39.48-1984. ∞™

10 9 8 7 6 5 4 3 2 1 (pbk)

Printed in the United States of America.

To Peter

CONTENTS

Foreword ix
Preface xi

Chronology 1
Introduction 11

1. Botticelli in Hollywood: *The Moon and Sixpence* (1942) 27
2. Dr. Look: *The Picture of Dorian Gray* (1945) 41
3. A Café Called Désir: *The Private Affairs of Bel Ami* (1947) 63
4. La Belle Dame Sans Merci: *Pandora and the Flying Dutchman* (1951) 81
5. Blessed Benightedness: *Saadia* (1954) and *The Living Idol* (1957) 101
6. The Mystery and Melancholy of a Scene: Albert Lewin as Auteur 117

Notes 127
Bibliography 141
Filmography 153
Photo Credits 159
Index 161

FOREWORD

Of all the contemporary arts, the motion picture is particularly timely and diverse as a popular cultural enterprise. This lively art form cleverly combines storytelling with photography to achieve what has been a quintessential twentieth-century phenomenon. Individual as well as national and cultural interests have made the film an unusually varied medium for artistic expression and analysis. Films have been exploited for commercial gain, for political purposes, for experimentation, and for self-exploration. The various responses to the motion picture have given rise to different labels for both the fun and the seriousness with which this art form has been received, ranging from "the movies" to "cinema." These labels hint at both the theoretical and the sociological parameters of film as a medium.

A collective art, the motion picture has nevertheless allowed individual genius to flourish in all its artistic and technical areas: directing, screenwriting, cinematography, acting, editing. The medium also encompasses many genres beyond the narrative film, including documentary, animation, and avant-garde expression. The range and diversity of motion pictures suggest rich opportunities for appreciation and for study.

Twayne's Filmmakers Series examines the full panorama of motion picture history and art. Many studies are auteur-oriented and elucidate the work of individual directors whose ideas and cinematic styles make them the authors of their films. Other studies examine film movements and genres or analyze cinema from a national perspective. The series seeks to illuminate all the many aspects of film for the student, the scholar, and the general reader.

Frank Beaver

PREFACE

The title of this study of Albert Lewin's films, "Botticelli in Hollywood," is borrowed from a short story Lewin published in 1925, almost twenty years before his career as a movie director was to begin, when he had been living and working in Hollywood for only two years. The story, which is discussed at some length in Chapter 1, shares with the films many of the qualities that attracted me to Lewin's work. It is an ironic and highly constructed—even affected—blend of allusions to "high art" and erudition with the more predictable and sensational appeals typically associated with Hollywood. The title "Botticelli in Hollywood" itself manages almost to sum up Lewin's preeminent concern with the visual in cinema, as well as his confessed equilibrism between two poles of culture that are often, though perhaps unfairly, referred to as "high" and "low." I am glad to have an opportunity to offer the first comprehensive description and analysis of the small but fascinating body of work that resulted from Lewin's tightrope act.

This book had an earlier and somewhat different manifestation, as the doctoral dissertation with which I completed my Ph.D. in art history at the Graduate School of the City University of New York in 1993. To all the individuals and institutions who contributed to that accomplishment, and who were thanked in that volume, I reiterate my gratitude. Of those, several require more explicit reacknowledgment. Foremost are Lewin's nieces, Linda Lewin and Ann Lewin Diament; the latter, especially, has been unceasingly generous with her archives, time, expertise, and interest. Others to whom I should like to repeat my thanks include Ned Comstock, of the University of Southern California's Cinema-Television Library and Archives of Performing Arts, where Lewin's papers are held; and Richard Koszarski, Curator of Collections at the American Museum of the Moving Image (AMMI), and editor of *Film History*, the journal in which an earlier version of the present Introduction appeared as "How High Was His Brow? Albert Lewin, His Critics and the Problem of Pretension" (vol. 7, no. 4). My thanks extend also to David Schwartz of AMMI, who invited me to organize a retrospective film series there on the occasion of Albert Lewin's centenary in September 1994.

I am extremely grateful to friends and associates of Albert Lewin's who contributed to my understanding of his career, including Shana Alexander, Noma Copley, Cyrus Gordon, Barbara Gray, Hurd Hatfield, John Hawkesworth, and Betty and Maurice Silverstein.

I owe immense gratitude and appreciation to those at Twayne Publishers who accepted my book for publication and helped me to bring it to fruition. The unwavering enthusiasm and respect for the project manifested by Mark Zadrozny, Editor-at-Large, and Frank Beaver, Series Editor of the Filmmakers series, have been inexpressibly rewarding. I am especially grateful to Susan Gamer, the book's editor; Lisa Chovnick, Twayne's Art Director; and my good friend Julie Metz, who designed the cover—each of whom has brought her considerable talents to turning my manuscript into a readable and attractive book.

Personal friends who have helped me significantly with various aspects of my work or the exigencies surrounding it include Abdallah Kahil, Sarah Lowe, Christine Newman, Richard Stohlman, Bruce Tyroler, and Pat Vitiello. My two families, the Fellemans and the Chametzkys, have continued through their love, interest, and assistance to support all of my endeavors. My son Benjamin has done little to help this enterprise, but, considering that he is just three, he should be applauded for doing equally little to hinder it. He is always a shining star on my horizon, as is my daughter Hallie, who has come into the world just ahead of this book. To Ben's and Hallie's brilliant, wonderful father, Peter Chametzky, I owe more than it would be seemly to express.

Susan Felleman

BOTTICELLI
IN HOLLYWOOD

Albert Lewin in 1915, upon his graduation from New York University.

CHRONOLOGY

1894   Albert Parsons Lewin born September 23 in Brooklyn to Marcus and Yetta (née Mindlin) Lewin, working-class Russian-Jewish emigrants. Albert (called Allie—pronounced "Ahlie"—by his family) is the third of three children; the others are William (Willie, or Will, b. 1889) and Sarah (Sadie, b. 1891).

1903   Lewin family moves to Newark, New Jersey.

1911   Albert Lewin graduates from Newark's Barringer High School, with honors, as valedictorian; receives four-year scholarship to New York University, Washington Heights.

1915   Graduates from New York University with bachelor's degree in literature, with honors, Phi Beta Kappa, as class historian and commencement speaker; wins the university's Sandham Prize oration contest with "The Golden Statue," a denunciation of war; is awarded a scholarship to Harvard University, where he begins in the fall.

1916   Earns master's degree in English literature from Harvard University, where he has been a charter member of the Harvard Poetry Society, founded the same year. Professor George L. Kittredge urges Lewin to undertake doctoral studies at Harvard, but he instead accepts an offer from the English department at the University of Missouri. In New York, Lewin is introduced to Charles Reznikoff, who studied at Missouri and who is to become an objectivist poet and one of Lewin's closest lifelong friends.

1917   Employed as instructor of English, University of Missouri, where he teaches composition and public speaking and coaches debates.

1918   Called up for military service. Leaves Missouri and serves briefly at Fort Dix while awaiting an honorable discharge (he is 5 feet tall—3 inches shorter than the army's minimum height). He is then employed by the philanthropist Jacob Billikopf as assistant director (a paid position) for the American Jewish Relief Committee in New York. On August 17 he marries Mildred Mindlin Jacobs (Millie), a maternal first cousin, who until her teens was reared in England. Lewin begins doctoral studies in literature at Columbia University.

1920   Teaches summer school at Newark's Central High School. Millie graduates with honors from Hunter College.

1921   Bernard Bergman, editor of the *Jewish Tribune* and a friend of Lewin's, offers him an unpaid position writing a column, "Playthings," for which he would review plays and films of his choice. Lewin accepts, admittedly mainly for the free tickets to theaters and movie houses. Through the influence of Jacob Billikopf, Lewin is hired as a New York reader for Samuel Goldwyn's film company. Millie earns a master's degree in economics from Columbia University.

1922	Lewin works at Goldwyn and at the American Jewish Relief Committee while continuing his criticism and his doctoral studies (completing all requirements for the Ph.D. except his dissertation); he then persuades Goldwyn to send him to California.
1923	In Culver City, Lewin continues as reader for Goldwyn, trains as script clerk, and works in the latter capacity for the directors King Vidor and Victor Sjöström (Seastrom). He also participates in the founding of Little Theater Films, an association of movie people interested in advancing "artistic quality" in cinema (other members include Curtis Melnitz, Paul Bern, and the directors Rex Ingram, Ernst Lubitsch, and Maurice Tourneur).
1924	Lewin moves to Metro as screenwriter and writes an adaptation of Charles Norris's *Bread*. A merger of three studios results in the founding of Metro-Goldwyn-Mayer (MGM), with Louis B. Mayer serving as vice president and general manager and Irving Thalberg (at age twenty-four) as vice president and production supervisor.
1925	Lewin continues writing continuity and scenarios for MGM silent films.
1926	Adapts James M. Barrie's *Quality Street* for MGM.
1927	Lewin, now head of MGM's story department, meets and becomes friends with the director Robert Flaherty, who is briefly involved with MGM; this will be a lifelong friendship, and through Flaherty, over the years, Lewin will make many other friends, including Jean Renoir, Mary Meerson, Hugh and Barbara Gray, and Ernestine Evans.
1928	Lewin is coauthor of the script for *The Actress* for MGM; he is promoted to Thalberg's personal assistant.
1929	Lewin is promoted to producer at MGM, responsible for projects in which Thalberg takes the closest interest, including Garbo's last silent picture, *The Kiss,* directed by Jacques Feyder. William (Will) Lewin (Albert's brother) organizes an educational sound film unit for Western Electric Company (later to become Encyclopedia Britannica films).
1930	Produces *Devil-May-Care* for MGM. Although very close to, and loyal to, Thalberg, Lewin mostly eschews personal friendships with other movie executives; among his close friends during his MGM years are the composer Herbert Stothart and his wife Mary, an artist (who, after her husband's death in 1949, would marry Paul Wescher, an art historian); Dr. Rudolph Marx and his wife Agnes; Frank Davis, a film editor at MGM and an amateur pilot; the opera singer Marguerite d'Alvarez; and the screenwriter Anita Loos, who gives Lewin, on his first trip to Europe, an introduction to Janet Flanner (correspondent for the *New Yorker*) and her lover, the journalist Solita Solano. Flanner and Solano will both become Lewin's lifelong friends and correspondents, as will another American in Paris, Djuna Barnes.
1931	Produces *The Guardsman,* the only talking film in which Alfred Lunt and Lynn Fontanne star. Lewin's father dies, September 4.
1932	Produces *Smilin' Through* for MGM. Lewin becomes very friendly with the Danish explorer and writer Peter Freuchen, who is employed by MGM on a production *(Eskimo,* 1933; W. S. Van Dyke, director) based on his own

books about his quarter-century among the Inuit in Alaska. In the coming years, Lewin will socialize and correspond with, among others, a coterie of colorful, adventurous, jocular men including Flaherty, Freuchen, Frank Scully, Jim Tully, Oliver St. John Gogarty, and Gobind Behari Lal.

1933   Lewin secretly explores the possibility of leaving MGM to set up an independent production company with Sol Grossbard, Anita Loos, John Emerson, and Jules Furthman, but the plan does not materialize. Lewin's brother Will receives a Ph.D. from New York University (his doctoral thesis is "Photoplay Appreciation in American High Schools").

1934   Albert Lewin produces *Red-Headed Woman* and *China Seas* for MGM.

1935   Produces *Mutiny on the Bounty* for MGM. He is now interested in being set up alone as an independent producer and negotiates again with Sol Grossbard, but this idea, too, comes to naught. His brother Will is now chairman of the English department at the new Weequahic High School in Newark; with Max J. Herzberg, Will founds Educational and Recreational Guides, Inc. (E.R.G.I.), which publishes the periodical *Photoplay Studies*.

1936   Lewin meets the Chinese writer Lin Yutang, who is consulting on MGM's production of *The Good Earth;* the two become friends and correspondents. Irving Thalberg dies. Lewin quits MGM and travels in Europe.

1937   Lewin's last MGM production, *The Good Earth,* is released. He is hired as a producer for Paramount, where he plans the epic *Gettysburg* (written by

Lewin house at 514 Ocean Front, Santa Monica; Richard Neutra, architect, 1939 (photo by Fred R. Dapprich).

Clifford Odets) and *Knights of the Round Table,* but he is forced to take on lesser projects, including *True Confession.* Albert and Millie Lewin commission Richard Neutra to build them a modern house on a narrow beachfront property they have bought in Santa Monica.

1938　Frustrated and dissatisfied at Paramount—where his second production, *Spawn of the North,* is released this year—Lewin brings his old friend, the poet Charles Reznikoff, from New York to assist him as a researcher and reader, mainly employing Reznikoff on preproduction research for his pet project, *Knights of the Round Table.*

1939　Lewin's third of his three Paramount productions, *Zaza,* is completed. Early this year, he and Millie travel to Europe again and tour Arthurian locations in Wales, Devon, and Somerset with Hugh and Barbara Gray. They also visit Paris, where they visit friends, view and buy art, and meet Marcel Duchamp. Upon returning to New York, Lewin, who has long suffered from progressive deafness, undergoes surgery to restore his hearing—it is only temporarily effective. The Lewins move to their newly completed

Albert and Mildred Lewin aboard a transatlantic liner, probably 1939.

house, designed by Neutra, at 514 Ocean Front, Santa Monica. Because war in Europe seems likely, Paramount cancels plans for *Knights of the Round Table;* Lewin, who still wants to make this film, negotiates unsuccessfully with Universal, RKO, and other studios. The mime, artist, and author Angna Enters spends most of the summer with the Lewins in Santa Monica and paints a portrait of Millie. In November, the Lewins visit Death Valley with their friends Rudolph and Agnes Marx.

1940   Lewin quits Paramount, abandoning, among others, a few projects he was working on with Preston Sturges. Lewin and David Loew found Loew-Lewin Productions. Loew-Lewin, in the hope of helping Britain and fighting Nazism, undertakes an adaptation of Erich Maria Remarque's *Flotsam* and buys the film rights to Nevil Shute's story of the RAF, *Landfall*. After the Nazis occupy France and Denmark, Lewin is much involved with helping friends and associates in both countries, including Jacques Feyder, Jean Renoir, Gilles and Claire Guilbert, and Peter Freuchen. At a dinner party given by the art patrons Walter and Louise Arensberg, Lewin meets Man Ray, who will spend the next decade in Los Angeles and will become one of Lewin's closest friends.

1941   Loew-Lewin Productions releases *So Ends Our Night* (based on Remarque's *Flotsam*), about refugees from Nazi Germany who are trying to escape occupied Vienna. Loew-Lewin is forced to defend the film before a panel of the House of Representatives investigating films for propogandiz-

Loew-Lewin's *So Ends Our Night* (1941). *Left to right:* Alexander Granach, Leonid Kinskey, Philip Van Zandt, Fredric March, and Glenn Ford.

ing American entry into the war, but the investigation is dropped when Pearl Harbor is attacked. Lewin plans to adapt Odets's *Night Music* and brings Odets back to Los Angeles to work on the script. Jean Renoir, with the aid of Lewin and Robert Flaherty, escapes from France and comes to Hollywood, where he meets often with Lewin, professionally and socially. Barbara Gray (the wife of Hugh Gray, who is now serving in the RAF) and her children, who have left London during the blitz, come to Los Angeles under Lewin's aegis and live with the Lewins for a time; Barbara is hired as a research assistant and British language consultant on Loew-Lewin's production of *The Moon and Sixpence*.

1942   Loew-Lewin Productions completes *The Moon and Sixpence,* written and directed by Lewin; this is Lewin's first film as a director. Millie does war work with the Red Cross Motor Corps, a canteen unit, and the Women's Auxiliary. The Lewins meet Peggy Guggenheim and Max Ernst during one of their visits to Los Angeles. David Loew dissolves his partnership with Lewin in order to do war work. Lewin is rehired by MGM and is assigned to direct *Madame Curie,* but he is taken off the production after ten days.

1943   Lewin starts to develop *The Picture of Dorian Gray* for MGM. After considering, among others, Salvador Dalí, Pavel Tchelitchew, and George Grosz, Lewin hires Ivan Albright (and Ivan's brother Malvin Albright) to execute the titular portrait. In April, Lewin makes a cross-country train trip, visiting the Albrights and the Devi Dja company (who perform an Indonesian gamelan dance in the film) in Chicago and Perkins Harnly (an artist who consulted on the Victorian interiors) in New York.

1944   Lewin struggles with the producer Pandro S. Berman over the production details, budget, and editing of *Dorian Gray.* Lewin becomes friendly with Sidney Janis, from whom he and Millie sometimes buy art for their growing collection.

1945   MGM releases *The Picture of Dorian Gray.* Lewin quits MGM after this production, because of artistic conflicts. Loew-Lewin is revived. Lewin begins researching and writing an adaptation of Maupassant's *Bel Ami;* he sets up a competition for a painting of *The Temptation of Saint Anthony* to appear in the film and persuades Darius Milhaud to compose and conduct the score.

1946   In March, the judges of the *Bel Ami* Competition select Max Ernst's painting as the winner; an exhibition of all the entries then goes on tour and is charged with obscenity in Boston. In October, the Lewins give a double wedding party for two newlywed couples: Man Ray and his wife Juliet, and Max Ernst and Dorothea Tanning. A friendship with Will and Ariel Durant begins.

1947   *The Private Affairs of Bel Ami* is released by Loew-Lewin through United Artists; in June, it is included in the Festival Mondial du Film et des Beaux-Arts, Brussels.

1948   The Loew-Lewin partnership splits up again. Lewin returns to Metro as an executive; he also researches and writes his next personal project, *Pandora and the Flying Dutchman.* (His contract with MGM allows him sabbaticals for independent projects.) The Lewins celebrate their thirtieth anniversary

Angna Enters, *A Party,* 1948. *Far side of table, left to right:* Juliet Man Ray, Van Leyden, Aelis Crosby, Karin Van Leyden, Floyd Crosby, Mary Anita Loos, Max Ernst, Dido Renoir, Dmitri Tiomkin, Marguerite d'Alvarez, Albert Lewin. *Near side, left to right:* Mildred Lewin, Man Ray, Mary Stothart, Jean Renoir, Dorothea Tanning, Hugh Gray, Angna Enters, Richard Sales, Barbara Gray, Helen Freeman, Herbert Stothart, Albertina Rasch.

	with a dinner party. One of the guests, Angna Enters, presents the Lewins with a painting of the dinner scene as an anniversary gift.
1949	Lewin is involved in a supervisory capacity in preproduction work on *Quo Vadis,* but only as long as John Huston is scheduled to direct it; both will soon leave the project.
1950	Lewin films *Pandora and the Flying Dutchman* on location in and around Tossa, a town on the Costa Brava in Spain; in Wales; and in studios in London. Man Ray executes a painting for the film, which is not used, and a color photograph of Ava Gardner, which is. While he is in London, Lewin spends time with Roland Penrose and Lee Miller, from whom he borrows a Man Ray chess set to appear in the film; through the Penroses he meets Dylan Thomas.
1951	*Pandora and the Flying Dutchman* is released. Man and Julie Ray move from Los Angeles to Paris.
1952	Lewin researches and writes the script for an adaptation of Henrik Ibsen's *Peer Gynt.*
1953	Lewin films *Saadia* in French Morocco, whose government will later honor him with a medal. He approaches various European studios (in France and Italy) about an independent production adapted from Albert Adès's *Un roi nu.*

1954   *Saadia* is released by MGM. The Lewins move from California to an apartment on Fifth Avenue in New York; somewhat later, Mae West buys the Neutra house in Santa Monica. Alfred Barr, James Soby, Andrew Ritchie, René d'Harnoncourt, and Dorothy Miller of the Museum of Modern Art (MOMA) all come to see the Lewins' art collection; a MOMA members' tour is held on May 12.

1955   In Mexico for his production of *The Living Idol,* Lewin meets or visits the artists Leonora Carrington, Remedios Varo, Wolfgang Paalen, Alice Rahon, and others, adding works by each to the Lewins' collection.

1956   Jean Renoir, Lewin, and the MGM producer Maurice Silverstein (who was head of MGM's Latin American unit when Lewin filmed *The Living Idol* in Mexico) discuss forming a production company. Lewin approaches Ingrid Bergman about a role in *Un roi nu,* which he hopes to film on location in Europe with this proposed company. Meanwhile, he begins work on an original script based loosely on the Faust legend: *Diana at Midnight,* conceived as a vehicle for Ava Gardner.

1957   *The Living Idol* is released by MGM. Lewin is approached about a faculty position by the Theater Arts department at UCLA, where his friend Hugh Gray is already on the faculty. He declines, and he and Millie travel to Europe (Rome, London, Paris, Bordeaux, Toulouse, Castres, Albi, Bayonne, Biarritz, Saint Jean de Luz); they spend most of the summer in Spain. In Spain, Lewin researches and writes a script for a biographical film about Francisco Goya; this script will eventually be sold to the producers of *The Naked Maja,* who use none of it.

1958   The Lewins spend several months in Europe, including Italy (Florence, Naples, Rome), considering locations for *Diana at Midnight;* England; and Paris, where the Cinémathèque Française holds an "Hommage à Albert Lewin." Lewin has become friends with Robert Graves while doing research on his project on Goya in Spain; he now corresponds with Graves about archaeology, anthropology, history, and literature. Lewin approaches Jerome Robbins about choreographing *Diana at Midnight,* which is to include a ballet sequence set against a background reminiscent of the Spoleto festival.

1959   Lewin suffers a heart attack. On his doctor's orders, he retires from films. He abandons the idea of filming *Diana at Midnight* but considers making it into a novel.

1960   Lewin's brother Will dies, August 24.

1962   Lewin writes a stage play, *Bed Without Pillows* (never produced).

1963   The Lewins travel widely in the near and far east (Turkey, Iran, Pakistan, India, Burma, Thailand, Cambodia, Hong Kong, Singapore, Japan).

1964   Around this time, Lewin begins an intensive correspondence and friendship with Cyrus Gordon, a scholar of ancient near eastern language and culture, whom Lewin met through Charles Reznikoff's wife, Marie Syrkin—an author, translator, and Labor Zionist editor who is a colleague of Gordon's at Brandeis University.

1965   Lewin's wife and his mother both die—Millie, of cancer, in February; and his mother in July. Angna Enters becomes his fairly constant companion, as she will remain until his death.

Jean Renoir with Paul Delvaux's painting, *The Summons* (1944), in the Lewins' New York City apartment, probably early 1960s (photo by A.P. Raisbeck).

1966	Lewin is honored by a tribute, an exhibition, and a film series at the Gallery of Modern Art in New York in March; he is also honored in London—and in Toronto, where the Gallery of Modern Art retrospective is repeated.
1967	*The Unaltered Cat,* Lewin's first novel, is published by the Harvill Press in London and Scribner in the United States. *The Picture of Dorian Gray* is selected to inaugurate the Festival of the Development of the Cinema in the United States, held at the American Embassy in London. Lewin and Angna Enters travel to London and the continent.
1968	In February, Jean-Luc Godard and François Truffaut solicit the help of Lewin (among others) for their campaign to save Henri Langlois and his Cinématheque Française. On May 9, Lewin dies of pneumonia. He is cremated and his ashes are mingled with Millie's in a favorite Ming vase; Charles Reznikoff delivers the funeral eulogy. Lewin leaves various sums of money and select pieces of his art collection to many friends and relatives, and his library to New York University; he has divided the balance of his estate between two charities: the Motion Picture Relief Fund and the Society of the New York Hospital. His art collection is auctioned in two sales by Parke-Bernet.

Albert Lewin—as always, impeccably dressed—at home. The painting, a work of a nineteenth-century Swedish folk artist, shows the parable of the wise and foolish virgins. The pile of art books is topped by a monograph about the self-taught African-American painter Horace Pippin. Lewin is reading *Transition Forty-Eight* (no. 2, 1948), a short-lived reprise of the prewar journal published by Eugene Jolas.

INTRODUCTION

> I always tried to make pictures that would please me and some of my intelligent friends and still please the general public enough to pay off.... I did it as a kind of tight-rope walking. I was a bit of an equilibrist.
>
> Albert Lewin[1]

Albert Lewin (1894–1968) was the director, in the 1940s and 1950s, of six films that were literary, artful, exotic, and odd. Lewin was known as one of Hollywood's few resident intellectuals; he had received his B.A. from New York University in 1915 and his M.A. from Harvard in 1916; had taught at the University of Missouri in 1917 and 1918; had been a doctoral student in English literature at Columbia University from 1918 to 1922; and had been a film and theater critic for *The Jewish Tribune* in 1921 and 1922.

It was in 1921 that Lewin had decided to enter films, after seeing *The Cabinet of Doctor Caligari*. Having swiftly worked his way up the ranks at the Goldwyn and Metro studios, he became indispensable to Irving Thalberg of Metro-Goldwyn-Mayer, as a writer, then as head of the story department, and finally as production supervisor on several prestigious MGM films, including *Mutiny on the Bounty* (1935) and *The Good Earth* (1937). After Thalberg's death (in 1936), Lewin left MGM. Not until 1942, when he was nearly fifty years old, did he undertake his first directorial project: his own adaptation of Somerset Maugham's novel *The Moon and Sixpence* for an independent production company he had started with his friend David Loew.

With *The Moon and Sixpence,* Albert Lewin began his strange career as an "auteur," writing and directing eccentric, self-conscious films that bear little witness to his long tenure under Thalberg. Lewin commissioned original artworks, songs, and dances for his films; filled them with metaphors and metonyms, signs and symbols; and—convinced that talking films had diminished the visual power of cinema—tried to develop methods of staging and filming that defied the conventions which had evolved in relation to synchronous dialogue. Lewin characterized himself as an "equilibrist" and said that his ambition was "to make a few pictures which will be both commercial and artistic, and which will have enough originality and distinction to be remembered for a little while."[2] The results of this endeavor were highly stylized, self-reflective, intellectually multilayered, and uneven by almost any standard, and their reception was also uneven; even *The Picture of Dorian Gray*—Lewin's most internally consistent and most highly regarded film—has met with mixed responses from the time of its release to the present day.

If the "novel of ideas" is rarely successful commercially and seldom well received critically, the "film of ideas" is likely to fare even worse, especially in Anglo-American culture. This is one of the main problems with Albert Lewin's directorial works. To a great extent, ideas were the stuff of which his films were made, and thus ideas became a focal point of reactions to them, and to him: his (Anglo-American) critics often called him a "middlebrow," disparagingly, or a "highbrow," sarcastically. Lewin himself did not hesitate to use these terms against others, though they are ultimately dismissive and futile, and their etymology underscores their dubious value as classifications. Both words originated in phrenology, a nineteenth-century pseudoscience:

> "Highbrow," first used in the 1880s to describe intellectual or aesthetic superiority, and "lowbrow," first used shortly after 1900 to mean someone or something neither "highly intellectual" nor "aesthetically refined," were derived from the phrenological terms "highbrowed" and "lowbrowed," which were prominently featured in the nineteenth-century practice of determining racial types and intelligence by measuring cranial shapes and capacities.[3]

Although these terms were already in use, they seem to have achieved their greatest visibility from a rather damning article written by Russell Lynes in 1949: "Highbrow, Lowbrow, Middlebrow." According to the criteria Lynes outlined, Lewin—as well as most if not all of Lewin's critics, and indeed Lynes himself—would all be classified as "upper middlebrows," along with other "principal purveyors of highbrow ideas" including "many publishers, . . . most educators, museum directors, movie producers, art dealers, lecturers, and the editors of most magazines which combine national circulation with an adult vocabulary."[4] One might not think this company particularly shameful, but highbrows, exemplified in Lynes's article by Clement Greenberg, and by his positions in the *Partisan Review*, hold middlebrows in contempt and blame them for "devaluating the precious, infecting the healthy, corrupting the honest, and stultifying the wise."[5] Lynes is rather hostile to such elitist rhetoric, implying that it is totalitarian (ironically, it does sound somewhat like the Nazis' vitriolic attacks on modern art[6]); still, he defends at least some highbrows on the ground that not all "are so intolerant or desperate as this, or so ambitious for authority."[7]

One might think that Lewin, who had very consciously pitched his own tent on the border between high and popular culture, would be loath to cast this particular type of aspersion; but in fact he was as ready as anyone else to use these slurs. He was outraged by James Agee's review of *The Picture of Dorian Gray* in 1945, and seven years later he was still fuming:

> The middle-brow critic has the notion that it is his function to serve as a bridge between the artist and his public. He is not a bridge at all, but a road-block. . . . James Agee . . . is one of the middle-brows I refer to who consider themselves stupendous highbrows. He said in his review that he had to thank me for making him read the Oscar Wilde book. He admired the book and despised the picture. While preparing the picture, I happened to have read the contemporary criticisms of Wilde's book. It was furiously attacked by people just like James Agee, who said things about the book not unlike things he said about the picture.[8]

It may well be true that in admitting to having been introduced to a minor classic of literature by a motion picture, Agee was leaving himself open to derision, but he was by no means alone in his dislike of Lewin's film. In fact, his review was much more sympathetic than many others to Lewin's aims, and he faulted the film more for its execution than its approach:

> A good movie might have been made from *The Picture of Dorian Gray*. Albert Lewin's version is respectful, earnest, and, I am afraid, dead. . . . The movie is just a cultured hor-

ror picture, decorated with epigrams and an elaborate moral, and made with a sincere effort at good taste rather than with passion, immediacy, or imagination.[9]

Agee did not despise *Dorian Gray* so much as pity it. He misconstrued the purpose of Lewin's fastidious evocation of fin-de-siècle aestheticism: whereas Lewin was creating an archaeological and psychological milieu, Agee mistook this for effortful "taste." And *The Picture of Dorian Gray* was meant to be a horror picture and, arguably, achieved this in no small part through its rather chilling, formal rigor. Agee missed this, too, though he was neither a philistine nor a snob.

Some other critics and viewers, though, really did despise Lewin's film. "*The Picture of Dorian Gray* is remindful of nothing so much as a Grosset and Dunlap edition of the Oscar Wilde work, editorially fumigated by Lloyd C. Douglas, and ornamented with illustrations from the brush of Maxfield Parrish," wrote Herb Sterne, invoking the most insidious tendencies of "middlebrow" culture.[10] Actually, if any illustrator should have been identified as an influence on Lewin's sets, it was not Parrish but Aubrey Beardsley. Beardsley had illustrated the edition (1893) of Malory's *Morte d'Arthur* that is shown, open to an illustration titled "How Sir Tristram Drank of the Love Drink," in Dorian Gray's library, and in this film, Lewin sometimes achieves a

The Picture of Dorian Gray (1945). A moment of profane illumination: Dorian Gray (Hurd Hatfield) in his childhood schoolroom, where he has just murdered his friend, the painter Basil Hallward (Lowell Gilmore).

cinematic equivalent of what one might call Beardsley's "post-Pre-Raphaelite" style. Lewin uses that style to meet both internal and external demands of the scenario: internally, to create an atmosphere associated with Wildean decadence; and externally, to achieve a kind of narrative dissociation from the story's amorality and perversity. But such visual meanings (which will be discussed further in Chapter 2), either eluded or offended many of Lewin's viewers. For example, the director Val Lewton—who saw the film in 1945 with another director, Mark Robson—thought it "a disgustingly pretentious piece of poopishness,"[11] and his reaction was not unique.

Lewin himself described the reactions to *The Picture of Dorian Gray* in a response (which he never actually sent) to James Agee: "The divergence of opinion regarding my film . . . is violent. Harry Hansen, Alton Cook, Howard Barnes, Eileen Creelman, Kate Cameron, and a number of others, approve of it with varying degrees of enthusiasm. At the same time it is a subject of amusement, contempt or condemnation by Bosley Crowther, John Mason Brown, the New Yorker, Time, P.M., and by you in the Nation."[12]

Although the reception of *The Picture of Dorian Gray* in America was divided, that was less true of Lewin's later films: American opinon regarding these was increasingly unanimous, and low. These later films were characterized by an odd combination of tragedy and irony, spectacle and ritual, pomposity and play, and thus they seemed to have a particularly "un-American" mien. Andrew Sarris's comments exemplify the response of many American critics to films that aspire to sophistication or literacy; in evaluating Lewin and certain other directors, he places them in the category of "strained seriousness": "talented but uneven directors with the mortal sin of pretentiousness. Their ambitious projects tend to inflate rather than expand."[13]

If there is any epithet more damning than "middlebrow," in our culture at large or in the microcosm of American film, it may be "pretentious." This term has a strong effect, but—beyond the simple fact that it is pejorative—it often goes unexamined, and it is often misused. It may fail to distinguish between genuine and feigned expertise; and it is inherently suspicious of the "literary" or the "artistic" and thus may indiscriminately dismiss any person or product that manifests or aspires to these qualities. Albert Lewin, whatever his failings as a writer and director, was not a pretender to the world of arts and letters—he was, as a scholar and critic, a part of that world. This has not, however, prevented a majority of his American critics from characterizing his films as vulgar and naive and condemning him as pretentious and snobbish.[14]

Aside from a few writers, perhaps, not many people in Hollywood, especially in its classic period, were likely to be accused of pretension or snobbery. Most European émigrés, even the best-educated, seem to have been to some extent exempted from such charges, no doubt for a complex variety of reasons. Among these reasons are the often tacit assumption on the part of many Americans that Europeans are more "cultured" than we are; the Europeans' tendency not to make blatantly "arty" or "intellectual" films; and the Europeans' general isolation from the rest of the community.

John Russell Taylor, in *Strangers in Paradise,* describes Lewin as one of the very few Hollywood figures "who appreciated the special qualities of the émigrés . . . whose strange devotion to European culture made them almost as much outsiders as if they were European non-joiners themselves." Taylor, however, shows the ambivalence or skepticism that is ubiquitous in discussions that must deal with intellect and American moviemakers in the same breath: "Lewin . . . had been a professor before being lured into movies—a fact that always enormously impressed those around [him], particularly Irving Thalberg. . . . Lewin was always very consciously and obviously an odd-man-out in Hollywood: it was in a sense his gimmick. With his Savile Row suits, his collection of Pre-Columbian artifacts (years before they were fashionable), his disdain (real or apparent) for commerce, his obsession with surrealism and his host of European friends, he was absolutely what then passed in Hollywood—and probably still would—for an intellectual."[15]

But Lewin was, by almost any definition of the term, in fact an intellectual. That was the crux of his problem. The criticism leveled at Lewin was often anti-intellectual; and even if anti-intellectualism was unusual and generally unnecessary in Hollywood, it was—and is—hardly unusual in American culture at large. Richard Hofstadter has written a definitive study, *Anti-Intellectualism in American Life*, identifying and analyzing this persistent animus in the American body politic, which often harbors the suspicion, he argues, that intellectuals "are pretentious, conceited, effeminate, and snobbish; and very likely immoral, dangerous, and subversive."[16]

As an intellectual, Lewin was not cloistered, or at least not cloistered enough to avoid charges from "above" of being a middlebrow or charges from "below" of being pretentious. This fact, I believe, goes far in explaining the vicissitudes of his reputation. The anti-intellectualism Lewin encountered in Hollywood was motivated from within and without. Not only did the industry cater to a "know-nothing" public, but it was itself fraught with anti-intellectualism. This is beautifully illustrated by an anecdote about Lewin's battles with MGM during the production of *The Picture of Dorian Gray*:

> The film went forward, not without difficulties since it ran over schedule and budget. Once [the producer Pandro S.] Berman spent most of the day watching Lewin set up just one characteristically complex shot: that which starts on Dorian, inclined to be contrite for ill-using poor innocent Angela Lansbury [Sibyl] and writing her a letter, then moves over to George Sanders [Lord Henry Wotton], who turns and walks away from the camera to deliver the crucial information that the girl has killed herself, then turns back at last, cynically, to observe the effect of his words. Berman watched all this with some mystification, then took Lewin aside. "Al, I don't see why you're complicating things for yourself. This guy's telling his friend the very sad and tragic news that his girl has died. Why don't you do it in a nice two-shot on the sofa, with over-shoulder close-ups?" Lewin felt there wasn't much point in explaining at length, so he said, "Well, Pan, that's my style, you see." Berman was puzzled. "Style, style, people are always talking about style. What is this style?" Lewin explained that it was the quality which told you at once that a Lubitsch film was by Lubitsch, or if you turned on a radio to Wagner made sure you knew at once it wasn't Mozart or Bach. Berman reflected. "Oh, so that's style. Well, I don't want it in any of my movies."[17]

Berman's response may be the quintessential anti-intellectual comment, but the discourse that provoked it reveals not only the pedant in Albert Lewin, but also the aesthete, two aspects of his character he made no attempt to subdue in Hollywood, where they were mightily out of place. And that reveals a third, and very interesting, aspect of his personality—his perversity.

Perversity, of a particular kind (not necessarily sexual), is evident in much that Lewin was and did and is inherent in all of his films, manifesting itself in all sorts of fascinating contradictions, paradoxes, and problems. As Lewin himself was wont to point out, his very choice of material for his films tended toward the perverse. About the choice of material for his first film, *The Moon and Sixpence,* for instance, Lewin once recalled in an interview: "Everybody felt we'd make, at most, an artistic flop. David [Loew]'s friends tried to dissuade him, but he was steadfast. They said the story of a disagreeable character, a painter whose paintings are burned and who dies of leprosy—this is entertainment?"[18]

And upon completing *The Moon and Sixpence* early in 1942, Lewin remarked in a letter to a friend, the poet Charles Reznikoff: "The general impression around here seems to be that it will make a fine picture and a commercial flop. My indurated contrariness finds this very encouraging."[19]

Additionally, Lewin's films often had perversity as a theme: cruelty, even sadism; sexual promiscuity (in several of them); deviance; manipulation. And they presented these perverse themes cinematically in a purposefully "detached, studied, symbolic style,"[20] which ran counter to many Hollywood conventions. Formally, Lewin's films were a perverse—or, if you will, paradoxical—combination of the primitive and the baroque: they were visually overloaded, yet the camera work was very restrained, almost static; and they were aurally overloaded, with a complex counterpoint of music and dialogue, yet dramatically circumspect. Finally, all this was achieved in a system carefully guarded by the censors of the Hays office.

In all his films, Lewin made compromises with Hollywood's self-censorship, as exercised by the Hays office, yet in many cases he seems to have made a point of somehow showing visually, or encoding, the material he was forbidden to relate as

A suggestive poster for *The Private Affairs of Bel Ami* (1947), the film that secured Lewin's reputation for "censor-proof depravity."

narrative. This appears most graphically in *The Picture of Dorian Gray,* whose strongly homoerotic subtext had to be suppressed, but which nonetheless manages to convey homoerotic content through metaphor, analogy, and other visual "tropes."[21] By the time he completed *Bel Ami* in 1946—a film based on Guy de Maupassant's story of a cad who advances professionally and socially through a series of sexual affairs—Lewin's treatment of taboo themes had earned him the "unrivaled reputation for bringing viciousness to the screen with the approval of the Production Code censors" and he was considered to have established a tradition of "censor-proof depravity."[22]

Though *Bel Ami* may perhaps have been censor-proof, it was not critic-proof. This film is evocative, in many respects, of the artists who inspired it—not only Maupassant, but Flaubert, Manet, and Degas, among others—and it is a marvelous examination of the ethos and ambience of the era it represents; but it was hardly a succès d'estime, as a few remarks will illustrate:

> The film is elaborate and expensively produced, but for all that, is dull, dated and a rather absurdly passionate piece of celluloid, seemingly designed to shock the easily shocked and titillate the amorously curious. It's far more ridiculous, however, than wicked.[23]

> Really, it is incredible that a picture could be made from a Guy de Maupassant novel and be as tiresome as this. . . . Everybody . . . acts as posily and pompously as they are compelled to talk. . . . The whole lot of them are as utterly artificial as the obvious paint-and-pasteboard sets.[24]

As is evident from such comments, the object of ridicule was not so much the problematic material that Lewin chose to bring to the screen, but rather the purposefully complex, formally distanced, artful manner in which he presented it. Lewin's manner, for which his films were so often condemned, is at odds with a prevailing idea of the American cinema. Any number of European films share many qualities with Lewin's: stylization, self-consciousness, historicism, literary allusiveness, and so on; examples include Michael Powell's *The Red Shoes* (1948), Alf Sjöberg's *Miss Julie* (1951), Max Ophuls's *Lola Montès* (1955), Ingmar Bergman's *The Seventh Seal* (1957), and Jean-Luc Godard's *Contempt* (1963). But it is hard to imagine these works being so readily dismissed as pretentious. They may well be better films than most of Lewin's, but that is not because their creators were less pretentious or more genuine "men of ideas": rather, it is probably because the creators were better, or more thoroughly, artists. Lewin was, perhaps, less of an artist precisely because he was more of an intellectual. His ideas often encumbered and undermined his artistry; a film by Lewin can seem almost annotated, with built-in criticism—like a teaching edition of a novel. Actually, this characteristic too can be found in some European films, and again, it is a quirk more readily forgiven in the work of Europeans—Antonioni, for instance, or Godard—than it can ever be in the work of their American counterparts. As is true of Antonioni and Godard, Lewin's earlier career as a critic gave his films a kind of critical reflexivity, but while Godard and Antonioni were likely to be praised for the complex imbrication that resulted from this, Lewin was more often excoriated. Tom Milne, one of Lewin's admirers, claims, in fact, that Lewin's "style of direction, elliptically elusive and allusive, anticipates the Antonioni-Godard revolution in having actors persistently deliver lines back to the camera or in avoidance of unequivocally direct communication."[25]

American film criticism has tended, for the most part, to cherish a fantasy about home-grown filmmakers (Griffith, Flaherty, Ford, Keaton, and Hawks, for instance), seeing them as representing a kind of unschooled, native genius; but it welcomes sophistication, erudition, and artifice from abroad. One exception to this rule was the cosmopolitan but nonetheless very American Orson Welles, who is now, of course, highly regarded by American film critics. However, even he was not greeted with unalloyed enthusiasm in Hollywood in 1940; rather, he was regarded with not a little suspicion and bemusement by the "regulars"—a phenomenon captured beautifully in one of F. Scott Fitzgerald's late stories, "Pat Hobby and Orson Welles." Hobby is a washed-up studio hack:

"Who's this Welles?" Pat asked of Louie, the studio bookie. "Every time I pick up a paper they got about this Welles."

"You know, he's that beard," explained Louie.

"Sure, I know he's that beard, you couldn't miss that. But what credit's he got? What's he done to draw one hundred and fifty grand a picture?"[26]

The Moon and Sixpence (1942). The painter Charles Strickland (George Sanders) inspects another artist's work at a Parisian café, observed by the writer Geoffrey Wolfe (Herbert Marshall).

And it was not only the man himself, with his signifying beard, who could alienate people. According to Arthur Knight, Welles's masterpiece, *Citizen Kane,* also flew in the face of American anti-intellectualism: "At a time when the big audience in America was still the small-town, grass-roots moviegoer, *Kane* proved a chill and forbidding experience, cold, objective and intellectual. Welles had so distanced all his characters that the kind of empathy most moviegoers then expected of a picture was totally lacking. They might be impressed, but they were rarely moved."[27]

The morbid and pessimistic *Weltanschauung,* the formal artifice, and the almost Brechtian distancing devices that Welles brought to *Citizen Kane* are equally characteristic of most of Lewin's films—certainly the three from the 1940s—however different Welles's and Lewin's particular conceits and overall approaches may have been.

Like *Citizen Kane,* Lewin's directorial debut, *The Moon and Sixpence* (released the following year), involved a retrospective attempt to reconstruct and understand the enigma of a great man. Charles Foster Kane was based on William Randolph Hearst; Charles Strickland—the character in Somerset Maugham's novel and Lewin's film—was based on the French painter Paul Gauguin. Like Kane, Strickland is a man of massive contradictions: hateful and seductive, brutish but brilliant, paradoxically naive and cynical. Again like Kane, Strickland is transformed in the course of the story: in this case, from a bland, witless London stockbroker and family man into an avant-garde and fiercely misanthropic painter. And Strickland's death, like Kane's, is central to the entire film. Finally, Lewin's solutions to the formal problems posed by Maugham's nonchronological first-person narrative—though not as dazzling as Welles's untraditional construction—are no less unusual:

> We bought it [rights to *The Moon and Sixpence*] from MGM for $25,000. The contract came out of the MGM legal department faster than any other contract in my experience, they were so glad to get rid of it. They thought we were screwy. But I had an angle. The reason it couldn't be adapted was that it was told in the first person and because the author at times became a participant in the action. The transposition was very, very hard to do, and the people who had tackled it never solved that problem. For this, I owe a debt of gratitude to Sacha Guitry, who made a wonderful picture called *The Story of a Cheat,* which used a narrative technique for the first time in a theatrical film. He told his story in the first person, the action carried it along, and at intervals when necessary, he talked again. I thought this was a most original and exciting thing.[28]

The Story of a Cheat (*Le roman d'un tricheur,* 1936), generally considered the best film of the French director Sacha Guitry, is "told entirely from the point of the leading character—Guitry himself—who describes the action in a running commentary while the characters act in pantomime."[29]

The art historian Erwin Panofsky observed that *The Story of a Cheat* betrays "a kind of nostalgia for the silent period and that devices have been worked out to combine the virtues of sound and speech with those of silent acting," in films that use voice-over to free the picture from the narration.[30] The theme of nostalgia is central to *The Moon and Sixpence,* and Lewin's borrowing of Guitry's technique reveals a similar yearning for what he felt were the greater (more imaginative, more dynamic, more dramatic) visual effects of silent cinema. To the end of his career, Lewin mourned for the loss of silent film, as is evident in this letter to the critic Dwight MacDonald:

> Inspired especially by "The Cabinet of Doctor Caligari," I started working in silent pictures because I thought the movies were an exciting new art. I was young, too, and I

wanted to take part in the development of this new art. I was betrayed by the inventors. With the use of synchronized sound, the movies ceased to be an art and have never recovered. I am still at it, but without hope of finding that "counterpoint," that non-synchronous co-ordination of visual and auditory images that Eisenstein was not permitted to experiment with. The simple truth is that an art exists *because* of its limitations, not in *spite* of them. The theorizers and critics clap their hands and jump up and down in joy whenever another limitation is removed and we take a further step in the direction of the last banality. The history of the movies has a happy ending if it is told backwards.[31]

That last observation might be made of Lewin's own career, were one to judge by either criticism or profits. By the time Lewin's most "original" film, *Pandora and the Flying Dutchman,* was released in 1951, his early reputation—earned under Thalberg—as a canny producer and a keen judge of scripts had been overwhelmed by his newer reputation as a rather fussy, impractical, expensive writer-director of risky, arduously ornate movies. After *Pandora,* Lewin failed to realize his most cherished projects (they included, among others, a film about Goya, an adaptation of Ibsen's *Peer Gynt,* and a Faustian fugue called *Diana at Midnight);* and the two films he did manage to

Pandora and the Flying Dutchman (1951). *(Back to camera)* Pandora Reynolds (Ava Gardner). She faces three admirers, suggestive of the holy trinity *(left to right):* Hendrick van der Zee, captain of a ghost ship (James Mason); a father figure, Geoffrey Fielding (Harold Warrender); and her fiancé, Stephen Cameron (Nigel Patrick).

make were deeply and inherently flawed and were further weakened by second-rate acting and by interference from the studio.

Pandora and the Flying Dutchman, about a woman unable to love and a man unable to die—a baroque synthesis of classical myth and Germanic legend set in Spain around 1930—met with mixed reviews. Few critics could deny its visual splendor (glorious Technicolor photography by Jack Cardiff of the Costa Brava, and of Ava Gardner), but most of the English-speaking critics could not accept its script, which they described as "confused and pretentious"[32] and "turgid."[33] Many French critics, on the other hand, generally more catholic in their tastes, loved *Pandora,* not only for its sensual beauty but also for its eccentric and literate blend of poetry and myth, tragedy and spectacle. Critics in the surrealist circuit and those of *Cahiers du Cinéma* were most rapturous. (*Cahiers* was the maverick French film journal out of which emerged "auteur" criticism and many French directors of the New Wave, including François Truffaut, Jean-Luc Godard, Eric Rohmer, Claude Chabrol, and Jacques Rivette.)

These contrasts in the film's reception are almost as fascinating and paradoxical as the film itself. When *Pandora* was shown in England in 1985, Tom Milne, an admirer, recognized both its link with surrealism and its impact on the New Wave but seemed unaware that the responses to the film had varied widely:

> Made a decade or two earlier, Lewin's marvellous fantasy might at least have stood some chance of being annexed to the surrealist pantheon. Instead critics, surprisingly unanimously, dismissed it as an embarrassingly arty aberration, a comedy of manners that was all too unintentionally comic and much too mannered. Characters who quote as liberally as Lewin's do always seem to be a source of unease—witness reactions to Godard's early work—as though mere quotation were itself a pretension. Yet as Godard realised (and if you consider *Le Mépris* [*Contempt*] in relation to *Pandora and the Flying Dutchman,* there can be little doubt where his debt lies), allusion is a rich source of texture, adducing tenuous parallels, reverberating echoes and mysterious insights in support of perspectives whereby (to quote Novalis) "The world becomes a dream and the dream becomes a world."[34]

Milne, who knew a great deal about the French New Wave, must have been thinking only of Anglo-American critics; in fact, *Pandora* was "annexed to the surrealist pantheon"—and to the New Wave pantheon—in France, where Ava Gardner as Pandora was described in deliriously surrealist prose under "G" in the *Cahiers du Cinéma*'s dictionary, "F comme femme," in its special number "La femme et le cinéma" (1953):

> Here Aurelia has the marine look and the salty tresses of Undine. . . . Ava Gardner's body is yet that of Pandora, the first woman, who, along with her hair, undoes the ties of all fatalities. . . . When the eyes of dawn open on the wet sands of an untouched beach, finally, when in the cabin mirror, Pandora reappears . . . now never to leave, . . . cinema, once again the magic lantern of our childhood, has borne us very far and very high on the wings of dreams.[35]

Ado Kyrou, France's most prolific late-surrealist film critic, also adored the film, characterizing Gardner's Pandora as, with Lya Lys (the star of Luis Buñuel and Salvador Dalí's *L'Age d'or*), "the only fiercely surrealist woman in all cinema."[36]

Even the detractors of *Pandora* have not all been unaware of its affiliation with surrealism, but some simply did not consider this a reliable endorsement. For instance, Russell Davies (who, like Milne, was reviewing it in London in 1985), described it as having been "received at the time with a barrage of maledictions ('utter poverty of imagination and taste' wrote C. A. Lejeune) but it appealed, so the re-releasers tell us, to the Surrealists. . . . It's the sort of mixture that commonly gets called 'high camp,' but it's much too inorganic and effortful to qualify. See it, by all means, in the company of a 1950s Surrealist, but remember—with rare exceptions, they were a notoriously po-faced lot."[37]

Pandora was, in fact, deliberately, and pointedly, surrealist, according to Lewin himself, who had become friendly with a number of surrealist artists, including Man Ray and Max Ernst, during the Second World War and who had, through them, begun collecting surrealist art.

> It was natural . . . that I should try to create a film with a deliberately surrealist intention. This desire took form in "Pandora and the Flying Dutchman." The surrealist practice of juxtaposing ancient and modern images, particularly evident in the work of de Chirico and of Paul Delvaux, especially moved me. . . . Among other surrealist incidents in the film I might call attention to the scene of the racing car on the beach—a modern machine being driven at great speed past the statue of a Greek goddess standing on the sands. As a matter of fact, it was this image which was the original thought that prompted me to develop the entire story and film of "Pandora."[38]

It was not only this visually surrealist orientation that interested many French critics, surrealists included, in *Pandora*. More generally, French intellectuals appreciated Lewin's attempt to reconcile the perceived contradictions between the "high art" of surrealism and the "low art" of Hollywood. Lewin, like André Breton, the father of surrealism, loved paradoxes and sought in all of his films to resolve "life and death, the real and the imagined, past and future, the communicable and the incommunicable."[39] As an author, too, he attempted to reconcile two aspects of his character that were always in tension in his films: the critic, ironic, academic, and skeptical; and the artist, sensitive, intuitive, and sincere.

Pandora's reception must be seen as a gauge of the success of this attempt. Its reception suggests that it was (and is) two different films: one a "masterpiece," the other a "supreme folly."[40] To many English and American critics—and (judging by its revenues) to audiences—it seemed to be virtually a travesty; but in France, critics and audiences saw something else. To this day, Americans persist in their discomfort with this unabashedly literary, self-conscious, and stylized work, while French audiences seem to appreciate the frisson created by the exercise of such self-consciousness within the studio idiom.

This disparity between the Americans and the French is not unique (though I do not want to equate it with their responses to either Jerry Lewis or Mickey Rourke). For instance, *Peter Ibbetson* (directed by Henry Hathaway) had "a mixed reception in 1935, when some critics thought that the elaborate dream sequences failed completely, but a few years later it was discovered by the French surrealists and claimed by André Breton as 'a triumph of surrealist thought,' using the cinema to 'turn our way of feeling upside down.'"[41]

One source of this discrepancy, no doubt, is language. Lewin himself described the problem in his eulogy for silent cinema, written on the eve of his debut as a director, "R.I.P.: Obituary for a Dead Art":

> It is probably true that since the invention of talking pictures not a single movie has been made which can be called a "work of art" in the unique and definitive sense in which the silent Chaplin pictures, "Caligari," "The Last Laugh" and "Potemkin" were works of art. . . . The only talking picture that approached being a work of art is "Maedchen in Uni-

form," and it may be that I think so only because I do not understand German. Foreign pictures often seem artistic to us because we do not understand the dialogue, and consequently are still regarding them as silent pictures.⁴²

This is a questionable observation generally, but it is obviously relevant to *Peter Ibbetson* and *Pandora,* two of the surrealist group's favorite Hollywood films. The often stiff, "unnatural" quality of the dialogue in these original and dreamlike fantasies cannot embarrass a foreign audience as it might a native one. The surrealists, and the French enthusiasts who came after them, clearly responded to the visual concreteness of the "dream work" in both of these films—not to the somewhat "creaky" scripts.⁴³

Hurd Hatfield with George Sanders in *The Picture of Dorian Gray* (1945).

Lewin's films are indeed characterized by their often disjunct combination of a verbose soundtrack with a highly mannered visual field, a result of Lewin's technique, which, as he himself and some of his more astute critics have noted, reflects his attachment to the aesthetics of silent film. As Sylvie Trosa remarks, "If a very pictorial, surrealist mise-en-scène seems related to the silent cinema . . . and has been lost, for some complex reasons, with the talkies and their realism, *Pandora* constitutes a sort of historic counterpoint, where, in a so-called 'Hollywood' production, Lewin risks the visual audacities of a poetry and of an invention that the talkies seem to have made impossible or at least 'silenced.'"[44]

This paradox—that a writer-director whose scripts were as "talky" as possible preferred and aspired to the qualities of silent film—is not as inscrutable as it might at first seem. There is a sense in which the excess of talk, especially in the form of voice-over narration, separates itself from the visual elements, as Richard Combs has suggested in his excellent analysis of *The Picture of Dorian Gray*:

> But to look for the seed of modernism in Lewin is to find it also in the most old-fashioned qualities of his cinema, in the strong trace of silent cinema where he (most loquacious of writer-directors) began after all. . . . The pile-up of dialogue itself begins to suggest another dimension, perhaps even to redefine the film altogether . . . towards a formal puzzle of appearances and reality, form and essence, body and soul. These are figured, as it were, in the interplay of vision and sound—or not so much an interplay, more an inconclusive confrontation. What the ceaseless epigrammatic wit of the dialogue seeks to describe, the visuals frame (like the portrait of Dorian Gray) mysteriously, "perfectly," impenetrably. *Dorian Gray* may be one of the few films that has actually weighed the value of a thousand words against that of a picture, and found the former infinitely distortable and the latter infinitely inscrutable. . . . The "picture" of Albert Lewin that emerges finally from *Dorian Gray* is not of a director who was a prisoner of his high-culture pretensions, but of one with a remarkable visual sensibility that has little to do with conventional notions of style.[45]

Today Lewin is, perhaps, on the verge of rehabilitation. Recent theorists have used the remarkable imagery of *The Picture of Dorian Gray*, in particular, to support certain complex notions about classical Hollywood cinema and the "cinematic apparatus" in general. Judith Mayne offers a particularly interesting argument about reflexivity and visual reflections in this film in her recent book, *Cinema and Spectatorship,* which devotes a chapter to the implications of portraits, mirrors, and other indications of specularity.[46] In an essay, Réda Bensmaïa concentrates on one stunning dissolve from *The Picture of Dorian Gray,* and goes on to argue, on this basis, that the cinema dissolve in general tends to present narrative content that is taboo, repressed, or disavowed.[47]

Intelligent and persuasive as these pieces are, however, both make certain common assumptions about the director as artist. Bensmaïa, with a sleight of hand all too familiar in structuralist theory, allows his own ignorance of Lewin's intentions to override the entire problem of intentionality: as a result, he takes Lewin's highly complex cinematic device not as the brilliant conceit of an individual author but rather as a typical cinematic function. Mayne is more cognizant of Lewin's part but remains uninterested in pursuing it, betraying two widespread tendencies in contemporary film theory: an unease with auteurism and a tendency to describe many effects of Hollywood cinema as functions of the unconscious—the author's, the spectator's, or the cultural unconscious. I do not wish to argue with the psychoanalytic view of the unconscious that underlies these two critics' premises, or with the notion that the unconscious plays a significant role in shaping the cinematic experience. For me these are givens. But in examining Lewin's works, I believe, his very assertive presence as author must be considered. Any view that neglects this presence is likely to overlook, and to misconstrue, much of importance.

"There are unconscious artists and others who are perfectly conscious," wrote Jean Renoir, just as the New Wave was about to begin. "The former are neither inferior nor superior to the latter. But the latter are indispensable in periods of transition. Albert Lewin is indispensable to our epoch."[48]

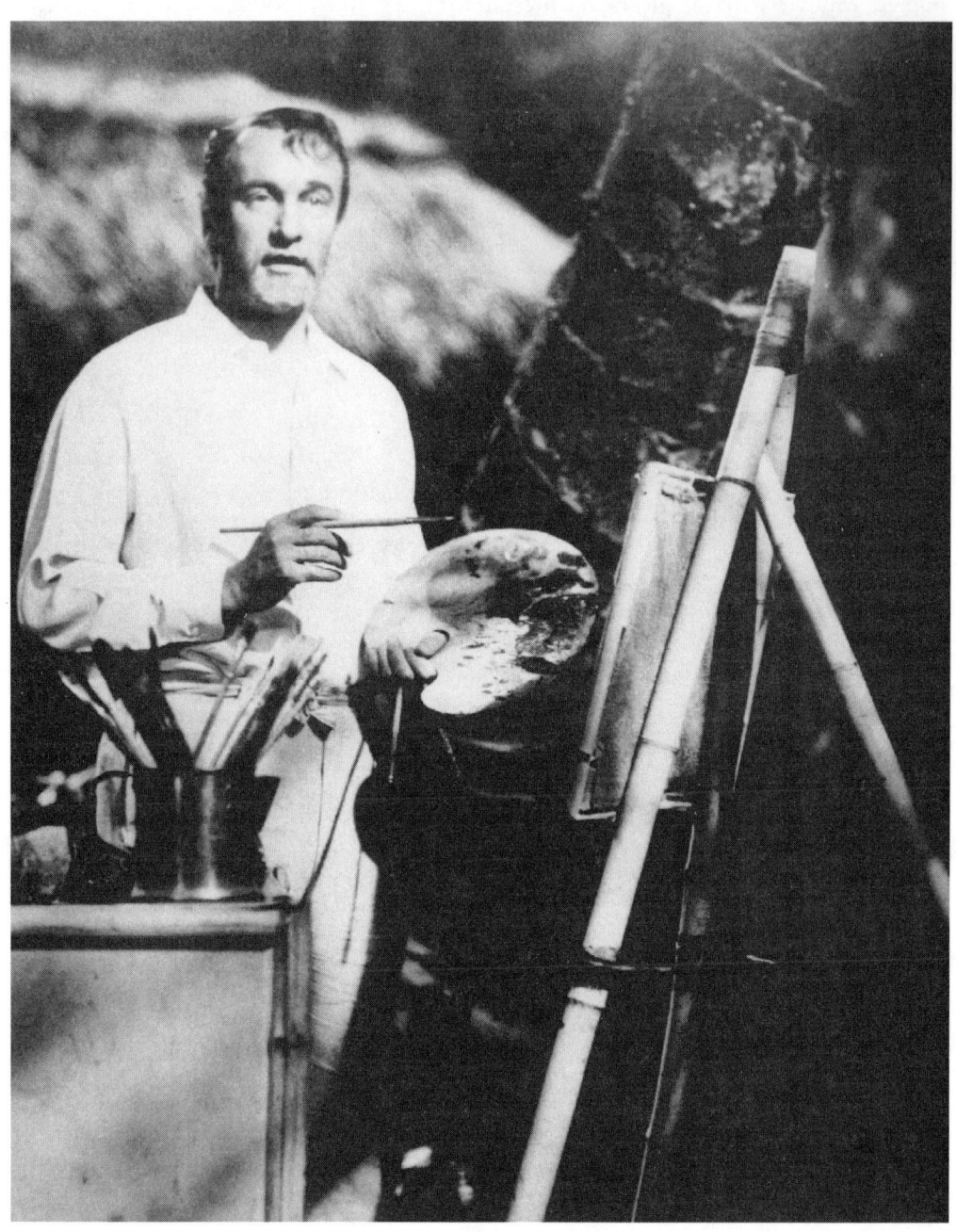

The Moon and Sixpence (1942). Charles Strickland (George Sanders) at the easel.

CHAPTER 1

Botticelli in Hollywood:
The Moon and Sixpence (1942)

> The Sears Roebuck catalogue had nothing to do with my delay in writing to you. I have begun to be a little busy at last with a book called *"The Moon and Sixpence."* The catalogue might make a very good movie, but it's all I can do to tackle a simple narrative.
> Albert Lewin, 1941[1]

Albert Lewin, who had been more or less successful and more or less satisfied as a producer at two major studios for almost fifteen years, embarked on his career as an auteur—as he would later often claim—for financial reasons. He and his old college friend David Loew had formed a small independent production company, and according to Lewin, Loew suggested that it would be cost-efficient for Lewin, who had once been a screenwriter, to undertake the adaptation of Somerset Maugham's novel *The Moon and Sixpence* himself: "I hadn't written a script for fifteen years. David wanted to save the price of a writer, so he turned to me, 'You're a writer. For God's sake, write.'" When Lewin had successfully accomplished that task, he later recalled, "we began looking for a director, but a big director in those days cost around $100,000. David said, 'Why the hell don't you direct it? Look at all the money we'd save.' This was a case of economic determinism."[2]

The Moon and Sixpence (1942) was shot quickly and inexpensively,[3] and because of its relatively low cost and its considerable popularity, it was more profitable than any other of Lewin's films. In a sense, it can be seen as a dress rehearsal for the two films that followed it in the 1940s, *The Picture of Dorian Gray* and *The Private Affairs of Bel Ami*. However, both of these later films would be planned and executed far more carefully and far more expensively; and *The Moon and Sixpence* is less consistent than either of them in its construction of a highly formalized, artificial mise-en-scène, less deliberate in its performances and pacing, and less daring in its anachronisms.

One important aspect of *The Moon and Sixpence* was unusual at the time it was made but may fail to strike us now—that is, its narration. In a note to a friend (Ernestine Evans), Lewin had described the novel as a "simple narrative," but it is hardly that. His solution to the problem of adapting it involved a relatively early instance of voice-over narration. Lewin was particularly pleased with this solution (as was Maugham himself)[4] and believed that he had actually introduced the technique to Hollywood.

The Moon and Sixpence

London, late nineteenth and early twentieth century. The events of the film are told retrospectively from the point of view of a narrator, Geoffrey Wolfe (Herbert Marshall), a successful English novelist. A newspaper article on a posthumous exhibition of the work of the painter Charles Strickland causes Wolfe to reflect on his acquaintance with Strickland, whose genius was recognized only after his death.

Wolfe first knew Strickland (George Sanders) as a dull stockbroker, the husband of Amy Strickland (Molly Lamont), a woman with literary aspirations who cultivated talented young people such as Wolfe himself. When her husband suddenly runs off to Paris, abandoning her and their two children, his wife, assuming there is another woman involved, asks Wolfe to undertake a mission to restore Strickland to his senses and his responsibilities. As much out of curiosity as loyalty, Wolfe obliges, finds Strickland in a shabby Parisian garret, and is surprised to learn that Strickland has always harbored a fervent wish to paint and has escaped his bourgeois life not for a woman but for art.

Strickland is not persuaded to return to his family, so Wolfe returns to London without him, and Amy soon files for divorce. In the ensuing years, Wolfe checks up on Strickland periodically and learns of the poverty, squalor, and moral dissolution that are the climate of the painter's devotion to his new vocation. When Strickland's destitution eventually leads to illness, his life is saved by Dirk Stroeve (Steve Geray), a Dutch painter of inferior gifts but great generosity and judgment who recognizes Strickland's otherwise unappreciated genius, takes Strickland into his home, and nurses him—against the wishes of his wife, Blanche (Doris Dudley), who abhors the cruel and misanthropic Strickland.

As Strickland recovers, his behavior toward Stroeve is selfish, ungrateful, and disparaging. It also becomes plain that Blanche's aversion to Strickland has been motivated in part by sexual attraction; she soon leaves her loving husband for Strickland, and when Strickland in turn spurns her, she commits suicide. Strickland, who has ruined the life of his one devoted admirer, and who has longed for "an island, somewhere off the map," leaves Paris and, after a time in Marseilles, ends up in Tahiti.

There, after Strickland's death, Wolfe learns about the painter's last years from three people: a retired seaman (Eric Blore); a Eurasian hotelkeeper, Tiaré Johnson (Florence Bates); and a local doctor (Albert Basserman). Strickland had married a young Tahitian woman, Ata (Elena Verdugo), gained a growing sense of peace and satisfaction, and then contracted and slowly succumbed to leprosy; thereafter, Ata—following his wishes—burned the hut containing his masterpieces: "indescribably wonderful and mysterious" murals painted while he was blind and in the last stages of his disease.

It is true that voice-over narration—a device which is now associated particularly with the rather self-conscious genre of film noir—had rarely, if ever, been used in the 1930s, for reasons having to do, above all, with the antinaturalistic effect of such techniques. Sarah Kozloff argues that the first decade of talking pictures was characterized by overidentification with theater, and that fascination with the novelty of synchronous speech militated against any use of external narration. However, using a very broad definition of the term "voice-over narration," she dates the widespread introduction of the technique in the United States to 1939, when "several major releases incorporating voice-over, including *Wuthering Heights, Juarez, The Roaring Twenties,* and *Confessions of a Nazi Spy,* simultaneously appeared, and the ice was broken. At the start of the 1940s the stream of narrated films deepened into a flood." By Kozloff's criteria, then, Lewin was mistaken in thinking that he had brought voice-over narration to Hollywood; nevertheless, few of the earlier films she cites were so structurally dependent on it as *The Moon and Sixpence.*[5]

The antinaturalism of voice-over narration is strikingly illustrated in the opening scene, which, in the final film, is realized very much according to Lewin's script:

> This introductory episode is played between the rich and famous popular novelist, Geoffrey Wolfe, and his valet [Maitland, whose] . . . activity primarily consists of picking things up—a movement which punctuates the monologue of the novelist. At no time do Geoffrey and his valet betray, by the slightest sign, that either is aware of the other's presence. Geoffrey's remarks are not addressed to Maitland and they are ignored by him. The monologue is a comment meant for the audience and Geoffrey and Maitland never once look at each other.[6]

In this scene, Geoffrey, the narrator, directly addresses the audience (that is, the camera) from unusual vantage points, such as his mirror (while he is shaving) and his bathtub. This is rather irregular for a character in a Hollywood drama, even for a narrator, who typically is omniscient and invisible (as is the case in Lewin's next film, *The Picture of Dorian Gray*) or addresses the narration, more naturalistically, to someone or something within the film itself. (An example of the latter is found in the framing scenes of Billy Wilder's *Double Indemnity,* 1944, when the character played by Fred MacMurray records a confession into a dictaphone, intending it to be heard by the investigator, played by Edward G. Robinson.) The opening scene of *The Moon and Sixpence,* then—which is also the opening scene of Lewin's directorial work—announces a singular disregard for certain conventions of Hollywood drama. For a character to look at the audience—the camera—so directly is rare in Hollywood cinema, and when it happens at all, the context is usually a special genre, such as a comedy or a musical, in which absorption in a naturalized dramatic scene is not the desired effect.[7]

Indeed, this opening scene, although it frames a very serious and disturbing story, plays much more like comedy than like drama, and that is also true of several other scenes. This equivocation—the sense that there is no definite commitment to humor or to gravity—may have originated in the literary source. *The Moon and Sixpence,* based loosely on the life of the French postimpressionist painter Paul Gauguin, is an equivocal novel. Maugham's narration has an arrogant, misanthropic tone, and the inherently dramatic tale of passion, genius, and degradation is told from a strangely ironic and supercilious distance. As I have discussed in the Introduction, Lewin's choice of this particular material for his film debut reveals what one might call a certain perversity.

In his review for *Commonweal,* Philip T. Hartung described *The Moon and Sixpence* as "a strange picture—perhaps as strange as W. Somerset Maugham's novel; and it is unusually faithful to the original novel, at least in spirit. It neither condemns nor defends Charles Strickland as it reveals the extraordinary story of the man who, at the age of 40 after many years of life as a prosaic London stockbroker, suddenly deserts his wife and children to go to Paris to become a painter."[8] Hartung remarks on what would become one of the most consistent themes in Lewin's works, the morally neutral or ambivalent treatment of deliberately shocking material. Especially in the films of the 1940s, Lewin's protagonists, exhibiting disdain and effrontery toward general mores, stand out in sharp relief against a carefully conventionalized social fabric.

George Sanders plays Strickland almost as two separate characters. The first character is a bland pillar of family and society, whose flaccid gestures and facial expressions (the voice-over narration allows this character to be seen but not heard in the pantomimed scenes that precede Strickland's transformation) betray a colorless, meager temperment. The second character—endowed with the superior, scornful voice for which Sanders became famous—is a man possessed. The transformed Strickland is so consumed by his desire to paint that he has abandoned all remnants of etiquette and propriety. His obsession allows or forces him to manifest an indiscriminate cruelty toward anyone and anything that impedes him. His worst cruelties injure the only person who recognizes his genius, Dirk Stroeve (played by Steve Geray), a Dutch artist of mediocre talents but excellent judgment; and a woman, Dirk's wife Blanche (Doris Dudley), who despite her better judgment desires Strickland passionately and fatally.

Strickland's cruelty is evident in his brutal, acerbic remarks and in his conduct, and it is also represented symbolically or, as Lewin put it (applying the term rather loosely), "metonymically." Lewin described one example as follows: "George Sanders is talking to this unfortunate Dutch painter, whose wife he has seduced and who has

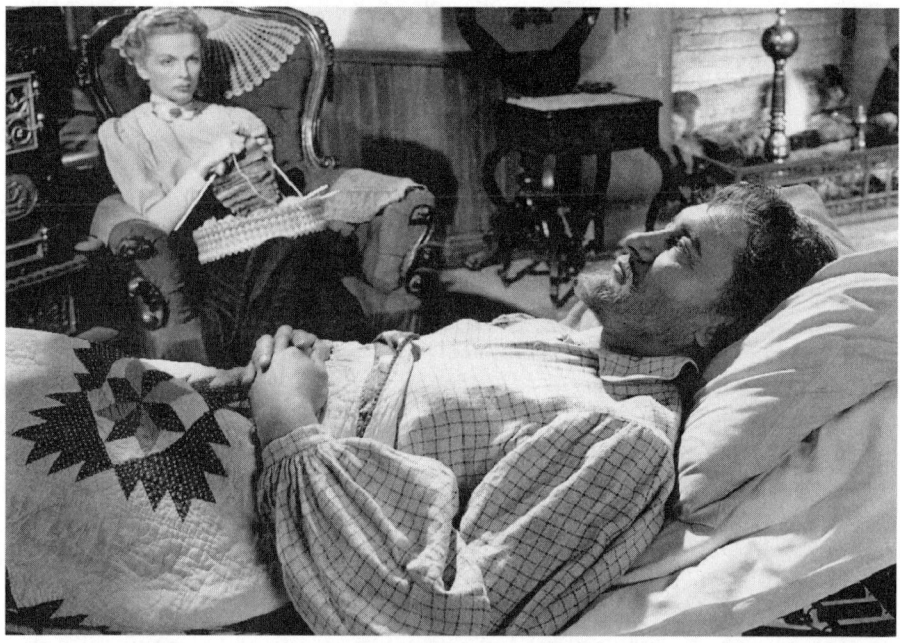

Strickland, during an illness, is watched over by Blanche Stroeve (Doris Dudley).

subsequently committed suicide. And he's a rather sadistic character. So during this scene I had him grinding paint in a mortar and I had him tightening a canvas on a stretcher. Well, that's perfectly normal business for a painter to do. However, in this situation it's what I would call a kind of metonymous symbolism."9

Blanche's fatal attraction to Strickland is echoed by that of the young Tahitian woman, Ata (Elena Verdugo), who becomes Strikland's second wife in his island paradise and shows her desire very plainly. (In the film, unlike the novel, for reasons dictated by the censors—that is, the Hays office—Strickland divorces his first wife and marries Ata.) These female characters are clichés in conception and realization, embodying a schism between the transcendent passion for art of the masculine "genius" and the immanent passion for love of the feminine sensibility; nevertheless, this film anticipates the startling focus on a male object of female desire that is central to Lewin's next two films.

The three films of the 1940s are characterized by tension between a compelling sense of self-agency in the female characters and a deep misogyny in the male characters, particularly in whichever character is played by George Sanders (Strickland in *The Moon and Sixpence,* Lord Henry Wotton in *The Picture of Dorian Gray,* and Georges Duroy in *The Private Affairs of Bel Ami*). But women seem weakest in *The Moon and Sixpence,* a film based on a deeply misogynistic novel, in which Blanche's and Ata's desire for Strickland is seen as instinctive and masochistic. One female character, Tiaré Johnson (Florence Bates), a good-humored, fat, middle-aged Eurasian hotelkeeper on Tahiti, is allowed a fairly robust sexuality, which is manifested in her keen reminiscences of her six marriages, in her aggressive matchmaking, and—during the scene of Strickland's and Ata's wedding feast—in a ribald dance of which she is the focus. In *The Picture of Dorian Gray* and *The Private Affairs of Bel Ami,* younger,

On Tahiti, the Eurasian girl Ata (Elena Verdugo) is introduced to Strickland by her aunt, Tiaré Johnson (Florence Bates).

more conventionally desirable female characters show active sexual desire and—like the films themselves—take a male character (the title character) as their object. This intriguing and quite unusual aspect of these films will be examined in more depth in Chapters 2 and 3; at this point, though, it should be noted that such treatment of sex roles and sexuality, perhaps inevitably, created friction between Lewin and the Hollywood censors, internal and external, whose business it was or who made it their business to protect innocent moviegoers from corruption and sin.

The following letter—which Lewin wrote, but evidently did not send, to the Reverend Patrick Masterson of the Legion of Decency—is an example of that friction:

> I am not entirely unfamiliar with the great Catholic writers, and I do not believe there is any incompatibility between Christian morality and good literary style. I still think that the final title in its present form is in execrable taste, whatever other virtues it may have. As a matter of fact, it is not only badly written, but gratuitous besides, since it says nothing which has not already been far more effectively shown in the picture....
>
> But if you are convinced that the bad rhetoric with which the picture now ends is necessary to save Christian morality in a world in which it is struggling so desperately for survival, I am prepared to make this slight sacrifice for so great a cause.[10]

The Legion of Decency was a Roman Catholic reviewing and rating body that exerted enormous pressure on the film industry to censor itself and threatened to boycott it if such censorship was not forthcoming.[11] Lewin's hackles were raised because the Legion of Decency had, over his strong protests, attached a moralistic "warning" to the opening and closing credit sequences of *The Moon and Sixpence*. "They made me put a terrible title on the front of the picture which read something like this: 'We don't want you to have the impression that the character we are telling the story about is an admirable character. He is not.' And then we had to repeat that at the end of the film. The phrasing wasn't even good English.... I rewrote the title.... They thought about it and read it and reread it and then decided to accept it. I was relieved.... I took the train to California. I got to my office and I found a letter on my desk. They had changed their minds. It went back to the original title. I guess they didn't trust me, even if they couldn't see why. Maugham hated it. Everybody hated it. It finally got lost on most of the prints."[12]

Lewin's protests notwithstanding, it is quite clear why the Legion of Decency was up in arms. Depravity was of considerable interest to Lewin; it is more than hinted at not only in *The Moon and Sixpence* but in all his films. Whatever else he may be, Charles Strickland is a pathological character—narcissistic, grandiose, utterly lacking in empathy, and given to acts of gratuitous cruelty.

Yet *The Moon and Sixpence* is not so much about a depraved human being as about an *artist*. Maugham's novel and Lewin's film both take the life of Gauguin as an exemplary instance of "genius" escaping its bonds, and each is an attempt to fathom the forces that might enable a "civilized" man to release himself from whatever is assumed to constrain or inhibit this genius. Both novel and film, however, reveal a certain cynicism, and neither succeeds in finding the germ or spark that could explain the mysterious workings of art. The investigative format, whereby Geoffrey Wolfe—rather like the reporter in *Citizen Kane*—interviews various people who had encountered Strickland during his years in Tahiti, allows Strickland's life to be reconstructed topically, but it leaves the ultimate questions unanswered. In *The Moon and Sixpence*, there is no "Rosebud," no symbol standing for something that has been irretrievably lost. If there is any comparable symbol, it is much more obscure: it stands, instead, for some-

At a café in Paris, Geoffrey Wolfe (Herbert Marshall) watches Strickland drawing an image of a Tahitian idol, as the painter confesses that he has "sometimes thought of an island, somewhere off the map. . . ."

thing that was never possessed at all and therefore could not be lost or was in a sense "always already lost."

In Strickland's bare, sordid garret in Paris, an idol stands—a Tahitian idol. This idol is not part of the narrative exposition, but it figures prominently in several scenes set in Paris. During the film's most probing dialogue, set in a café, Strickland obsessively sketches the idol as Geoffrey seeks explanations. "Don't you want fame?" Geoffrey asks. The painter answers, "I've sometimes thought of an island, somewhere off the map, where I could live and work in a hidden valley, among strange trees, alone, in silence"— and as he speaks, he sketches the Tahitian idol from memory. In discussing this film years after it was made, Lewin characterized this idol, perhaps paradoxically, as signifying Strickland's "nostalgia" for Tahiti, a place where Strickland has not yet been: "The symbol was not at all metonymous, it was actual. You see, in Somerset Maugham's brilliant book, there was nothing that I could actually photograph that represented the nostalgia of this painter for the tropics. So very early in the film you will observe there was this image. This image was carved by a very talented Icelandic sculptress named Nina Saemundsson, deriving, however, from an actual painting by Gauguin, and it is a Tahitian goddess, and the painter acquires this even in Paris. And you see at the end of the sequence, I drew the camera back and this image came up very prominently in the foreground."[13]

Although Lewin's choice of the word "nostalgia" may seem paradoxical, it was certainly deliberate, as is suggested by the fact that the later scenes set in Tahiti were filmed in sepia, as opposed to the standard black-and-white of the scenes in London and Paris. This use of sepia is surprising: one might suppose that if the palette shifted at all, Strickland's island paradise would be shown in color. In Tahiti, Strickland finds liberation and vision—the clarity and freedom that he had sought and that enable him to paint masterpieces whose vivid color has been implied—and so color (much like Dorothy's dream in *The Wizard of Oz*) would seem appropriate, in opposition to the black-and-white prosaism of the world he has left behind. But in *The Moon and Sixpence,* color is reserved for a brief glimpse of Strickland's Tahitian paintings; the island paradise itself is rendered in the softer sepia tones generally associated with age, with photographs of the irretrievable past. The nostalgia whose object is always absent—because it has never been possessed and thus was "always already lost"—provides the palette that turns the world to sepia. Visions that are meant to be "indescribably wonderful and mysterious . . . tremendous, sensual, passionate, . . . horrible . . . primeval . . . terrible . . . magic . . . beautiful and obscene" images of the birth of the world, painted by a blind man in the last stages of leprosy,[14] take their color and vividness from the strength of something internal—and also from something eternal, something that seems to be a union of memory, desire, and phylogeny.

In passages such as this, Maugham's novel and, somewhat more ambivalently, Lewin's film articulate a myth of modernist primitivism strongly associated with Gauguin. As Abigail Solomon-Godeau has described it: "Gauguin's voyage of life was perceived in both the most literal and gratifyingly symbolic sense as a voyage ever further outward, to the periphery and margins, to what lies outside the parameters of the superego and the polis. . . . Common to both the embrace of the primitive—however defined—and the celebration of artistic originality is the belief that both enterprises are animated by the artist's privileged access, be it spiritual, intellectual or psychological, to that which is primordially internal. . . . The artist 'recognizes' in the primitive artifact that which was immanent, but inchoate; the object from 'out there' enables the expression of what is thought to be 'in there.'"[15]

At the end of the film, when Strickland's work is seen for the first time, Lewin had intended to reproduce an actual Gauguin painting, *Where Do We Come From? What Are We? Where Are We Going?* (1897). He had obtained permission from the Boston Museum of Fine Arts, but as the production was about to get under way, he was threatened with a lawsuit by one of Gauguin's sons and had to abandon the plan.[16] Lewin satisfied himself with translating Gauguin's pictures into some of his own filmic compositions. For instance, several shots of Ata recall Gauguin's paintings of Tahitian women seated on the ground. One scene, set in the darkened hut after Strickland's death, shows the grieving Ata lying facedown in the dark, suggesting Gauguin's *Manao tupapau* (1892) or *Nevermore* (1897). A Tahitian man is seen in the exact pose of *Man with an Ax* (1891). The wedding feast recalls *Upaupa* (1891).

But without Gauguin's paintings, Lewin was faced with the problem of finding suitable pictures to show when Strickland's exotic masterpieces, the wall paintings in his Tahitian house, are revealed in color at the climax of the film. To produce these paintings, he hired a young Russian painter named Dolya Goutman, who "had to create works of genius in about a week. I knew that Dolya Goutman, or Leonardo da Vinci, could not . . . and so what I did was this: I got a copy, a photograph, of a very famous painting (well, there's probably no more famous painting except the Mona Lisa). The painting was [Sandro] Botticelli's *Spring,* and I had Botticelli's *Spring* blown up until it was the size of a whole wall and then I said to Dolya Goutman that he should repaint all the classical figures, not change the composition a bit, but to make all the figures Tahitian girls, . . . and the cypress trees . . . all palms. And Dolya did that. . . . And we did another painting, on the other wall, by a pupil of Leonardo's named Bernadino Luini, of Milan. It was called *The Bath of the Nymphs.* It was a rather neo-

Strickland at his wedding feast in Tahiti.

classical canvas with nymphs around a formal pool. And that became a Tahitian pool, with Tahitian girls around it and palm trees, too. Of course that wasn't so dangerous because he wasn't quite so well known a painter, but I was terribly worried about Botticelli. So when the picture came out, finally, I was waiting in fear and trembling for someone in the audience to jump up and cry out, 'Botticelli, Botticelli!' And not a single person *ever* discovered it—no critic, nobody in the audience, nothing!"[17]

In fact, Goutman's murals are not particularly distinguished paintings; they hardly could be, considering the circumstances under which they were made. Not only were they executed in a week (if Lewin's account is accurate), but they were destined to be burned to the ground, along with the hut for which they were made, in the final Tahitian scene—in which Strickland's widow, Ata, acting on his prior instructions, runs from his grave with a torch and sets the whole place afire. Nor were the murals well received by the critics who bothered to remark on them, and (as Lewin observed) none of these critics recognized Botticelli. Philip Hartung, who rather liked the film, considered the paintings its "greatest flaw . . . showing us some third-rate art in technicolor near the film's end and telling us that this is the work of a great artist. Why, if we must be shown the products of this film's supposed genius, couldn't we be shown something approaching competence?"[18]

Actually, Technicolor was not used for the color insert, although virtually every critic described it as Technicolor. As Lewin later explained:

> Technicolor at that time had a monopoly on color in Hollywood, and they were able to dictate exactly what they would do. They saw no particular percentage . . . in putting a Technicolor insert in a black-and-white picture. They refused to do it . . . and we were determined to have color anyhow. Actually, the color scenes . . . were photographed in

A detail of Strickland's "masterpiece." This pastiche, based on Paul Gauguin's "primitivism" and a Botticelli composition, was executed on the back lot by a young Russian artist, Dolya Goutman (photo from *Life* Magazine).

16mm Kodachrome. The original Kodachrome was very beautiful, but of course we couldn't make prints from it. The problem was to transfer to a negative from which prints could be made and we had to do that in a two-color, rather than in a three-color process, and the loss of quality was enormous.[19]

Whether it was a "masterpiece" or a "travesty," the painting used to illustrate Strickland's achievement returns us to the question of nostalgia. Although Gauguin had been Lewin's first choice as Strickland's surrogate, his second choice—Botticelli—was perhaps not made at random. The superimposition of exotic detail over a Renaissance composition that itself relied on a mythic reconstruction of the classical, whatever its aesthetic failings, expresses rather well the complex origins of such seemingly unmediated pictures as Gauguin's Tahitian work.[20] In a letter which was written a few

Sandro Botticelli. *La Primavera (Spring)*, c. 1480

years after the film was made, and in which much consideration is given to the beauty of the lost medieval French of the *Tristan et Yseut* by the trouvère Beroul (c. 1190), Lewin digresses toward the Renaissance:

> How is it possible to carry over this extraordinary language, not merely the verse, but the language itself, in which all the syllables are softly spoken, the word-endings so feminine as to be downright erotic? I imagine Italian is a little like this lost language, as tender and golden as infantile excrement—a brief and felicitous interlude between Latin and French, as fleeting as Villon's neiges d'antan.... The women of Botticelli are full of his never-slaked yearning for the model, Simonetta I think her name was, who found him what the French call "sympathique," which means that they like you but prefer to go to bed with someone else. In Botticelli's case, perhaps it was just as well; he put his yearning into the painting instead of the model. His rivals had Simonetta, but didn't paint her as well. Botticelli would understand the nostalgia of Tristan and his language—the neo-romantic suffused with classic souvenirs. Nostalgia is the clue to a great deal. Love is the nostalgia of the embryo—instinct the nostalgia of the will—sleep the nostalgia of the anatomy itelf. In our dreams our ontology goes home to its philogenetic mother. We swim again, and fly, or break the penitentiary seed-pods in the ooze. This is the enchantment which the early de Chirico understood, and toward which the surrealists strain.[21]

Here Lewin, at his most romantic, waxes transhistorical, ranging across centuries of humankind and of western art, and expresses a somewhat morbid faith in the inchoate and undifferentiated preservation of traces of the past, both cultural and biological, in the aspirations and accomplishments of the greatest art. No distinction is made between desire and nostalgia; they are both described as ineffable, unfulfillable, ultimately objectless states. And these states are seen as symptoms of an existential condition, which the greatest of art somehow evokes. This is very close to the myth of modernist primitivism that Solomon-Godeau demystifies, a myth that is itself a permutation of earlier myths of artistic genius. Yet sometimes in his films, as well as in his writings, Lewin betrays a strain of doubt or skepticism regarding the cult of genius that at other times he seems to support.

Lewin had already put this ambivalence into words in 1925, in a published story, "Botticelli in Hollywood," about the pathological possibilities of the cult of genius carried to its most horrible extremes.[22] The narrator describes an encounter in a Hollywood restaurant with a young artist who is literally and deliberately "starving," denying himself nourishment while surrounding himself with the most luscious foods, in order to paint a sea bass, "as if it were the one final and quintessential fish," or "an orange that would have lived forever as a symbol of all oranges, the genius and Deucalion of its race, rich, sweet, flooded internally with the delectable juices of the golden citron."[23] As the artist explains to the narrator:

> It was because he could not possess her himself that Botticelli was able to arrest and suspend the ideal Simonetta sub species aeternitatis for the delight of all the world.... I am disciplining myself to be nothing more or less than the Botticelli of the dining room wall—where Botticelli was denied the possession of the woman he loved, I consciously deny myself possession of the food which I crave, and as from his denial flowered Spring and The Birth of Venus, from mine shall some day be expressed the imperishable projection of the spirit of food.[24]

In its language, "Botticelli in Hollywood" is very literary—some would say "arty" or "pretentious." One suspects, however, that the author of this story about the question of whether "to eat or not to eat" might have had his tongue in his cheek. Using Botticelli as the paradigm of an artist whose genius not only transcends but actually feeds upon his desire—that is, what in psychoanalytic terms is called sublimation—Lewin goes on to travesty this paradigm, and perhaps also to travesty Hollywood. The actual Botticelli's desire is for a beautiful woman and is transformed into the perfection of works such as *The Birth of Venus* and *La Primavera (Spring);* but in "Botticelli in Hollywood," the artist's desire is for food, and the perfect paintings of food that he would make are blank canvases. His desire is "lower," or so to speak more "vulgar," than Botticelli's, just as commercial cinema was considered by many to be lower and more vulgar than theater and the other plastic arts. Toward the end of "Botticelli in Hollywood," Lewin invokes Edgar Allan Poe's story "The Oval Portrait," in which a young bride's "blood lent color to the painter's brush until her own life passed into his ideal creation—the obverse to the classic story of Galatea and Pygmalion."[25] The sense of awe and horror that Lewin's narrator conveys is countered by rather parodic "purple prose," as in the story's penultimate line: "Oh brave, true Botticelli of the entrails, you merit a more distinguished encomium than mine."[26]

This is not an isolated instance of self-conscious excess. A faint aura of travesty surrounds all of Lewin's work. It is a quality to which critics such as Andrew Sarris have responded with distaste, assuming it to be naive, vulgar, snobbish, or pretentious. What I call travesty,[27] and others call vulgarity, might be interpreted as an inevitable result of Lewin's avowed aspiration to make films "both commercial and artistic," an aspiration many see as pure folly. I am inclined, however, to see it also as a function of two other tendencies that were in tension throughout Lewin's directorial career: first, to evoke the magic, horror, and beauty of art and of the natural and cultural world; but, second, to draw back, to place himself at a distance from and adopt a skeptical and analytic attitude toward art, toward convention, and even toward himself. Lewin the equilibrist was also an equivocator. He wanted to eat his cake and have it: to indulge in the sensual delights of cinema and to criticize these as well.

The Picture of Dorian Gray (1945). Dorian (Hurd Hatfield) enters the Two Turtles, a tawdry London pub, with "Dr. Look" visible behind him.

CHAPTER 2

Dr. Look: *The Picture of Dorian Gray* (1945)

If something cannot be done to check, or at least to modify, our monstrous worship of facts, Art will become sterile and beauty will pass from the land.... The moment Art surrenders its imaginative medium it surrenders everything.... As a method realism is a complete failure.

Oscar Wilde[1]

In going from the spectacular to the real the movies are losing something for which they will not be compensated until they go on from the real to the symbolic. The danger in the commonplace is dullness. People want to be thrilled.

Albert Lewin[2]

In its characteristic tension between artistic "sincerity" and critical irony, Lewin's work echoed not only Maugham, but also the authors of the other two works Lewin adapted in the 1940s, Guy de Maupassant and, especially, Oscar Wilde. Barbara Charlesworth claims that Wilde can be best understood "by separating him, as he separated himself, into several selves (each, however, watching the other selves and offering comments upon or even engaging in dialogues with the self at stage-center), remembering always that the man and his work are inextricable, though the work too is a mask."[3] Wilde and Lewin shared not only their highly introspective, rather fractured self-criticism, but also several literary opinions. High among these was their disdain for realism, which had been the dominant literary mode in Wilde's time and was the dominant filmic mode in Lewin's. Max Tessier nicely expresses this by describing Lewin as having "entered the delicate and poisonous universe of Oscar Wilde with the ease of a gentleman of the same spiritual family, dissatisfied with the world as it is and little interested in undertaking to modify it."[4]

But *The Picture of Dorian Gray,* a film made in 1945 under the auspices of one of Hollywood's largest and most conservative studios, was under a good deal more pressure to conform to conventional realism than a novel could be, particularly the novel on which it was based—written by Wilde in 1890, when he was already famous, or infamous, as an aesthete.[5] And this film, Lewin's second directorial project, was criticized at the time of its release, and has been criticized ever since, for literary pretentiousness, for making compromises with Hollywood, or for both.

The Picture of Dorian Gray

London, 1886. Lord Henry Wotton (George Sanders) drops in on a friend, the painter Basil Hallward (Lowell Gilmore), and finds him finishing a portrait of a beautiful young man, Dorian Gray (Hurd Hatfield). As Dorian poses, Henry seduces the youth with his wit and his cynical, hedonistic worldview. When Dorian sees the completed portrait, he wistfully makes a Faustian bargain: he would give up his soul to remain always as he appears in the portrait, while the painting should age instead. Under Henry's influence, and following his own obscure, now unleashed impulses, Dorian seeks out new and sensual experiences. At a tawdry pub in London's "half-world," he is charmed by an innocent young singer, Sibyl Vane (Angela Lansbury), with whom he falls in love. Learning that Dorian has proposed to Sibyl, Henry diabolically suggests that Dorian test her virtue by asking her to spend the night with him. Dorian, though initially shocked by the suggestion, succumbs to its appeal; Sibyl consents and thus "fails" the test; Dorian then heartlessly breaks off their engagement. A glance at Basil's portrait then reveals it altered by a touch of cruelty. Reflecting, Dorian has regrets, but before he can rectify the situation he learns of Sibyl's suicide. He is briefly remorseful but soon "recovers" and throws himself into a dissolute life of pleasure and sensation.

Nearly twenty years pass. Rumors about Dorian's degeneracy abound, but his friends, seeing only his unmarred, youthful beauty, cannot believe ill of him. Gladys Hallward (Donna Reed), Basil's young niece, has come to love her uncle's handsome friend, despite the attentions of her suitor David Stone (Peter Lawford). Dorian, who retains a vestige of virtue, cherishes Gladys's esteem but keeps her at arm's length. When Basil visits Dorian to confront him with his wicked reputation, Dorian is stirred to reveal the picture of his corrupt soul that has long been hidden away. As Basil, in shock, implores Dorian to repent, Dorian is overcome by fear that his secret will be divulged, and by hatred for the painter. He murders Basil and then blackmails an acquaintance, Alan Campbell (Douglas Walton), into disposing of the body. The mystery of Basil's disappearance remains unsolved, and Dorian is never connected to it. But with Campbell's subsequent suicide, Dorian's culpability for two more deaths is etched in blood on the portrait.

Hoping that her goodness will redeem him, Dorian becomes engaged to Gladys, but still he cannot resist the lure of transgression. In a den of iniquity, Dorian encounters an embittered acquaintance who identifies him to James Vane (Richard Fraser), Sibyl's brother, who has long burned to avenge Sibyl. When Vane is accidentally killed while stalking Dorian at his country estate, Dorian feels a last pang of decency. Resolving to spare Gladys, he leaves her and returns to London, hoping to see his sacrifice as a slight erasure upon his portrait. Then, wishing to undo the diabolical compact, Dorian assaults the painting. But when he thrusts a knife into the breast of the monstrous figure portrayed, he falls over dead. When his body is discovered, it has assumed all the ravages of the portrait, and the portrait has reverted to its original, pristine state.

Nonetheless, *The Picture of Dorian Gray* is certainly Lewin's most critically acclaimed film and is arguably his best. While avoiding the dangers of the commonplace, it remained subject to the dangers of Lewin's tightrope act, his equilibristic attempt to reconcile intellectualism and artistry with commercial viability; but these unavoidable dangers constitute much of its historical importance and its fascination. In several ways, this film is a striking mediation between Wilde's perhaps effete aestheticism and Hollywood's conventional realism: in its visual presentation of a text that was not very visually descriptive; in its divergence—often necessitated by the Production Code—from Wilde's narrative; and in its representation and symbolization of content that was explicitly disallowed or formally problematic.[6] Above all, *The Picture of Dorian Gray* is notable for its preoccupation with visuality—a thematic concern of Wilde's novel and, of course, the very essence of cinema. In fact, this film is an almost clinical case study of the specular: of mirrors and mirror images. Exactingly yet lovingly, virtually every frame is designed as an affront to conventional cinematic pleasures, an affront that is at the same time seductive.

In Wilde's novel, the pursuit of aesthetic pleasure and the fatal desire to possess it are depicted as material and sensuous; in contrast, cinema is by its very nature intangible: its picture moves and mutates. Like the enchanted picture of the title—the portrait of Dorian Gray—cinema can be neither fixed nor held. Because of this evanescence, Lewin's film tends to focus on visual pleasures and on visualized pressures (gazes, reflections, fetishes), rather than on Wilde's more catholic array of Epicurean pleasures where they border on sensual passion and folly.[7] Many critics would be inclined to investigate the visual qualities of Lewin's film as examples of cinematic excess—as material from outside the story itself which represents a return of something usually repressed for the sake of narrative homogeneity.[8] But knowledge of Lewin's entire body of written and cinematic work, consideration of Wilde's novel, and a close scrutiny of the film itself lead to a different impression: a consistent, concerted theme of visuality, one that lingers deliberately and connectedly below the surface, or perhaps above the surface, and becomes a disturbance in the visual field of the version of the narrative that is dictated by convention.

The extravagant specularity of *The Picture of Dorian Gray* has many motives, one of which seems to have been evasion of censorship. "Those who find ugly meanings in beautiful things are corrupt without being charming," Oscar Wilde wrote in his preface to *The Picture of Dorian Gray*. "There is no such thing as a moral or an immoral book. Books are well written, or badly written. That is all."[9] Contrast this with the position of Joseph Breen, who enforced Hollywood's Motion Picture Production Code: "Art can be morally good. . . . Art can be morally evil. It has often been argued that art in itself is unmoral, neither good nor bad. This is perhaps true of the THING which is music, painting, poetry, etc. But the thing is the PRODUCT of some person's mind and the intention of that mind was either good or bad morally when it produced the thing."[10]

It might be predicted from such assertions that a film version of *The Picture of Dorian Gray* made in Hollywood would be bound to present problems, aside from any inherent problems of adaptation. As with *The Moon and Sixpence,* then, Lewin again had problems with the censors (and he probably would have worried if he had not). Even so, Lewin's film, like the novel, manages to advance troubling propositions and disturbing questions about human nature, desire, sexuality, and morality; in fact, to the extent that these are implicit in the narrative content of the novel, they are generally maintained in the film. However, it is largely in the visualization of the story that they are most provocatively presented.

The film's most significant alteration of Wilde's plot is the addition of two new characters: Gladys, who is the niece of the painter Basil Hallward; and David, who is her suitor. There is a Gladys in Wilde's novel who, like the Gladys in the film, wants Dorian. But unlike the film character, she is not Basil's niece, she is not virginal—she is a married woman, the duchess of Monmouth—and she plays a relatively small role. In Lewin's version, Gladys is a child of only five or six when the portrait of Dorian is painted but at that point is already enamored of him; much later, some twenty years after the death of Sibyl Vane, Dorian will again contemplate marriage, this time to Gladys, now a grown woman. In this regard, it is interesting to consider a scene that is incidental to the plot but central to the film's elaborate layering of visual information: the scene in which the child Gladys enters her uncle's studio just as the portrait is completed. Here the composition is clearly based on Velázquez's *Las Meniñas* (*Ladies-in-Waiting,* 1656), though it is not an exact imitation; the child is in the foreground, the canvas and painter are at screen left, and Lord Henry is in the background, at the door.[11]

Dorian—described by the critic Parker Tyler as "the first male erotic somnambule who is a beauty rather than a Dracula, . . . the detached object of love, not its subject"—provokes the painter Basil Hallward (Lowell Gilmore).

Gladys's early, naive adoration of Dorian, at a point when he is as yet uncorrupted, persists in her adulthood. Dorian is then morally depraved, though physically unchanged, and has become infamous; but despite the rumors of his indulgences and his cruelties, Gladys will not hear a word against him: she believes that beauty is truth. She pursues Dorian (almost brazenly) and her gaze, like Sibyl's before her, lingers on him. This gaze seemingly defies Victorian mores (it would also be considered as defying some recent feminist theory); but Gladys (unlike Sibyl Vane) is not punished for it.

Dorian, the object of her desire, is to Gladys what a *femme fatale* is to the male protagonist in film noir: sexually alluring but enigmatic and potentially treacherous.[12] As an object of desire—ultimately even to himself—Dorian has an ambiguous sexual identity, and this is underlined by the ambivalence with which he is described and characterized.

For instance, Parker Tyler observed in a contemporary review that Dorian, as enacted by Hurd Hatfield, is a curiously effeminate and narcissistic creature: "I could not help noting that in certain scenes of the movie, Mr. Hatfield's face and manner of speaking strongly suggested the romantic adolescent style of Katherine Hepburn.... It is not only that the structure of Mr. Hatfield's face is similar to Miss Hepburn's, but that the use of his lips and a muted monotone also resemble hers.... I mention this only to show that by happy coincidence, screen history provides a handy index to the effeminate defensiveness of Dorian's style. His is a passive, dreamy mask.... Not only does Hurd Hatfield create the first male erotic somnambule who is a beauty rather than a Dracula, or such as the denizen of Caligari's cabinet, but he is the first Great Lover who, despite all Hollywood handicaps, manages to seem more loved than loving.... For the meaning of Dorian's life is that he is the detached object of love, not its subject; the beloved, not the lover."[13] In characterizing Wilde's Dorian, Tyler wrote, "Wilde was the prince of an alien and socially aggressive philosophy, and Dorian Gray was his 'Mata Hari'—a man not in the service of another country but of another sex."[14]

Tyler could not have known how appropriate his analogy to Mata Hari actually was: if Lewin and Greta Garbo had had their way, Garbo, who played Mata Hari in 1932, would have played Dorian. "One day I received a message from Cedric Gibbons," Lewin later recalled, "who wanted to see me on a matter of urgency and secrecy. Gibby was the only close friend of Garbo around the studio at that time, and he had been deputed to tell me that Garbo wanted to play Dorian. Indeed, it was the only role she would come back to the screen for. Of course I moved heaven and earth to set it up. But everyone had a fit: the censorship problem, formidable anyway, would become insurmountable with a woman *en travesti* playing the role. I had to give up, but I've always regarded that as one of the screen's great lost opportunities."[15]

As it happened, casting the title role in *The Picture of Dorian Gray* was evidently no simple matter. Under regulations established by the British War Office, English actors could not be released for roles in the United States.[16] Among American actors, Lewin was interested in Montgomery Clift and Gregory Peck, who—when they were approached in 1943—were stage actors with no screen credits. Both of them turned the role down. Clift gave it some thought and decided that it was "not the type of role or script for his debut in pictures."[17] His screen debut would not occur until five years later, in Fred Zinnemann's *The Search*. Peck's debut, in Jacques Tourneur's *Days of Glory*, came sooner, in 1944. It is of some interest that Clift and Peck each chose to make his debut as a soldier (albeit a "sensitive" soldier) rather than as an exquisite aesthete. This was perhaps wise: compare Peck's and Clift's subsequent film careers with Hatfield's. Hurd Hatfield, who was eventually chosen, was another dark young American actor with no screen credits at the time Lewin cast him, although Hatfield did make another film, *Dragon Seed* (1944, directed by Jack Conway), during the long time that *Dorian Gray* was still in preproduction.

The effeminate narcissism that Tyler saw in Hatfield's performance is at least in part a reflection of Lewin's own view of Dorian Gray; in the novel, Dorian is a wholesome type, blond and robust. Whatever its source, though, Dorian's narcissism is repeatedly emphasized in the film: as he stands before the portrait of himself, at the beginning, and as he stands before mirrors. And although the homosexual subtext of the novel is suppressed,[18] the film makes it clear that Henry and Basil Hallward are as captivated as Sibyl and Gladys by Dorian's static, delicate beauty.

The ambiguity of Dorian's sexual appeal and its almost fetishistic nature seem to be symbolized in one of the film's early and most striking images. Dorian has just met Lord Henry at the home of Basil. While Dorian stands, immobile, posing for the portrait Basil is painting, Henry is in pursuit of a butterfly. As he doggedly and dispassionately follows the butterfly around the studio, Henry imparts his hedonistic philosophy to Dorian: "A man should live out his life fully and completely, give form to every feeling, expression to every thought, reality to every dream. Every impulse that we sup-

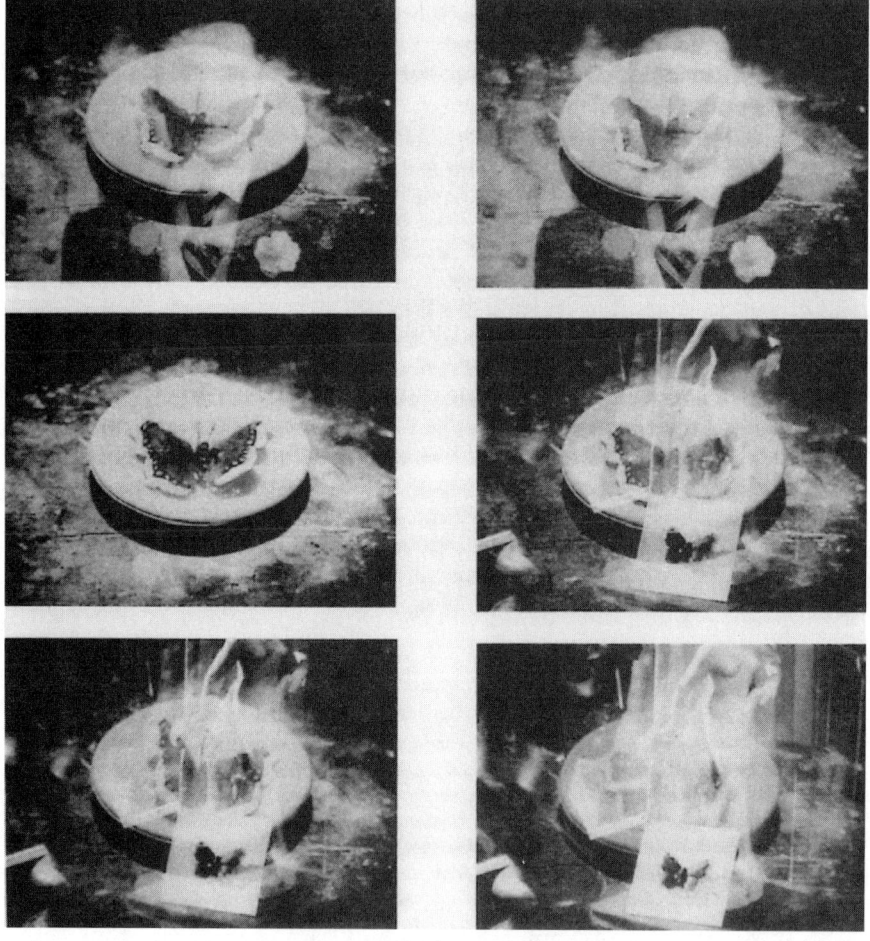

Six frames of a dissolve that merges Dorian's visage with a captive butterfly, then suggestively superimposes the butterfly upon a sexually ambiguous arrangement of objets d'art.

press broods in the mind and poisons us. There's only one way to get rid of a temptation, and that is to yield to it [he captures the butterfly under his hat]. Resist it [pouring alcohol into a dish], and the soul grows sick with longing for the things it has forbidden to itself. There is nothing that can cure the soul but the senses, just as there is nothing that can cure the senses but the soul. . . . What the gods give, they quickly take away. Time is jealous of you, Mr. Gray. Don't squander the gold of your days. Live. Let nothing be lost upon you. Be afraid of nothing. It is such a little time that your youth will last. And you can never get it back. As we grow older, our memories are haunted by the exquisite temptations we hadn't the courage to yield to. The world is yours for a season." The younger man is enthralled by Henry's monologue, as the film's narrator confirms: "The creed of pleasure soared into a philosophy of life, while Dorian stood as if he were under a spell. It was as if he were learning to know himself for the first time; as if a stranger had revealed his own most secret thoughts to him."

The symbolic use of the butterfly begins on a rather obvious note—the beautiful Dorian succumbing to Henry's verbal seduction as the lovely butterfly succumbs to a physical pursuit—but it soon becomes more complicated. First, a close-up of Dorian's face dissolves into a close-up of the dying butterfly, then another dissolve reveals the butterfly, now dead, pinned to a card and propped against a figurine in a third close-up, an arrangement of objects on a table. The figurine represents Venus leaning on a structural element, apparently a branch (this is the first "legible" part of the still life as it fades in), which is undeniably phallic and in turn points toward the mouth of a sexually indeterminate bronze bust. For a fleeting moment during the dissolve, this phallic form and the close-up of the butterfly are superimposed, provocatively suggesting a conflation of the male and female genitalia—specifically, a penis emerging from a vagina. The dissolve uses objects that, on the face of it, simply signify the tasteful milieu through which Dorian, Basil, and Henry are moving; but it uses and combines them in a way that quietly suggests fetishism, perversity, and polymorphic sexuality. These suggestions are echoed after the dissolve, when Lord Henry presents the butterfly to Dorian and leans over to blow it dry.

Réda Bensmaïa has observed that this dissolve provides a concentrated image (in Freudian terms, a "condensation") of what is fetishistic and perverse in Dorian Gray's character and notes that its content—its actual meaning—was therefore profoundly censorable. From this observation, Bensmaïa proceeds to propose that the cinematic dissolve as such tends to convey taboo, repressed, or disavowed aspects of a narrative.[19] Although this particular dissolve in *The Picture of Dorian Gray* certainly has that effect, there is little basis for Bensmaïa's generalization, other than his evident conviction that Hollywood films are made in large part unconsciously. The dissolve in general does not seem to have the function he suggests: a survey of dissolves would be unlikely to find many in which such stunning content is advanced; most are used as simple transitions between shots or scenes, often denoting a lapse of time. And although Lewin's dissolve in the butterfly sequence does indeed articulate content that had to be suppressed in the story line—a "psychosexual lapse"—this is hardly inadvertent; rather, it is the director's very intentional and efficient way of obliquely slipping this content past the producers and the censors.

Another image—or index—of Dorian's sexual ambiguity and primary narcissism occurs later in the film. In a scene with Gladys, Dorian, who has his back to the camera, appears to be directly facing a mirror as he speaks to her, but what is reflected in the mirror is not Dorian but a bronze copy of Verrocchio's *David* (c. 1470). This *David*, which is part of Dorian's extensive and eclectic art collection, is prominent in many scenes set in his drawing room; similarly, a copy of Donatello's *David* is featured

Gladys Hallward (Donna Reed) gazes at Dorian, while a mirror reflects not Dorian but a Renaissance bronze of the biblical David, by Verrocchio (c. 1470).

in a scene set in Dorian's club.[20] These two Renaissance bronzes are highly meaningful: they are iconographic references to youth in general, and to sexually ambiguous, narcissistically erotic, adolescent youth in particular; and their meaning literally "reflects" Dorian himself. There is something statuesque about Dorian, as portrayed by Hurd Hatfield; and his every move, gesture, and expression is produced with considered, self-conscious circumscription, as though he were (in Parker Tyler's words) a somnambule or an inanimate object brought to life—like Galatea in the legend of Pygmalion, or like E.T.A. Hoffmann's Olympia (from his story "The Sandman," 1816) and Villiers de l'Isle-Adam's "future Eve."

Dorian Gray's likeness to these female figures suggests the "inversion" that is evident in Lewin's concept of him: Dorian is (as Tyler puts it) "the detached object of love, not its subject." In an article on Villiers's science fiction novel *L'Eve future* (1885), Raymond Bellour quotes the following passage, in which "Thomas Edison," inventor of the android Alicia, addresses Lord Ewald, who has fallen in love with her: "The creature whom you love, and who for you is the *sole* REALITY, is by no means the one who is momentarily embodied in this transient human figure, but a creature of your desire. . . . What you love is this *phantom* alone; it's for the *phantom* that you want to die. That and that alone is what you recognize as unconditionally REAL." Bellour comments: "The 'ideal-double' whose possibility Edison suggests to Lord Ewald is none other than the ideal-double of himself, projected through Alicia. We shall call this encompassing of doubles the Narcissistic double. It is born from the subject's concern for his own image, and for the conditions necessary for its formation."[21]

But Dorian is no ordinary "somnambule," nor is he simply an animated statue or a living doll. He is represented not only by the figures of David, but also, because of the repeated use of mirrors in the film, by his own inert beauty and by his portrait. The blending and blurring of these stable reflections—David, Dorian, the portrait of Dorian—are a key to what Dorian sees in the mirror. In the post-Freudian terms of the French psychoanalyst Jacques Lacan, it is a primal, infantile "misrecognition": "This image is a fiction because it conceals, or freezes, the infant's lack of motor co-ordination and the fragmentation of its drives. But it is salutary for the child, since it gives it the first sense of a coherent identity in which it can recognize itself. For Lacan, however, this is already a fantasy."[22] Thus when Dorian first sees the finished portrait, his rapture at this revelation almost perfectly illustrates Lacan's concept of the "mirror stage." The portrait, along with Lord Henry's exhortation to grasp transient youth and beauty, induces a "self-consciousness" that Dorian has, until now, lacked. From the moment he perceives his representation, Dorian is fatally seduced by a fiction—for a representation, like a mirror image, is unreal. He is undone by the myth of a perfect, stable, and coherent self.

Dorian Gray's portrait is, of course (like Stevenson's Jekyll and Hyde, and many other literary figures), a variation on the theme of the double. This literary phenomenon has been analyzed, also in Lacanian terms, by Mladen Dolar, who describes the structural features of the theme as follows:

> The subject is confronted with his double, the very image of himself (that can go along with the disappearance, or trading off, of his mirror image or his shadow), and this crumbling of the subject's accustomed reality, this shattering of the bases of his world, produces a terrible anxiety. Usually only the subject can see his own double, who takes care to appear only in private, or for the subject alone. The double produces two seemingly contradictory effects: he arranges things so that they turn out badly for the subject, he turns up at the most inappropriate moments, he dooms him to failure; and he realizes the subject's hidden or repressed desires so that he does things he would never dare to do or that his conscience wouldn't let him do. In the end, the relation gets so unbearable that the subject, in a final showdown, kills his double, unaware that his only substance and his very being were concentrated in his double. So in killing him, he kills himself.[23]

Lewin was certainly aware of the history of the double in literature; in fact, he made an interesting discovery while doing some research on diabolism for *The Picture of Dorian Gray*. He found in his own library a beautifully illustrated edition of Lady Wilde's translation of Wilhelm Meinhold's *Sidonia the Sorceress*. The preface, by Henry Gustavus Schwalenberg, included a description of a portrait of Sidonia done when she was a young and beautiful woman, to which was later added, behind the original figure, another—made when she was a hideous old witch about to be beheaded and burned for her sins. Meinhold's story, according to Richard Ellmann, "makes much of a painting of Sidonia which proves to be a double portrait: in the foreground, executed in the style of Lucas Cranach, is a woman golden-haired and richly gowned, while in the background lurks the ravening sorceress in the garments worn at her execution, done in the manner of Rubens. The search for sources of Wilde's *The Picture of Dorian Gray* is unending, but here is another analogue to the benign portrait of Dorian by Basil Hallward, and the malign one of Dorian as drawn by his own soul."[24] Although the story of Sidonia does not exactly involve doubling, the portrait described certainly does.

Lewin was quite certain he had discovered an important source for Wilde's novel in this translation by Wilde's mother, and he confirmed it to his own satisfaction when he read the following in one of Wilde's reviews: "Lady Duff Gordon's *Letters From the*

Cape, and her brilliant translation of *The Amber Witch,* are, of course, well known. The latter book was, with Lady Wilde's translation of *Sidonia the Sorceress,* my favourite romantic reading when a boy."[25]

In Wilde's variation on the theme of the double and—even more—in Lewin's version, the schism between the two selves is relocated: it moves from the realm of morality and psychology to the realm of the visual and the specular. Instead of splitting Dorian into two conflicting selves, Wilde and Lewin split only his visual aspect. The bodily Dorian becomes a static, unvarying visual simulacrum of a fantasy—the original misapprehension. Meanwhile, the portrait, although it is no more "real" than the body, records visually the immaterial "substance" of Dorian's evil deeds. This device might be considered a sort of cinematic trope—the counterpart of a figure of speech. Its effectiveness depends, obviously, on the fears and the magical thinking of childhood; as children, we imagine, and are often led to believe, that our bad deeds will somehow be visible on our bodies. A child is often warned not to "make faces" because "your face will freeze that way," or is told that secret thoughts and deeds will manifest themselves in bodily symptoms. "The double," Leo Braudy has remarked, "expresses in terms of theme and plot something of the inner aesthetic of films, the double exposure, the fleeting insubstantiality of the image, its potential lack of authority even at the moment of greatest assertion."[26]

At a den of unspecified iniquity at Blue Gate Field, Dorian encounters the ruined Adrian Singleton (Morton Lowry), who draws Dorian's portrait in chalk, framing it with a hangman's noose, while a companion of Adrian's, Kate (Lillian Bond), looks on.

The fact that visuality is the locus of the disturbances central to this construction of Dorian is further demonstrated in *The Picture of Dorian Gray* by means of a host of indices. Foremost are the innumerable references within the film to framing: windows, doors, mirrors, screens, signs, and paintings permeate its mise-en-scène. These frames are sometimes used to delineate particular visual messages, and often it is Dorian himself who is framed, in mirrors, in doorways, and in pictures. Basil's is not the only "picture of Dorian Gray." Near the end of the film, when Dorian encounters the ruined and dissolute Adrian Singleton in a den of (unspecified) iniquity at Blue Gate Field, Adrian draws a caricature of Dorian in chalk on the table, then "frames" the picture with a gallows and noose. (This hangman's iconography echoes some inexplicable and fleeting glimpses of a noose early in the film, in the scene where Dorian is introduced to Lord Henry.)

In other instances, references to frames are less about that which is framed than about framing itself. These are often scenes in which the narrative exposition is extrinsic to the visual scenario, as in the film's second shot: Lord Henry Wotton is shown inside his carriage, reading a book (Baudelaire's *Les fleurs du mal*), while through the carriage's window, which fills over half the screen, the viewer observes the graphic shadow of coach and coachman "projected" by harsh sunlight onto the "moving image" of a London street.[27] As the scene continues, the point of view shifts to above that of the coachman, who opens a hatch on the top of the carriage in order to speak to Henry. Through the frame of this hatch, we observe Henry from above. As the coachman informs him that he has reached his destination, the house of his friend, the painter Basil Hallward, Henry begins to move.

In these first two shots, the film establishes its characteristic mise-en-scène—that is, a conspicuous tension between static, manifestly "composed" compositions and cinematic movement. This tension is generally effected in one of three ways: (1) by the circumscription of movement within an otherwise static scene, as in the first shot; (2) by temporal contiguity, as in the second shot, which progresses from stasis to movement; or (3) by movement of the camera in a static scene. There is very little simultaneous use of camera movement and dynamic mise-en-scène (i.e., the typical tracking or panning shots that follow an action). Indeed, when camera movement and character movement are simultaneous, they tend *not* to be coordinated. For instance, in a scene in Dorian's drawing room, a sudden, rapid horizontal tracking movement of the camera serves to bring a static figure—an Egyptian statuette of a cat—to center screen while Dorian himself has moved slowly to the depth of the set on an orthogonal, through the drawing room doors, closing them: that is, in a compositionally vertical direction.

In that this use of the camera often has nothing to do with the actual narrative, in that its reference to a frame is often gratuitous (at least in terms of immediate expository requirements), and, most important, in that it draws attention to itself in a manner quite at odds with Hollywood's typical effacement of technique, it functions always both as Lewin's stylistic "signature" and as a signal of style—as an antinaturalistic device. It refers at once to the artifices of Dorian Gray and his aesthetic environment and to those of cinema itself. The extent to which this "style" was at odds with Hollywood practice is evident in Pandro S. Berman's alleged dismissal of the very idea of "style" in any film of his (see page 15).

In the film's many interiors, in particular those in Dorian's and Basil Hallward's homes, Lewin's conspicuous framing is elaborated by his lavish use of artworks. These sets are crowded to overflowing with large and small sculptures and figurines, prints, paintings, and decorative objects, including, at Dorian's home, a book illustrated

Basil Hallward, Dorian Gray, and Lord Henry Wotton (George Sanders) at Basil's house, which is filled with art.

by Aubrey Beardsley, some identifiable reproductions of Renaissance masterpieces, nineteenth-century neoclassical sculptures and reliefs of Hellenic and Florentine types, copies of antique statuary, and numerous Asian antiquities. The homes of these aesthetes are clearly distinguished from the two or three other homes represented, in which the decoration is less profuse and generally more banal, in a late Victorian, neorococo style.

The aesthetes' homes are also composed and photographed in a distinct manner. Scenes that take place in Dorian's home, in particular, display arrangements—often symmetrical—that are highly artificial and are photographed equally artificially. There, for instance, most doorways, windows, mantels, and the like are flanked by complementary sculptures, paintings, or panels; and Dorian himself is often shown moving delicately and deliberately on an orthogonal over patterned floors in symmetrically composed shots set up with the picture plane parallel to the rear wall of the room, recalling the strict one-point perspective of fifteenth-century Italian painting. This very formalized treatment of Dorian's environment clearly conveys the artificial nature of Dorian's character and his beauty. It is quite contrary to the conventions of Hollywood drama, which has usually favored more oblique camera angles and seemingly haphazard compositions that effect a sense of verisimilitude.

While in general the plethora of art functions as an extension of Dorian and his exquisiteness,[28] on occasion—as in the symbolic use of the statues of David—the artworks serve as more than indices of Dorian's taste and its historical context. In particular, Lewin's predilection for the art of Egypt, the near east, and the far east represents a significant embellishment, actually an alteration, of Wilde's story. Whereas Wilde's Dorian is a connoisseur and collector mainly of western cultural oddities (religions, music, gems, and textiles), Lewin's Dorian involves himself with eastern art and litera-

The Devi Dja dance company performs a Buddhist parable, accompanied by an Indonesian gamelan orchestra, in a scene of a party at Dorian's home.

ture as well (as does Basil Hallward). Some of Lewin's most conspicuous amendments to Wilde's plot, in fact, have a flavor of the oriental. One is the Egyptian cat figurine, which appears next to Dorian in his portrait, whose magic is implicated in the metamorphosis of the painting, and toward which the camera seems to gravitate at portentous moments of revelation, or to be attracted as if by a magnet.[29] The implied power with which this cat is imbued underlines the extent to which art operates in the film as a function of the irrational and the imaginary.

Another bit of orientalism, one of the film's most unusual scenes, is the Balinese-Javanese dance and gamelan performance at Dorian's house. This was an abbreviated version of the scene, Lewin having fought, and lost, a strenuous battle over the editing. The original scene included a narrative dance about the Buddha, in which he "sits in meditation under the Boddhi Tree, while the Courtesans, who came to beseech him to return to his princely life, sit on one side.... Then come the dancing girls. Buddha replies and in dance and other symbolic gestures spurns them. Disappointed they all leave him, when he returns to his original posture of meditation under the Tree."[30] As Lewin later described the cutting of the scene, "It was quite a fine dance, all about the temptation of Buddha. But the preview audience laughed at one of those sideway head-turns as executed by lead dancer Devi Dja. I fought for the number, begged producer Pan Berman to take the film to a big first-run house in San Francisco.... It was one battle I didn't win. Most of the number was cut. I took a trip to Chicago to explain it to the dancers."[31]

It is probably not a coincidence that the Buddha dance illustrates female desire for a male object; this would have echoed Gladys's desire for Dorian, about which the larger scene revolves. Immediately after the performance there is a private scene between Gladys and Dorian. While she woos him, she studies a book illustrated by

Aubrey Beardsley, "How Sir Tristram Drank of the Love Drink," from his illustrations for an edition of Thomas Malory's *Le Morte d'Arthur* (1893–1894). A volume of this book is seen in Dorian's library, open to this page, and Dorian is associated with the ill-fated knight throughout the film.

Aubrey Beardsley that is open on a table before a mirror, in which she keeps an eye on Dorian. The book is Sir Thomas Malory's *Le Morte d'Arthur* (Beardsley illustrated an edition of 1893). It is open to the illustration of "How Sir Tristram Drank of the Love Drink."

The image of Tristan and Iseult recalls Sibyl Vane's print of Sir Tristan, with whom she identified Dorian. The equation of Dorian with the medieval knight is reinforced by many details, including a toy figure of a mounted knight prominent in the schoolroom where Dorian hides the portrait. The toy knight is knocked down when the portrait is installed, and Dorian stands it upright again only at the film's conclusion, when he repents, just before stabbing the portrait through the heart—thus making plain the knight's symbolic relationship to the condition of his soul, to the state of grace he has lost.

This symbolic relationship is also shown, in this same scene, by the organization of a child's set of alphabet blocks on the floor. A large D—for Dorian—is surmounted by a somewhat smaller 8, and the 8 by a small pyramid consisting of the letters L, H, and W: Lord Henry Wotton. On the floor around the D are several groupings of small

Near the end, a repentent Dorian is seen in the schoolroom where he has concealed the horrible picture of his soul. Surrounded by symbolic reminders of his past, he sets upright a fallen toy knight.

blocks with the initials of Dorian's victims: J-S-V, for James and Sibyl Vane; A-C, for Alan Campbell; B-H, for Basil Hallward; and S-T, for the "good" part of Dorian's soul (perhaps his alter ego), Sir Tristan.[32]

In Wilde's novel, Sibyl describes Dorian as Prince Charming, a name from fairytales rather than from Arthurian legend. In addition to its intrinsic relationship to the narrative, Lewin's alteration is reminiscent of his efforts to bring the *Knights of the Round Table* to the screen in the late 1930s, and it also refers to a theme prevalent among the decadents. Lewin's equation of Dorian with Sir Tristan, however, cannot be taken only as a cliché of knightly virtue, although that cliché may represent Sibyl's and Gladys's delusion. The story of Tristan and Iseult, as was well known to Lewin,[33] is neither simply about passionate love and desire nor about chivalry. As Eugène Vinaver describes it, it "is a tale of tragic love, enacted as it were above the level of the characters' consciousness: a tale of a disaster caused by the clash of irreconcilable forces, human and supernatural. The magic of the love potion is no less powerful than the sense of feudal and moral allegiance binding the lovers to the world . . . a world from which there is no final escape but death."[34]

The conflict between supernatural and societal forces, between the mythic or sacred and the civic or profane, is one that is explored in many ways in Lewin's work, often through characters whose actions seem curiously overdetermined, or predetermined, and detached from psychological causality. Thus, the analogy drawn between Dorian and Tristan, even as represented by the highly cultural and contextualized Beardsley image—in a manner more circuitous than the use of the Egyptian cat—refers also to the ineffable, magical forces of mysticism and the occult, which in the world of the film are subtly interwoven with the themes that derive more directly from Wilde.

In other words, while the influence of the Egyptian cat is patently ineffable and mystical, Beardsley's picture, at least prima facie, betokens a more culturally determined influence. And not only does the picture of Tristan and Iseult in the scene with Gladys symbolically suggest her attitude toward Dorian; Sibyl Vane has already overtly associated Dorian with Tristan, who is pictured in a popular pseudo-pre-Raphaelite print beside her dressing table. Sybil's print is a lower-class version of the same icon that is associated with Gladys, and so Gladys is revealed to be as vulnerable to an elevated notion of "beauty as truth" as Sibyl—her lower-class counterpart—was to a mass-produced image of the same value. These images, then, function on two levels: the idealistic, romantic level at which the female protagonists project them onto Dorian, and, more subtly, by reference to a story in which desire is the result of magic and the cause of tragedy—a parallel to the narcissistic desire to which Dorian falls prey and to which he is magically bound.

The environment in which Sibyl's fantasies of chivalrous knights develop is another of Lewin's inventions. Wilde's Sibyl Vane is a Shakespearean actress in an East End theater, whereas Lewin's Sibyl is a singer in a pub or cabaret. Parker Tyler objects to this substitution; but the "low" environment of the pub gave Lewin stunning opportuni-

As he wanders the streets of London's "half world," Dorian is approached by "Dr. Look."

Dr. Look: *The Picture of Dorian Gray* (1945)   57

ties for amplifying his visual hypertrophy. The scene in which Dorian first visits the "Two Turtles," the pub where Sibyl performs, contains the film's most clinical dissection of visual plenitude.

When Dorian wanders the strange streets of London's "half-world" (as it is described by the narrator), a figure wearing a sandwich board enters the frame; and while Dorian contemplates entering the Two Turtles, this figure crosses the scene. Having entered the pub, Dorian closes the door, in which a window distinctly reveals the center of the sandwich-board advertisement—an enormous, disembodied eye with the words "Dr. Look" beneath it. Around this window, printed on the door itself, appears the enjoinder, "Eat, drink, and be merry." Looming above the doorway is a gruesome gargoyle that gazes fiercely out toward the camera. The sandwich board appears again later in the scene, without its bearer, propped against the wall, its awful eye focused uncannily upon Sibyl Vane (or Dorian, or the viewer) amidst a host of embodied eyes—those of the audience in the pub.

The disembodied eye is one of the most ubiquitous elements of surrealist iconography. It appears in works by, among others, Giorgio de Chirico, Man Ray, Max Ernst, and René Magritte.[35] Coincidentally, another Hollywood film released in 1945 features more explicitly surrealistic disembodied eyes—Alfred Hitchcock's *Spellbound,* for which Salvador Dalí designed a dream sequence that includes curtains covered with bodiless eyes. *Spellbound,* in turn, especially when a scissor cuts through the curtains and the eyes, recalls Dalí and Buñuel's 1929 surrealist classic, *Un chien andalou (Andalusian Dog),* in which a woman's (actually a cow's) eye is sliced by a razor. The appearance of a disembodied eye, then, at the Two Turtles, a locale full of details worthy of a surrealist (a squirrel nutcracker, libidinous puppets, a menacing gargoyle),

Malvolio Jones (Billy Bevan), "chairman" of the pub, counts his receipts as he watches his wellborn visitor during a performance by Mr. and Mrs. Ezekiel—a puppet-and-xylophone act—at the Two Turtles.

confirms that Lewin's familiarity with surrealist imagery must have played some role in the staging of the scene.[36]

Inside the Two Turtles, a bizarre cabaret act is under way, but the manager of the pub interrupts it upon Dorian's entrance, announcing to the entire establishment that they are "honored by the visit of a gentleman," whereupon everyone turns to stare at Dorian, who smiles blandly and condescendingly takes a seat. The performance resumes. A Mr. and Mrs. Ezekiel perform a xylophone-and-puppet act, displaying their own heads above limp puppet bodies that hang in front of a black screen. The puppets' feet contain otherwise hidden sticks or mallets, so that when these are manipulated from behind the screen, the puppet bodies dance on the xylophone and appear to be playing it. The performance ends hysterically, or orgasmically, with the female puppet opening and closing her legs frantically as the music rises to a fevered pitch. Not a curtain, but a screen, falls and the next act, Sibyl Vane, is announced. The flat, abrupt movement of the screen as it falls and rises distinctly recalls its famous counterpart, the "silver screen," as well as the "wipe," a cinematic technique in which one shot supersedes another. As the screen lifts to reveal Sibyl, posed amid artificial snow, an sudden cut to above the stage reveals a theater employee casually dropping handfuls of white confetti onto the stage.

Sibyl's performance of a sentimental song, "Little Yellow Bird," is briefly but dramatically interrupted by her almost stunned silence when she meets Dorian's gaze as she moves out and about the audience. As she nears the end of the song and moves toward the stage door, she passes a table on which is standing the very statuette of Venus that has been seen in Basil's studio. Its presence in this environment is dissonant, yet it will appear again in the Two Turtles, in a different location, when Dorian returns with Lord Henry and Basil.

The visually overloaded atmosphere of the pub, which is as packed with props, placards, tchotchkes, and other lower-class icons and artifacts as Dorian's home is with high art, is the site of unabashed spectacle. Dorian's function as spectator is undermined by the emblematic and clinical gaze of Dr. Look, by the stares his entrance inspires, and by Sibyl's sexually charged, desirous gaze. He sees—but even more, he is seen. The artificiality of the spectacle; the presence of an audience inside the pub; the omnipresent Dr. Look, whose disembodied eye recalls the "evil eye" of the middle east as well as the surrealists' psychosexual use of the same image; the explicitly sexual performance of Mrs. Ezekiel; and the inexplicably transposed Venus with her phallic support—all inundate the film's viewers with uncomfortable reminders of their own position.

The visual scrutiny by Dr. Look is echoed in two details in subsequent scenes. In one scene, after informing Dorian of Sibyl Vane's suicide, Lord Henry picks up a stereopticon, which he plays with while Dorian reacts in horror (albeit temporary). "You must learn to see it in its proper perspective," Henry says, peering into the viewfinder.[37] In a later scene, after Dorian has murdered Basil Hallward (and arranged for the thorough disposal of the body), he visits Scotland Yard with Gladys to discuss Basil's disappearance with a detective. While reporting to them, Sir Robert—the detective—examines what are probably forensic slides in front of a light box. In each of these scenes, the optical apparatus intensifies the audience's already heightened consciousness of the cinematic apparatus. At the conclusion of the scene in Scotland Yard, we learn that Sir Robert has apparently been investigating evidence related to the suicide of Alan Campbell, the acquaintance whom Dorian has blackmailed into disposing of Basil's body. Thus both scenes create a link between "looking machines" and suicides in which Dorian is implicated. The equation of death and vision—a link that is not necessarily obvious—expresses the mortality of sight, an important theme

Ivan Albright, *The Picture of Dorian Gray* (1943–1944).

of *The Picture of Dorian Gray*.[38] It should be noted here that Dorian's private reveries before the portrait, in the schoolroom where it is hidden from the world, are discreetly commented on by a Latin sentence written on a chalkboard: *Non ignoravi mortalem esse* ("I am not unaware that I am mortal").[39] Trapped in a narcissistic purgatory, as he obsessively compares his unmarked face in the mirror with the monstrous visage in the painting, Dorian denies the implications of the signs around him: his lost innocence and his certain death.

The hyperbolic visuality of *The Picture of Dorian Gray*—its obsessive and exquisite compositions and montages; its discomforting mirrors, literal and figurative; and its insistent correlation of sexuality with visuality—is brought into focus on the central image of the picture of Dorian Gray itself. The use of portraiture in films represents a potential disturbance of the viewer's relationship to the narrative: what has been called the "suturing" of the viewer to the narrative—that is, the means by which the viewers' absorption into and identification with the film is secured, at the same time as they are permitted to forget or "disavow" their actual, rather voyeuristic, act of watching. The self-conscious presentation of the portrait's subject threatens this "illusory absence."[40] *The Picture of Dorian Gray* doubly assaults the viewers' impunity, first by the very use of portraiture and then by "returning the repressed" in the transformed portrait. Although the original portrait (which was done by Henrique Medina) has been shown, the metamorphosed portrait (by Ivan Albright) is not seen until the second half of the film, but then it is revealed to its creator, Basil—and to the audience—in a shocking Technicolor insert.[41] In the transformed painting, Dorian has become a hideous, writhing mass of lurid, wormlike excrescences. Wilde's notion that the portrait is of Dorian's soul bodes darkly, in the film, for Dorian's fate; an uglier portrait is inconceivable. In its presence, Dorian is overcome with hatred for its innocent creator, and so he kills Basil.

But Dorian Gray's assault on the artist is not, of course, the end of his attack on art. The film ends with Dorian assaulting the picture itself, driving a knife through its subject's heart, and thus, inevitably, through his own heart. He falls dead, and the painting metamorphoses back to its original—seemingly banal and benign—form while his body takes on the the horrible characteristics of the picture.[42]

As the structural raison d'être of the narrative, the picture of Dorian Gray is the defining image of the film. In Wilde's novel, the concept of this phenomenon necessarily takes precedence over its function as a visual sign, but in the film the picture must predominate. Thus, the fastidiously disgusting color image of the transformed painting casts a shadow over the exquisiteness of the black-and-white film. The idealistic western notion that beauty is truth—the implicit credo of the aestheticized sphere of Basil, Henry, Gladys, and Sibyl, and of Dorian himself—is revealed as fallacy. In fact, the truth is uglier than could have been imagined.

The fate of Dorian Gray warns us that the eyes can be deceived and that visual duplicity can threaten our very subjectivity. Oscar Wilde notes that ugliness, as well as beauty, is in the eye (or mind) of the beholder. Albert Lewin's *Picture of Dorian Gray* suggests further that beauty is seductive and that it is a construction—that it is a fiction of wholeness and plenitude propagated by mirrors, paintings, movies, and ideologies. It may be in the eye of the beholder, but the beholder does not fully possess the sight with which the eye sees. Sight yields to culture, to the imperatives of a social and linguistic order. By disrupting the flow of the narrative with reflexive signs, Lewin's film pushes the audience's anxiety to the fore, confronting the viewer with the disturbing mysteries of art, representation, and vision itself. By contrasting the bloody colors of the transformed portrait to the artificial harmonies of the black-and-white mise-en-scène, and by employing objects from cultures in which the power of art is not differentiated from the power of the spiritual, the film hints at a sight that is separate from vision—a sight that bypasses the eye and refers to the mind, to the psyche, to the spirit. This kind of seeing may not, finally, render truth visible, but it denies the primacy of vision, implies the symbolic function of beauty and taste, and challenges the lure of illusion.[43]

> Like Christopher Columbus who, on the verge of discovering the Antilles, believed he was on the road to India, so in the twentieth century the painter found himself confronted by a new world before it had occurred to him that he could depart from the old. This old world was the reproduction of nature in accordance with visual perception, influenced more or less by the emotions. With some rare exceptions, most of them inspired by occult tradition or by religious mysticism, the artist remained the prisoner of external perception and envisaged no means of escape. . . . The eye and its satellite, the mirror, [were] soon to be accused of *despotism* (André Breton).[44]

How deeply this corruption of taste had eaten into the German mind was shown in the material submitted for hanging by artists in the *House of German Art*. There were pictures with green skies and purple seas. There were paintings which could be explained only by abnormal eyesight or wilful fraud on the part of the painter. If they really paint in this manner because they see things that way, then these unhappy persons should be dealt with in the department of the Ministry of the Interior where sterilization of the insane is dealt with, to prevent them from passing on their unfortunate inheritance. If they do not see things like that and still persist in painting in this manner, then these artists should be dealt with by the criminal courts (Adolph Hitler).[45]

It must not be forgotten to what ends classical male beauty and classical cinematic narrative were being put in 1944. The surrealists' skepticism concerning visual pleasure was to be historically justified by the heinous misrepresentations of the Third Reich's cultural program. "Official" taste in Nazi Germany had not a little in common with the fin-de-siècle neoclassicism of Dorian Gray's milieu. Hitler's and Breton's differences reflect questions about representation and visuality—questions in which ideology and culture overlap—and these questions are an integral part of the background of the production of *The Picture of Dorian Gray*.

Visual culture was a battlefield before and during the war years, in Europe and America, a field in which images were mobilized on behalf of ideology. Breton's hostility toward the despotic eye was matched by Hitler's faith in a kind of pure and righteous vision; but Hitler, unfortunately, was in a better position to proselytize. With the fine arts, cinema, and every level of visual kitsch employed in propaganda; with visual signs upended, beauty redefined and reinterpreted, and evil and sickness imputed to artistic practices by Hitler's Reich, Breton's accusation had to be taken to heart. Thus, the possible reading of Dorian as—whatever else he might also be—an allegory for a civilization conquered by the thrall of youth, beauty, and a promise of immortality cannot be overlooked. In this context, the horrible picture of Dorian's soul seems a prescient sign of evil yet to be revealed.

In any event, Albert Lewin's *The Picture of Dorian Gray* performs exactly the kind of tightrope act in which its maker imagined he was engaged. It is a thrilling horror story, balletically staged, lurid and risqué, at once beautiful and horrible. Lewin's friend Charles Reznikoff, the poet, gave him the following account shortly after the film had opened at the Capitol Theater in New York: "I came at the end of the picture. The audience was what the Bible might call a 'mixed multitude'—many Egyptians among the Israelites. . . . A very young fellow, obviously an intellectual, seemed lost in thought as the last of the picture faded out, and then murmured, 'Excellent!' I am not as good a judge of an audience's reactions as Mr. Le Baron [head of production at Paramount while Lewin was there], for example, but its interest, I thought, was definitely held: they laughed at the right places, were properly silent, and gasped and shrieked at the colored picture and the dummy on the floor. A woman behind me—after the murder of the painter—kept saying, 'Uh, uh!' at each twist in the plot. After a while, I became part of the audience myself and followed the picture with interest. I still think it very good. When I left there was a riot to get into the theatre."[46] The film did very well indeed at the box office and would have made a considerable profit, had Lewin not spent a considerable fortune making it look just right. At the same time, it is, if not a subversion, at least a rather disturbing contemplation of the very forces that ensured its success—the seductiveness of beauty and the thrill of spectacle, and the perils of succumbing to these.

The Private Affairs of Bel Ami (1947). Georges Duroy (George Sanders) and Virginie Walter (Katherine Emery) with Max Ernst's *The Temptation of Saint Anthony* (1945).

CHAPTER 3

A Café Called Désir:
The Private Affairs of Bel Ami (1947)

> I know that Dorian Gray has been excessively admired and detested, which makes me suspect that there may be a strange beauty in it. But it seems far away and long ago, and I am a little vague about it. In a few years I may have the curiosity to look at it again. Now I am involved in "Bel Ami," which, since I am hopelessly entangled, seems very thorny. Every morning I take a deep breath and leap into my briar bush. I bleed from a thousand scratches and am aghast at my own fortitude.
>
> Albert Lewin, November 16, 1945[1]

If one has seen *The Moon and Sixpence* and *The Picture of Dorian Gray,* one experiences a sense of déjà vu upon viewing *The Private Affairs of Bel Ami.* Again, one is in Europe at the end of the nineteenth century. Here again is George Sanders, playing a scandalous dandy. Here again are Angela Lansbury, Richard Fraser, and Albert Basserman. Here again are refined, patterned, black-and-white interiors, designed by Gordon Wiles. Here, too, a painting—this time one by Max Ernst—explodes from the screen in color.

There is a fictional painting in Guy de Maupassant's novel *Bel-Ami:* "by the Hungarian artist, Karl Marcowitch, . . . representing Christ walking on the water. The art critics enthusiastically declared this canvas the most magnificent masterpiece of the century."[2] However, it is probably safe to assume that a painting praised by Parisian art critics in the 1880s would have little in common with Max Ernst's work of 1945, *The Temptation of Saint Anthony,* a lurid, apocalyptic vision of torment, with brutal colors and frenzied forms that burst into the rarefied black-and-white mise-en-scène of *The Private Affairs of Bel Ami* with an effect bordering on violence. In fact, in 1947, when *The Private Affairs of Bel Ami* was reviewed by Bosley Crowther for the *New York Times,* Ernst's painting was hardly more digestible than it would have been sixty years earlier: "Blame the whole mess on Albert Lewin, who not only directed but wrote the screenplay—and who presumably was responsible for sticking into the film a close-up in color of a painting which is downright nauseous. It is called 'The Temptation of St. Anthony,' but it looks like a bad boiled lobster. Could this, maybe, be symbolic of 'The Private Affairs of Bel Ami'?"[3]

The purpose of the Ernst painting in this film is more obscure than that of the equally hideous painting in *The Picture of Dorian Gray*—Ivan Albright's transformed

The Private Affairs of Bel Ami

Paris, 1880. Georges Duroy (George Sanders), decommissioned from the Sixth Hussars after serving in Morocco, has recently come to Paris, where he is employed in a low-level, low-wage position in the railroads. At a café one evening, while attracting the attention of a dancer named Rachel (Marie Wilson), and contemplating the expenditure of his last centimes, he encounters Charles Forestier (John Carradine), a fellow officer in his regiment who now works for a newspaper, *La Vie Française*. Forestier tells him of an opening at the newspaper, invites him to a dinner party where he may cultivate the publisher, and lends him money to rent evening clothes. Georges uses some of the money to "entertain" Rachel.

At the dinner, Georges secures an opportunity to apply for a spot on the paper by writing an article about his experiences in North Africa, and also makes a striking impression on the women present, including his benefactor's wife, Madeleine Forestier (Ann Dvorak); the publisher's wife, Virginie Walter (Katherine Emery); the Walters' daughter, Suzanne (Susan Douglas); and a young widow, Clotilde de Marelle (Angela Lansbury), whose wish to go slumming at one of Paris's rather common dance halls impresses Georges. While M. Walter (Hugo Haas) and the caricaturist Jacques Rival (Albert Basserman) are amused by Georges, the influential and ambitious Laroche-Mathieu (Warren William) is decidedly not.

Georges struggles with his article all night in vain. When he arrives at Forestier's home the next morning, his friend refers him to his wife and departs. Madeleine Forestier—who, it is implied, is the talent behind her husband's success—ably assists Georges with his article, and he wins a place on the paper. Soon he is involved in a love affair with Clotilde (whose little daughter Lourine also adores him), even as he admires Madeleine. Charles Forestier, a consumptive, becomes increasingly ill; at Forestier's deathbed, Georges and Madeleine form a kind of contract; they are soon married. Georges's affair with Clotilde, who has felt betrayed by his marriage, soon resumes, while his rather more businesslike relationship with his bride continues, and he also begins the seduction of Virginie Walter, a pious matron.

Exploiting the women around him, all the while behaving derisively toward women and propriety in general, Georges advances his career and his ambitions. Only one woman, the virtuous Marie de Varenne (Francis Dee), wife of the newspaper's blind music critic (David Bond), is immune to the charms of "bel ami." Georges entraps Madeleine in a compromising position with his enemy, Laroche-Mathieu, divorces her, and then plots to secure the fortune that young Suzanne Walter will inherit by seducing Suzanne and coercing her father into permitting the engagement. Embittered and vengeful, Virginie Walter seeks out Philippe de Contel (Richard Fraser), the last member of a noble family whose title Georges intends to buy. Philippe challenges Georges to a duel, in which Georges is killed. With his dying breath, Georges declares his love for Clotilde and Lourine.

portrait of Dorian, which graphically (probably more graphically than Oscar Wilde could have dreamed) realized the soul's corruption. In Maupassant's novel, the painting plays a relatively insignificant role: Madame Walter (Viriginie, played by Katherine Emery in the film), the wife of the publishing magnate who has bought it, obsesses over the resemblance of Christ to her "bel-ami," Georges Duroy, the protagonist (Sanders's role). In Lewin's film, the theme of the painting was, by necessity, changed, and therefore its relation to the narrative was altered as well. As Lewin later wrote:

> In de Maupassant's book the subject of the painting was "Christ Walking on the Waters." But the Code Authority . . . advised me that this subject was unacceptable. Censorship does not permit the physical portrayal of Christ on the screen. Moreover, de Maupassant used the image of Christ in an ironical way, making the face of Jesus resemble that of "Bel Ami," a very bad man. So cynical an implication was out of the question in my movie.
>
> I was not disheartened by these difficulties. I had already conceived the idea of inviting an outstanding contemporary painter to do the canvas for my picture, and I knew that the subject of "Christ Walking on the Waters" had never been especially tempting to painters. The only great painting of this theme that I could easily recall was the beautiful one of Tintoretto. It occurred to me that for the purpose of my story, which is a dramatization of the struggle between good and evil (particularly as applied to the character of Madame Walter, who had a strong religious conviction), the theme of *The Temptation of Saint Anthony* was more fitting as well as altogether acceptable to the censors. I was also aware that, in choosing this subject, I was taking a theme which has never failed to fascinate the greatest of painters since medieval times.[4]

The anachronism of a contemporary painting in a period drama is more startling in *Bel Ami* than it was in *Dorian Gray*, where the plot justified the strangeness of the painting. And Lewin's handling of Maupassant's tale up to the point at which the painting is introduced does absolutely nothing to prepare the audience for the eruption of the shocking image—unlike his treatment of Wilde's story, which begins with the execution of the portrait and necessarily refers to it throughout, effectively withholding the revelation of its metamorphosis long enough to ensure a moment of gratifying, anticipated horror. In *Dorian Gray*, the contrast between the portrait and the elegant, rarefied setting was exactly the point. In *The Private Affairs of Bel Ami*, the function of the painting is either more subtle or more arbitrary.

The latter possibility—that the Ernst painting functions to some extent arbitrarily—is suggested by the curious fact that neither Lewin nor anyone else directly involved with the production actually chose it. It appeared in the film as part of the prize in an art competition, and although Lewin had conceived the competition,[5] he was not among the judges: Alfred H. Barr, of the Museum of Modern Art; Marcel Duchamp, an artist; and Sidney Janis, a gallerist. But Lewin was involved in choosing the field of competitors. They were, in addition to Ernst: Ivan Albright, Eugene Berman, Leonora Carrington, Salvador Dalí, Paul Delvaux, Leonor Fini, Louis Guglielmi, Horace Pippin, Abraham Rattner, Stanley Spencer, and Dorothea Tanning. All of them, except Fini, submitted their paintings on time and were entered in the competition. Max Ernst's submission won, in what the judges described as a very close vote.[6]

Undoubtedly, the idea of the competition was in large part motivated by publicity. The Albright picture in *Dorian Gray* had been quite a hit and had given both the artist and the film extraordinary exposure. Here, the plan was more ambitious: all the sub-

Albert Lewin examining several paintings in the *Bel Ami* competition, 1946; *(left to right):* by Ivan Albright, Dorothea Tanning, Abraham Rattner, Max Ernst, Salvador Dali, and Horace Pippin (photo by William Leftwich).

missions to the contest were to be featured in a special exhibition that would go on tour in the United States and Europe for two or three years under the auspices of the American Federation of Arts.[7]

An unexpected boost to the publicity campaign was provided by Mayor James M. Curley of Boston, who, "arguing that the paintings were offensive on a religious-moral basis . . . banned their exhibition" at the Copley Society, where the show had gone from New York. Loew-Lewin responded to Curley's censorship with a $200,000 lawsuit; the Stuart galleries in Boston confronted Curley by agreeing to display the paintings; Curley referred the matter to the police, who declined to act on it; and ultimately, the whole issue was dropped.[8]

The varied group of contemporary artists chosen for the competition—men and women from Europe and the United States, of different ethnic and racial backgrounds, working in a range of styles from surrealist, magic realist, and expressionist to naive—reflected Lewin's relative openness to the sort of image that would be featured in his film: his readiness to have the film "disrupted" by an image whose particular form and content were not designed to fit in. In fact (with only two possible exceptions), none of the artists in the competition, although all of them worked in representational modes, employed stylistic means similar to those Lewin and Wiles used in composing the film.

The film's mise-en-scène relies heavily on a very artificially composed, graphic rendering of architectonic layers in depth. Surfaces are patterned. The physical movements of the characters are charted and paced according to constraints imposed by the music, the dialogue, and the sets. The interior state, or psychology, of these characters (enacted by the cast with a restraint remarkable in Hollywood films), rather than

Abstract patterns and shifting spatial registers contribute to the psychological alienation of Madeleine (Ann Dvorak) and Georges as they dress for a party.

being played out dramatically, dynamically, or with affect, is suggested by their relationships to one another within spatial registers. Often, as in Lewin's two previous films, characters are deployed like chess pieces on a checkered floor,[9] but in *Bel Ami* they are manipulated more psychologically—that is, less existentially.

Georges and Madeleine (Ann Dvorak), for instance, are often shown in separate but adjoining spaces, with a vertical division between them; this effects a kind of psychological tension or alienation that is similar to what Edgar Degas achieved in his portrait of the Bellelli family (c. 1860), in which the mother and daughters, standing, form a pyramidal group that is separated by a series of vertical elements from the father (Baron Bellelli), who is seated and rather indistinct. In other instances, as in the chilling scene at the deathbed of Charles Forestier (John Carradine), Georges and Madeleine move in and out of shadows, which cast black marks across their faces and figures or leave them entirely obscure. The characters' subjective states are sometimes, as well, revealed by their relation to props that have inherently, or assume, a metonymic or symbolic psychological meaning. (These include mirrors, for instance, and objects the characters handle: Madeleine's wedding ring, which she fingers nervously, and her cigarettes and scissors; Georges's Punch and Judy puppets, his cup and ball, his playing cards, and his razor; Madame Walter's knitting.) "The result," remarks Douglas McVay of such a technique, "is a kind of Brechtian cinema, in which the formalized, detached yet contemplative images furnish a visual equivalent of Maupassant's sardonically unsparing yet humanely understanding verbal analysis."[10]

By contrast, the paintings of Saint Anthony submitted for the competition were with few exceptions much more affecting, immediate, and direct. Ernst's winning picture and the entries by Albright, Berman, Carrington, Dalí, Spencer, and Tanning each

In the film's opening scene, at a café called Désir, Georges, playing with Punch and Judy puppets, is admired by a dancer from the Folies-Bergère, Rachel (Marie Wilson). His old friend Charles Forestier (John Carradine) looks on.

represent torment, desire, madness, and temptation in more or less concrete terms. Most of them are characterized by hallucinatory vividness and dynamic color, composition, and execution. Only Delvaux, Guglielmi, Pippin, and Rattner rendered the theme with somewhat more restraint, and only the entries by Delvaux and Guglielmi—which relied on deep, graphic, architectonic compositions—shared any pictorial characteristics with the film.

If the style of Max Ernst's winning painting appears anachronistic in *Bel Ami*, its theme is somewhat less so. *La tentation de Saint Antoine (The Temptation of Saint Anthony)* was the title and theme of the novel which Gustave Flaubert called "l'oeuvre de toute ma vie" ("my whole life's work") and which—after over a quarter of a century of writing, involving several versions—he published in 1874.[11] Paul Cézanne's painting of this subject (1867–1869) had predated the publication, although not the conception, of Flaubert's work by five years. After Flaubert, the theme was taken up by many other artists, although it appealed more to symbolist and decadent painters—such as Moreau, Redon, Khnopff, and Ensor—than to those who were rather more academic; and one would assume that Maupassant's Karl Marcowitch belonged among the latter.

> Messieurs les démons,
> Laissez-moi donc!
> Messieurs les démons,
> Laissez-moi donc!

"Demons, leave me alone!" These were the lines that Flaubert set down at the beginning of his first manuscript version of *La tentation de Saint Antoine,* which, according to the translator Kitty Mrosovsky, "he insisted he must finish before setting off to Egypt with his friend Maxime Du Camp" in 1849. "This deferential pleading with tormenting familiars [the demons are actually addressed as "Sirs" or "Gentlemen"] plainly echoes the saint's popular trials. Years after his childhood, Flaubert enjoyed bringing George Sand to see the marionette theatre run by Père Legrain at the fair of Saint-Romain at Rouen. A fifteen-minute *Saint Antoine* would end with the saint's legendary pig taking flight with its tail on fire."[12]

Lewin's *Bel Ami* refers many times to popular puppet shows such as Flaubert enjoyed, particularly Punch and Judy. The closing shot of the film, after Georges has lost his duel in the rain and has died in the carriage bearing him away, pans across the lonely park and stops on a sign for Le Petit Guignol, which shows Punch beating another character with his stick, while a voice sounding like that of the film's virtuous Norbert de Varenne (played by David Bond), a fan of the Petit Guignol, whispers, "We are all no more than puppets unless we believe."

Indeed, there is little doubt that both Lewin and Ernst had Flaubert's *Tentation* in mind in, respectively, electing and executing this theme. Lewin admired Flaubert and was very well-read in French literature.[13] It is clear, too, that he diligently researched his period films, reading (and looking) widely and carefully in and around the particular time and milieu represented. The visual traces of his research are recorded not only in the (albeit highly mannered) accuracy of his period detail, but in references to contemporaneous artworks within the scenes. The most obvious "quotation" in the film is to Edouard Manet's *Bar at the Folies-Bergère* (1881–1882) in a scene set at the Folies; another example is the strangely disjointed, puppetlike dance that Georges and Clotilde de Marelle (Angela Lansbury) perform when they go slumming at a rather louche nightclub, La Reine Blanche—their steps resemble the movements captured in certain images by Toulouse-Lautrec.

"Lewin's consistently superb collaboration throughout the film with cinematographer Russell Metty and art director Gordon Wiles rises to especial heights in this

Georges and Clotilde de Marelle (Angela Lansbury) slumming at La Reine Blanche, a plebian dance hall, in a scene reminiscent of period images by Auguste Renoir and Henri de Toulouse-Lautrec.

sequence," writes Douglas McVay, "the mastery of crowds, camera movement and cutting, the virtuoso counterpoint of plastic composition and music, remind us of Minnelli—or more nearly, of Renoir in *French Cancan*. One moment is unforgettable: a chanteuse raising her tipsy face from a tabletop, then weaving slowly through the waltzing pairs whilst she warbles the languorous 'Bel-Ami' ditty."[14] McVay's comparisons to the work of other directors, particularly Jean Renoir, who was Lewin's close friend, are apt, although *French Cancan* is a rather later film (1955) and the Minnelli musicals he alludes to are in general much more colorful and joyous than this somewhat ambivalent scene. For an art historian, anyway, comparisons to Auguste Renoir's paintings of dancing couples, and especially to Degas's and Toulouse-Lautrec's rather more acid views of Paris nightlife, are more appropriate. McVay fails to note one of the most atmospheric details in this scene: on the table where the chanteuse sits, drooping over a glass of liqueur (perhaps absinthe) before being prodded into performing, a black cat nurses a litter of kittens, an image that no doubt is meant to express something of the profligacy and promiscuity of her environment.

In any case, Lewin and Flaubert were, in aesthetic and philosophical terms, kindred spirits. "Nineteenth-century decadence, masochistic and morbid, is the context in which Mario Praz placed *Saint Antony*, suggesting that it influenced D'Annunzio and Swinburne and that Oscar Wilde skimmed from it some rare rhyme-words for *The Sphinx*," Kitty Mrosovsky notes in the introduction to her translation of Flaubert's *Tentation*.[15] One cannot help being reminded of Lewin's *The Picture of Dorian Gray*, a compendium of decadence, with its references and allusions not only to Wilde's *Sphinx*, but also to Baudelaire, Huysmans, Beardsley, the Buddha, *The Rubáiyát*, and many other literary and figurative touchstones of the fin-de-siècle. These two spirits—Flaubert and Lewin—seem even more closely related, however, when one considers the strange "shifting tableaux" which alternate, or layer, lyricism with irony, sensuality with austerity, and deeply moral inquiry with indurate cynicism, and which characterize Lewin's work as much as Flaubert's.[16]

Ernst must, too, must have known this most surreal of Flaubert's works, this "genealogy of desire" that its author described as a "metaphysical howl,"[17] and I think that it must have been a source for the powerful, metamorphic torment of Ernst's picture, along with the obvious precedents in northern medieval and Renaissance painting (Matthias Grünewald's, of course; Jacques Callot's; and others, including a version in Genoa which may have inspired Flaubert's work and which in his day was attributed to Pieter Brueghel the Younger[18]). The wondrous monsters of Ernst's version have as ancestors not only Grünewald's "dream-monsters of surpassing obscenity, grotesque, repulsive, . . . the cthonic image of evil,"[19] but also the marvelous menagerie of Flaubert's book: the Chimera, Astomi, Nisnas, Blemmyes, Pygmies, Sciapodes, Cynocephales, Sadhuzag, Martichoras, Catoblepas, Basilisk, Griffin, Unicorn, Beasts of the Sea, and more:

> A thousand voices answer him. The forest trembles.
> And all sorts of frightful beasts spring out: the Tragelaphus, half stag and half ox; the Myrmecoleo, lion in front, ant at the rear, and whose genitals are back to front; the python Aksar, sixty cubits long, which dismayed Moses; the great weasel Pastinaca, which kills trees by its smell; the Presteros, whose contact induces imbecility; the Mirag, a horned hare which inhabits the isles of the sea. Phalmant the leopard splits its stomach by dint of howling; the Senad, a triple-headed bear, tears up its little ones with its tongue; Cepus the dog splashes the rocks with blue milk from its udders. Mosquitoes start to drone, toads to leap, snakes to hiss. Lightning flashes. Hail falls.

There come squalls, full of wonderful anatomies. There are alligators' heads on roe-deers' feet, owls with snakes' tails, swine with tigers' snouts, goats with donkeys' rumps, frogs as furry as bears, chameleons as big as hippopotamuses, calves with two heads, one of which weeps while the other bellows, quadruple foetuses linked by the navel and waltzing like tops, winged stomachs hovering like gnats.

They rain from the sky, they spring from the ground, they flow from the rocks. Eyeballs are everywhere flaming, and mouths roaring; there are bulging breasts, elongated claws, gnashing teeth, the smack of flesh on flesh. Some give birth, others copulate, or in a single mouthful eat each other up.

Stifled by their numbers, multiplying on contact, they crawl over one another—and they all heave around Antony with a regular movement, as if the ground were a ship's deck. Across his calves he feels the trail of snails, on his hands the chill of vipers; and spiders spinning their webs enclose him in their mesh.[20]

And Ernst's painting is as dense and feverish as Flaubert's prose, evoking in visual terms the writer's synesthetic sense of mind-numbing noise and palpable agony. The writhing, red-clad figure of Saint Anthony arches out toward the viewer in the lower foreground, pinned down and surrounded by the leers and laughter, the gaping, screaming maws, beaks, tongues, the sharp horns, fangs, teeth, claws, and the dilated, bulging eyes of feathered, furry, scaly, webbed, gooey, prickly hybrids, who probe his eyes, nose, and mouth with their talons, caress his throat with bony paws, nibble his fingers, tickle his side, and nuzzle his genitals with spiny tentacles. Painted with hallucinatory clarity, this foreground scene is set off from the background by a stagnant lake of acrid green, beyond which a throbbing, decalcomaniacal,[21] mirage-like land-

Max Ernst, *The Temptation of Saint Anthony* (1945).

scape seems in the process of metamorphosing the snaky limbs of a tree into a voluptuous nude, while another nude, with her head covered, has sprung up on a pillar in the sand.

Ernst's statement in the catalogue for the exhibition reads: "Shrieking for help and light across the stagnant water of his dark sick soul, St. Anthony receives as an answer the echo of his fear: the laughter of the monsters created by his visions."[22] Harriet and Sidney Janis, in their contribution to the catalogue, interpret the nudes as a "presentation of the theme of sacred and profane love—in the lush center the figure of an earthly temptress; to the right, high on a pedestal, the figure of woman exalted."[23] I suspect that the nudes are meant to embody the psychoanalytic "return of the repressed" as described by Sigmund Freud: "A well-known etching by Félicien Rops illustrates this fact . . . through the model case of repression in the lives of saints and penitents. An ascetic monk has sought refuge, most likely from the temptations of the world, near the image of the crucified Savior. Then, phantom-like, the cross sinks and in its stead, there rises shining the image of a voluptuous unclad woman, in the same position as the crucifixion."[24] Rops's "ascetic monk" is, in fact, Saint Anthony.

But all this passes before the viewers of *The Private Affairs of Bel Ami* in an instant. One moment we are watching the stately movements of Parisian society at an evening party, and the next moment the soundtrack is silent but the screen is filled with the harrowing Technicolor din of this unlikely image—the return of the repressed. After its appearance, Madame Walter's young daughter, Suzanne (Susan Douglas), tells Georges (who is also her "bel-ami") how ironic she finds it that her mother—a dull, virtuous, devout matron—has become so obsessively enthralled by the painting; Suzanne remarks that Madame Walter has even claimed to understand the saint's temptation as no one else can. Georges, who has seduced and then spurned Madame Walter, knows perfectly well whence her guilty obsession derives. Even he, callous as he is, is manifestly struck by the picture as soon as he lays eyes on it. One even wonders whether the horrific image might be a projection of Georges's unconscious—a subjective distortion created by unacknowledged guilt. But within minutes he is plotting his next moves: the betrayal of his wife, Madeleine; a divorce; the acquisition of a noble title; and the acquisition of Suzanne, heiress to forty million francs.

Georges's demons are greed and ambition—not lust, not desire. These latter are inconvenient impulses, likely to cloud his clear vision of his future. Sex and desirability are his means to his venal ends. He suppresses his occasional pangs of conscience; espouses an ethos of pitiless, unfeeling self-interest; holds others in utter contempt; and blithely uses and abuses the women who desire him. In *The Private Affairs of Bel Ami* it is women who desire, and they all, inexplicably, desire Georges Duroy. (In the novel, their desire makes more sense: Georges, recently discharged from the Sixth Hussars, is young and dashing, tall, well-built, and fair, with bright-blue eyes, a curled moustache, and curly reddish-blond hair parted in the middle. According to Maupassant, he resembles the heroes of popular romances[25]—rather unlike George Sanders, who in this film looks no younger than his forty years and is quite leaden; of actors who were prominent at the time, David Niven would have been more to type.) But there is an existential insight in the otherwise inexplicable lure of this cold, awkward, leaden Lothario for the passionate women and girls who flock to him.

By detaching the passion, the desire, from its object—or rather, by directing it toward an "inappropriate" object—*Bel Ami* focuses on what Flaubert called the object of Saint Anthony's contemplation: the "larva of desire."[26] Georges is, in this sense, something of a "blank slate"—an empty screen onto which something that lacks a real object is projected. His contempt for the women who love him, his indifference, only intensifies this effect; as Claude Arnaud has observed: "'Your cruelty is dearer to me than the love of others,' says Clotilde to Bel-Ami incessantly (her masochism is illustrated in a poster for the film). This is the credo of all Lewin's characters who love indifference because it allows them to love, above all, their loving."[27] The image of desirous women, frustrated and diminished by a milieu in which they are destined for propriety (Clotilde, the young widow), devotion (Virginie Walter, the matron), restriction (Suzanne, the daughter), or abuse (Rachel, the "dancer"—in this context an implicit euphemism for "prostitute"), is both multiplied and telescoped.

There are only two women in *Bel Ami* who do not fall victim to this plague of masochistic desire, in which the object seems chosen precisely in order to punish the desire. One is the virtuous Marie de Varenne (Frances Dee), who loves her husband; the other is Madeleine, Georges's wife, who is the widow of his friend Charles Forestier and who may not love either of her husbands. Madeleine is a feminist. When, at her first husband's deathbed, Georges proposes marriage, Madeleine responds, "It is necessary that you should understand what *sort* of woman I am. Marriage for me is not a charm but a partnership. I must be free—perfectly free—as to my ways, my acts, my comings and goings. I must be an equal, an ally, not an inferior or an obediently submissive wife."

Madeleine, it turns out, is a journalist and politician, but she is forced to take cover behind her men and to act through them. Madeleine is plainly responsible for the article which earns Georges a job at *La Vie Française* and her authorship of both Forestier's and Duroy's articles is suggested when Laroche-Mattieu (played by Warren William) needles Georges, "accidentally" calling him by his dead friend's name and remarking upon the uncanny similarity in their writing styles. Georges's response is extreme; he brings into the offices of *La Vie Française* a mannequin that resembles Laroche-Mattieu and shoots it through the head and heart with a pistol. The film depicts the *sort* of woman Madeleine is not only by her sublime composure, but also

Madeleine, with her scissors, and Georges, disposed like pieces on a chessboard.

by her frequent fidgeting with her wedding ring; once, when Georges's vanity and venality have come to the fore, she removes the ring and places it between the open blades of a pair of scissors. So literal an image of the castrating female has rarely been devised. (Madeleine removes the wedding band permanently, dropping it into her husband's mug of beer, after having been entrapped by him into an affair with Laroche-Mattieu, which she thought politic but he wished to use to obtain a divorce with impunity.)

Madeleine and Georges are equals who use one another, and who use their sex, for equally rapacious ends. When, shortly after their marriage, Georges enters his wife's salon one afternoon, Madeleine watches with calm amusement as Virginie Walter and Clotilde de Marelle shoot passionate, pained glances his way, which the camera catches with quick, searing close-ups. When Clotilde then asks Madeleine whether she "will allow me to call him bel-ami, still?" Madeleine, who knows of the previous attachment, responds with swift, dispassionate composure, "I will allow whatever you please."

The witty yet hateful misogyny that Sanders displays in *Bel Ami,* as in *The Moon and Sixpence* and *The Picture of Dorian Gray* (and in many of his other roles, as well; he seems to have been well-suited to the task), is, then, double-edged. Without naming him, the film critic Cecelia Ager was surely describing her friend Albert Lewin when—in an article in a popular magazine about film producers' appeals, and their failures to appeal, to female audiences—she brought up "the case of a certain independent movie producer who tries to straddle the issue. He happens to be a henpecked fellow in his private life, so the movies he makes always show the man triumphant, picking his way through a clutter of supine female bodies with outstretched arms and submissive eyes. But he also happens to be a knowledgeable little chap who understands why he does what he does. 'To stave off my own compulsion,' he confesses, 'and snatch what women for my audience I can, I make it a practice always to include a singularly articulate character who denounces women unmercifully. Curious, but this always seems to fetch them.'"[28]

But Lewin's attitudes toward the sexes were certainly more complicated than this. First, he believed that audiences took a cathartic and constructive pleasure in representations of hateful, evil, and lurid deeds. Lewin stated this position most bluntly (albeit with his tongue often in the vicinity of his cheek) in a letter to the columnist Lowell E. Redelings:

> We seek in entertainment a vicarious outlet for our smothered frustrations. In his preface to the *Comédie Humaine,* Honoré de Balzac . . . takes it as a matter of course that villains are more entertaining than virtuous characters. . . .
>
> I must confess that I agree with him thoroughly. And yet, I have to admit, not without a sense of shame, that I myself am a hopelessly virtuous man. I am innocent of murder, arson, theft, mayhem—and I even commit conventional hypocrisies, lies, intrigues, gluttonies, briberies and common treacheries with a reluctance which often makes me feel that I am headed for a pauper's grave.
>
> Nevertheless, I am always prepared to read a book about a scoundrel, or see a movie about one; and a story of infidelity attracts me much more than one of deathless love. My literary ear and my movie eye are cocked for scandal and sin.
>
> Is this because I am by nature a bad man, in spite of my notoriously virtuous character? I am sure this is exactly the case. I am full of original sin, which I have repressed all my life out of sheer cowardice—fear of discovery—fear of punishment—fear of ridicule—fear. Consequently, I am saturated with an inhibited sinfulness incapable of

direct expression, and longing for vicarious release. When I see wickedness therefore in art, literature, the theater and the movies, I am happy. I am entertained. My soul enjoys a much needed purge—a psychic catharsis, which makes it possible for me to continue my prudent and exemplary existence less painfully.

I long ago gave up the notion that there is something unique about this combination of evil desires and irreproachable performance in my life. I am satisfied that it is the normal state of men and women."[29]

Lewin's hackles were always raised by any implication that films had a particular obligation to be moral or pedagogical. This was evident, again, in his response to a question posed to a variety of people in the film industry by Klaus Mann's short-lived journal *Decision:* "Do you think that the films have a pedagogical mission for the masses? If so, has Hollywood production over the last decade lived up to it?" Lewin's tongue was in his cheek here too:

Since the idea of discipline in education has been for some time a dead cat and the fashionable criterion of epistemology is now exclusively eudaimonistic, one can be only momentarily shocked by the suggestion that the movies have a pedagogical mission. With the schools becoming centers of entertainment, it is perhaps not too much to expect the movie-houses to be places of instruction. One can even imagine a time when the public will be compelled to attend the movies a minimum number of hours, but will have to buy tickets of admission to an entertainment classroom.

No doubt this is a long view. For the moment, one wonders why a question is asked of the movies which is not asked of the other arts.... If Shakespeare wrote *Hamlet* for a course in Danish history or *Macbeth,* in Scottish; if Sophocles wrote *Oedipus Tyrannos* for a text; if Dostoievsky designed *Crime and Punishment* as a lesson in psychopathology, then the movies should have a pedagogical mission. It is more likely that their mission will be to entertain the "masses."[30]

Lewin's ire (which he shared with Flaubert and Oscar Wilde) at the implication that art should offer up role models or in any other simplistic way cater to a morally prescriptive view of the world tends to obscure the fact that his view of sexual relations was essentially moral and principled. It is true that he gave Sanders's characters rather free rein, especially to make vicious pronouncements, but it is equally true, amusing as these characters could be, that their views are treated, in his films, as folly—as very grave folly indeed. Of the three, only Lord Henry Wotton even lives to regret the results of his heedless epigrammatic philosophy. Charles Strickland and Georges Duroy see the light only shortly before the moment of death. These are strong, often amusing, but unsympathetic characters. In all three films, sympathy is reserved for others—not for indisputably "good" characters (the few that are featured are rather flat[31]), but for characters who struggle with good and evil and with their conscience: in *The Moon and Sixpence,* Dirk and Blanche Stroeve; in *The Picture of Dorian Gray,* Dorian himself, as well as Basil Hallward, both Sibyl and James Vane, and Adrian Singleton; and in *Bel Ami,* Virginie Walter and Clotilde de Marelle.

It is particularly those women characters who suffer for a desire that is forbidden and seemingly beyond their control who are treated most sympathetically; Blanche, Sibyl, Clotilde, and Madame Walter are abused by their lovers and are all more or less tormented by conflict and guilt that is linked specifically to their sexuality. This is not altogether uncommon in Hollywood films, I should add, although women who commit adultery are usually not allowed to go unpunished—unlike, for instance, Clotilde, who suffers for Georges and loses him but is not driven mad with guilt (as Madame Walter is) or driven to suicide (as Blanche and Sibyl are for their "sins").

What is most unusual about Lewin's treatment of the sexes in his films is, however, not a moral view of sexual relations but an unlikely psychosocial view. Lewin's concentration on a multiplicity of desirous women disposed around one rather empty male object of desire (Blanche and Ata around Strickland; Sibyl and Gladys around Dorian; Rachel, Clotilde, Virginie and Suzanne Walter, and, marginally, Madeleine, around Georges Duroy) has the most in common with a formula of film noir: men drawn to a femme fatale as moths to a flame. But Lewin essentially reverses this formula. It is the male object of feminine desire that is represented, fetishistically, at the center of each of these three films. This is most prominent in *The Private Affairs of Bel Ami,* which begins at a café actually called *Désir,*[32] where Rachel (Marie Wilson), the dancer from the Folies-Bergère, develops a sudden passion for Georges, at whom she glances as a vender passes selling the sheet music to a popular song, "Bel Ami." One female character is used to make Georges's status as a fetish literal. This is Lourine, Clotilde's young daughter, who, like her mother, adores "bel-ami," and who is never shown without her toy soldier—a stiff doll, approximately eight inches tall, wearing the uniform of Georges's regiment. (The uniform is a coincidence, but Georges remarks that it reflects the child's good taste.) After Lourine's first encounter with Georges, the doll appears with the words "Bel Ami" embroidered on its jacket, and Lourine clings to it as she sleeps. In strictly psychoanalytic terms, there is no such phenomenon as a female fetishist, because of the etiology of this presumed "perversion": the fetishist (male) denies that females lack a penis; his denial is manifested by finding a substitute for what is lacking; and that substitute is the fetish. Still, I think it is reasonable to suggest that the phallic substitutes Lewin associates here with females, such as Lourine's doll (which was his invention) and Madeleine's cigarettes, represent a displacement that is comparable to a fetish and deserves to be called one.

Clotilde and Georges are introduced by Madeleine at the Forestiers' dinner party.

From the viewpoint of the most influential feminist analyses of representations of sexual differences in Hollywood films, and with regard to the possibilities for identification offered by these representations,[33] *Bel Ami* is a problem. The male characters in this film—the protagonist and others—offer male or male-identified viewers little with which to identify. Georges Duroy is a mechanistic, puppetlike vacuum whose attractiveness and wittiness are touted but not really discernible, and his sadistic actions are too hateful, repulsive, automatic, and enigmatic for any viewer to be inclined to empathize with them.

Georges is frequently identified with (and, indeed, identifies himself with) Punch, a puppet, on the basis of his rather mechanistic view of the world—and perhaps of sexuality. It is established during the Forestiers' dinner party early in the film that Georges appreciates Punch for his "amorous inclination," a phrase to which Douglas McVay—correctly, I think—adds: "with Punch's big stick invested with phallic connotations." Jacques Rival (played by Albert Basserman), the caricaturist for *La Vie Française,* promptly draws a cartoon of Georges as Punch, which reappears periodically to signify Georges's folly.[34]

As for the other men, Charles Forestier is a consumptive cuckold; Laroche-Mattieu—posed in the scene in which he is introduced rather like the figure in Ingres's portrait *M. Bertin* (1832)—is a pompous boor; and Monsieur Walter (Hugo Haas) is, as his wife puts it, "not a man. He's a cash box." The remaining male characters are minor; and of these, the most compelling, Norbert de Varenne (David Bond)—composer, organist, and music critic for *La Vie Française*—is blind: that was Lewin's invention and, given his focus here and elsewhere on the "gaze," not an arbitrary one.

In Lewin's *Bel Ami,* it is the female characters who are more fully realized and whose complex feelings and focused gaze offer more for the viewer—female or female-identified—to identify with. In fact, with his representations of female desire, Lewin achieved something that, in Hollywood films, was considered taboo—so much so that theorists have been led to describe it as "impossible." Perhaps it was only very difficult. Lewin effected it through complex, condensed, symbolic, literary and pictorial means—as he did in *Dorian Gray,* where not only female desire but also homoeroticism and male narcissism were represented, for example in the perverse "butterfly dissolve" (see page 46). In *The Private Affairs of Bel Ami,* female desire—another "desire that dare not speak its name"—is represented variously.

The guilty, morbid "larva of desire" explodes from a netherworld that has been rigorously held down in Max Ernst's painting. In the painting, Anthony is stroked, stimulated, and explored by gestures which on their own suggest a certain tenderness or erotic playfulness (tickling, nibbling, nuzzling, caressing), but which are delivered by a host of horrible, mutant demons. More transparently, in one scene (how this escaped the censors is hard to understand) the unrepresentable erotic life of women is conveyed through a dream. This is the scene in which Virginie Walter, who has succumbed to Georges's opportunistic seduction, meets him for luncheon in a private room at a restaurant; she is scorned, rebuffed, and humiliated by him, but she endures it and indeed seems almost to relish it. As he eats his dessert, she sits on the floor beside him and, discreetly winding a strand of her hair around his coat button (a gesture taken from the novel), she says:

"I shall tell you about a dream I had of you last night. I was traveling on a train at night through a mysterious forest. It was a very long train, but I seemed to be the only passenger. We stopped at a deserted station surrounded by dark trees. I hurried to close my suitcase and stepped down to the platform looking about for you because I knew that you would be there to meet me." At this point, Madame Walter is interrupted by Georges, who, irate about a piece of political intrigue of which she has informed him, leaps up in anger, yanking from her head the hair she had been winding around his button. In a prolonged close-up, the camera focuses on her blissful expression of pain. Then the pinched, middle-aged face of Madame Walter, with its expression of ecstatic agony, dissolves into the young, sensual, open visage of Clotilde, who—in the next scene—duplicates Madame Walter's position; sitting on the floor next to Georges, who is comfortably seated in an armchair, Clotilde, too, relates a dream:

"I dreamed that we were taking a journey together across the desert. We were riding on two camels and we'd taken some sandwiches wrapped in paper and some wine in a bottle. But it annoyed me, because we were too far off from each other on our separate camels and I wanted to get down." Georges remarks, "I want to get down, too," with a somewhat leering smile, before Clotilde discovers, to her immense chagrin, that hairs have been wound fastidiously around all his coat buttons.

While Clotilde's dream was derived from Maupassant's novel,[35] Madame Walter's was Lewin's invention. And while Clotilde's sensual journey has distinctly erotic overtones, it is Madame Walter's that, in the most elementary of Freudian terms, represents sexual intercourse, with its very long train (the penis) traveling through (penetrating) a mysterious forest (the vagina), to a deep, deserted station (the obscure interior of the female genitalia), its protagonist hurrying to shut her suitcase (in dreams, according to Freud, such cases always symbolize the female genitalia—thus this suggests the "closure" of orgasm) while rushing to meet her lover.[36]

Thus, through means that are poetic and, if not exactly subtle, were indirect enough to elude the Hays office, *The Private Affairs of Bel Ami* endows its female characters with a range of subjective desires (including Madeleine's intellectual and political

In the film's concluding duel, Georges must stand in place for two minutes while his wounded opponent, Philippe de Contel (Richard Fraser), is given an opportunity to return his fire.

aims, as well as Clotilde's and Virginie's erotic ones)—and with substance which makes them, however much they may suffer, the agents of his story. They, after all, take away Georges Duroy's name and substitute for it another, *bel-ami*—"handsome friend"—which objectifies him, just as women are so often objectified and diminished. These women are all disappointed, betrayed, or humiliated, but they survive Georges, who dies in a duel.

This duel was of Lewin's devising, in accordance with an imperative from the Hays office, but it does not have the tacked-on quality of so many other scenes devised to placate the censors; rather, it is rendered with atmospheric and ironic aplomb. It takes place in pouring rain, and Georges retains his umbrella throughout. His shot strikes his antagonist, Philippe de Contel (Richard Fraser), a member of the fallen nobility fighting for his family name, who—though severely wounded—is given two minutes to retaliate, while Georges must remain in place on the field. These two minutes, at the very end of which Georges is fatally shot, are in real time—a conceit that was considered remarkable when Fred Zinnemann used it (more extensively) in *High Noon* (1952) and was still noteworthy two decades later, when Ingmar Bergman used it in *The Hour of the Wolf* (1968).

When, after Georges's death, the camera—which gives an effect of lone movement through the empty park—shows (as if at random) a sign for La Petit Guignol and a disembodied voice (the film has had no narrator; the voice, as noted earlier, sounds like David Bond, the actor who played Norbert de Varenne) tells us that "We are all no more than puppets unless we believe," one can only wonder in what we might believe. Madame Walter's vindictiveness (it is she who informs Philippe de Contel that Georges has "stolen" his title) discredits her Christian piety. Madeleine's ambitions have been foiled, along with Laroche-Mattieu's. Clotilde, perhaps, has been salvaged by her ability to love. This last possibility is suggested in the short but eloquent scene, set at the Cathedral of Notre Dame, in which Marie de Varenne quietly gives voice to a transcendent love. Here, and in a handful of other scenes in Lewin's films—as will be discussed in Chapter 6—irony gives way with surprising lyricism to a sort of experimental sincerity.

Pandora and the Flying Dutchman (1951). The title characters (Ava Gardner and James Mason) express their mythically inevitable love amid antiquities on the Costa Brava in Spain—on what Albert Lewin once described as "that charnel-house, the Mediterranean, . . . stuffed to its shores with the bones of men and ships."

CHAPTER 4

La Belle Dame Sans Merci:
Pandora and the Flying Dutchman (1951)

If it weren't for my love of form, I might perhaps have been a great mystic.
                                                                Gustave Flaubert[1]

What I hear is valueless; only what I see is living, and when I close my eyes my vision is even more powerful.
                                                                Giorgio de Chirico[2]

It is nevertheless perhaps not useless to persuade ourselves that this idea of a unique love comes from a mystic attitude.
                                                                André Breton[3]

The materialist says that only appearance is real. The mystic (or realist, in the medieval sense) says there is a reality beyond appearance. Appearance, in fact, may not only be not a clue to reality, but a barrier. How many senses do we need to perceive reality? None; since many more than five would still not suffice. The beginning of knowledge is blindness, deafness, the absence of taste, touch, smell.
                                                                Albert Lewin[4]

Although Albert Lewin had begun work on his original screenplay *Pandora and the Flying Dutchman* as early as 1946,[5] and had researched the legend of the ghost ship even earlier, his film was not produced until 1950 and not released until 1951. And its appearance gives the impression of what one might call a "sea change" in Lewin's work and in his world. As has been noted, the three films that Lewin directed in the 1940s are bound together by a number of consistent visual, thematic, and structural attributes. They clearly represent one body of work, the exploration of one nexus of concerns, constructed within the restraints of the studio system (although two of the three were independently produced). When one considers their fastidious black-and-white interiors crafted under Lewin's and Gordon Wiles's supervision, their European fin-de-siècle settings, their pathologically attractive male protagonists, their explosions

Pandora and the Flying Dutchman

Esperanza, a village on the Costa Brava in Spain, about 1930. The events of the story are narrated by Geoffrey Fielding (Harold Warrender), an archaeologist and an expert in the history of this mythic stretch of Mediterranean coast. Geoffrey is among the admirers of Pandora Reynolds (Ava Gardner), a beautiful American chanteuse who is the erotic center of a mainly British expatriate community in Esperanza. Another of Pandora's admirers, Reggie Demerest (Marius Goring), kills himself in drunken despair over his unrequited love. Yet another, the racing driver Stephen Cameron (Nigel Patrick), manages to obtain her promise of marriage by sacrificing his beloved car for her.

The night of her engagement to Stephen, Pandora becomes intrigued by a splendid yacht in the harbor. On a whim, she disrobes and swims out to it; aboard, she finds its lone, brooding occupant, Hendrick van der Zee (James Mason). Hendrick is, inexplicably, finishing a painting of the mythical Pandora—the darling of the gods—that bears a striking resemblance to Pandora Reynolds. Mystified and provoked, Pandora lashes out at the picture, literally defacing it, but Hendrick is unperturbed.

Hendrick becomes part of the social life of Esperanza. Soon its most famous native, the toreador Juan Montalvo (Mario Cabre), returns on a visit; Juan was once a suitor of Pandora's, and now his passion is rekindled. Stephen, who has recovered and repaired his mangled car, succeeds in breaking a speed record. At the party to celebrate this, Pandora confesses her love to Hendrick, who seems torn between love and some more ineffable impulse and finally rebuffs her.

Geoffrey discovers Hendrick's true identity, which Hendrick himself admits—that he is the legendary Flying Dutchman, a sea captain who was condemned for the murder of his innocent young bride, and for blasphemy, to wander the seas until judgment day unless he could find a woman willing to die for him. Pandora, he says, is the reincarnation of his murdered wife and is the woman who can redeem him; but to spare her life, he will give up his own salvation.

Juan Montalvo sees that it is Hendrick—not Stephen—who is his real rival for Pandora's affection, goes to Hendrick's bungalow one night, and (so it seems) kills him. Pandora, who has been awakened, evidently by a premonition or dream, runs to Hendrick and finds him alive but the bungalow a shambles and his little dog dead. The next day, when Montalvo is performing in the bullring and looks up at Pandora in the crowd, he sees Hendrick arrive and calmly take a seat beside her. Paralyzed by astonishment, Montalvo is gored by the bull; before dying, he confesses his crime to Pandora.

On the eve of her marriage to Stephen, confused by her dream and Montalvo's confession, Pandora tells Geoffrey her troubles. Geoffrey, believing Hendrick to have sailed, divulges the Dutchman's secret. But the yacht has been becalmed. Pandora swims to Hendrick and, in a moment of suspended ecstasy, they declare their undying love. A thunderclap presages a sudden squall, and the yacht founders. Several days later, after a violent storm, their bodies are recovered, their hands interlocked.

of paintings in color, their crafty symbolism, and their dense ironies—and other features that need not be enumerated—it is clear that Lewin's first film of the 1950s represents a radical shift in terms.

Pandora and the Flying Dutchman at first glance seems to invert all the abiding traits of the three earlier films. This film is set largely out of doors, on the Costa Brava in Spain, where it was filmed in luxurious Technicolor by Jack Cardiff.[6] The mythical, romantic story (in which irony is relegated to a different role) is set in the twentieth century—about 1930, a period that must have been chosen at least in large part because of its contemporaneity with the height of surrealism. Further, not only is the central figure (and, one is tempted to exclaim, what a figure!) of this film a woman but, as embodied by Ava Gardner, she is presented almost as a cliché of the "eternal feminine": she is "Woman"; she is Pandora, the first woman; she is Eve, Pandora's Judeo-Christian equivalent; she is Eva (or Ava) Prima Pandora[7]—a "gift" to men from the gods, a "deadly delight," a *"beau mal."* Her allure is fatal. Men will sacrifice anything to possess her, including their lives. She is *la belle dame sans merci*,[8] an avatar of that mystic femme fatale who emerged in the romantic period and came to haunt a whole strain of late romanticism—to which Lewin himself was so attracted—that included Gustave Flaubert and Théophile Gautier, symbolists such as Gustave Moreau and Joris-Karl Huysmans and, ultimately (although they altered her form), the surrealists in France, as well as Keats and then the decadents, including Wilde, Swinburne, and Beardsley, in England.[9]

Against this original, fatal female, Lewin sets an eternal man: the Flying Dutchman (Hendrick, played by James Mason), Heine's "wandering Jew of the sea,"[10] the Ulysses of the north.[11] And he becomes fatal for her, yet saves her from the deadly, anesthetized indifference of her life—the curse of being loved but not able to love—while she saves him from his curse: eternally to be "blown back and forth between Death and Life, neither of the two willing to claim him; his sorrow as deep as the sea upon which he drifts, his ship without anchor and his heart without hope."[12] Thus, the two redeem each other from a hopelessly barren existence, from parallel purgatories: life without love and life without death. Eros and Thanatos, in this scenario, are inexorably linked, interlaced like Pandora's and Hendrick's hands—which are all that can be seen of them when their bodies, entangled in and obscured by a fisherman's net, are brought in from the sea in the opening, framing scene of the film.

This mystical union, or reunion, is played out in terms of excessively material sensuality, amid scenes and spectacles that juxtapose antiquity and modernity: archaeological ruins, deep-sea fishing, flamenco dancing, bullfights, beach parties, automobile races. The setting is a fishing village cum expatriate resort called Esperanza ("Hope"), where, according to the film's narrator, the archaeologist Geoffrey Fielding (Harold Warrender), an ancient treasure lies on the bottom of the sea. The treasure can be construed, mythically, as hope itself, the one blessing that remained at the bottom of Pandora's box (or krater[13]) after it was incautiously opened. And it is hope that Pandora and Hendrick find in Esperanza when they find one another.

Hope is the companion of love in Ferdinand Alquié's analysis of what he calls the "philosophy of surrealism."[14] And surrealism was, in fact, the starting point of *Pandora*. "It was natural," Lewin later claimed, "that I should try to create a film with a deliberately surrealist intention."[15] The relationship of *Pandora* to surrealist concepts of woman (*femme-enfant*, "child-woman"), of love (*l'amour fou*, "mad love") of fate (*hasard objectif*, "objective chance"), of space, of time, and of the "marvelous" accounts in large part for the wild discrepancies between the responses of the film's fervent advocates—who have been mostly French—and its detractors (almost everyone else). Visually, this

The film's narrator, Geoffrey Fielding (Harold Warrender), an archaeologist, reconstructs a Greek krater, in a metaphoric parallel to the narrative he relates.

strangest of Lewin's films is extravagant, fetishistic, and oneiric, traits that derive in equal and often indistinguishable parts from surrealism and from Hollywood; aurally, it has a top-heavy script in which literary pastiche is interwoven with mythic melodrama and which is spoken with rhetorical restraint and sometimes agonizing languor by the actors.

But to explain what some critics have called a "masterpiece" and others a "supreme folly" in terms of its obviously mixed parentage—surrealism and Hollywood—is, although necessary, still inadequate. It is nearly impossible to convey the oddness of this film: its almost flat recitations of lines alternately lyrical, pedantic, and cloyingly melodramatic; its juxtapositions of lavish, dynamic spectacle, and simple, static compositions; its very sensual denaturing of nature's sensuous beauty, with Ava Gardner clad in another dazzling gown in each scene, and with the Costa Brava seen by the synthetic moonlight of day-for-night photography (which uses filters in daylight shooting to give an effect of night).

The costume designer (Beatrice Dawson); the cinematographer (Jack Cardiff); the writer-director (Lewin); the daylight of the Mediterranean; the day-for-night phosphorescent moonlight, and the Technicolor photography—all these conspire to dissolve any difference between a movie goddess and an actual deity. It should be noted that Ava Gardner had already blurred this particular boundary: three years before, in the comedy *One Touch of Venus* (1948, directed by William Seiter), she had played a goddess come to life (like Galatea—a myth with which Lewin was fascinated) through a tacky statue in a department store. And with rather uncanny symmetry, she was to perform this feat in reverse three years after *Pandora,* in *The Barefoot Contessa* (1954, directed by Joseph Mankiewicz), in which she played a Spanish dancer who becomes a Hollywood star and finally, after her tragic death, a grave monument. Perhaps, though, these three films are not so much a coincidence as a sort of trilogy. According to James Mason, Mankiewicz—who, like Lewin, was given to making very wordy, self-conscious films—had been "deeply impressed" by *Pandora*.[16]

Despite the claim of some critics that *Pandora* must be loved or despised,[17] its ambiguities and contradictions are more likely to elicit ambivalence. The excesses of admiration and contempt that are found in the critical responses to the film are reactions to something essentially paradoxical and therefore unnerving—and to a whiff of travesty that led one of Lewin's French admirers, Raphaël Bassan, to describe *Pandora* as "almost a distanced documentary about the magnetism of stars, perhaps the first 'camp' film."[18]

> Everything tends to make us believe that there exists a certain point of the mind at which life and death, the real and the imagined, past and future, the communicable and the incommunicable, high and low, cease to be perceived as contradictions (André Breton, *Second Manifesto of Surrealism*).[19]

Pandora and the Flying Dutchman is set in coastal Spain in the same period in which the *Second Manifesto of Surrealism* appeared, a time when two Spaniards—Salvador Dalí, who created many hallucinatory images of nearly the same stretch of coast; and Luis Buñuel, director of the first really ambitious surrealist films—had emerged as major new figures among the surrealists, and were a particular influence on André Breton, whose avowed ambition to dissolve Cartesian oppositions could be considered a raison d'être for Lewin's film.

Lewin had become increasingly involved with surrealism during its wartime exile, through his friendship with Max Ernst and Marcel Duchamp, and especially through his friendship with Man Ray, who lived in Hollywood from 1940 to 1951, years during which he and Lewin became very close, as they were to remain until Lewin's death. Indeed, with the possible exception of Giorgio de Chirico, Man Ray is the most persistent influence on the imagery of *Pandora and the Flying Dutchman,* in ways both subtle and obvious. Moreover, there is a sense in which *Pandora* must be seen as a sort of tribute to Lewin's friendship and intellectual kinship with Man Ray—an artist who, although he was deeply involved with the surrealist movement from its inception, managed to retain a certain ironic distance from it. So similar were the two men, in many respects, that Jane Livingston might have been describing Albert Lewin when she wrote of his friend: "Never a dogmatic partisan or a fully credulous ideologue, Man Ray continually expressed a studied empathy with his peers, even while he diverged from them. He could be the most subtle and inventive of collaborators, the securely authoritative artist; also at times he veered inexplicably into some realm of doubt, becoming heavy-handed, aggressively banal. He was deeply clever and blithely naive, . . . perhaps too much the reflexive, dualistic, Western thinker, too much the pragmatist and too much the invested classicist, ever to capitulate totally to surrealism's cultural agnosticism."[20]

"Dear Man," wrote Albert Lewin to his friend from London in February of 1950, "I have just returned from a wonderful trip to the Costa Brava in Spain. It is just as if

Hendrick van der Zee and Pandora Reynolds prepare to meet their common destiny. In the foreground is a photograph by Man Ray that plays the "role" of a miniature portrait painting of Pandora's earlier incarnation—a Renaissance woman who was Hendrick's original bride.

God read 'Pandora' and made Costa Brava for my decor."[21] Lewin goes on to discuss some business regarding the film, for which he had commissioned Man Ray to make both a photographic and a painted portrait of Ava Gardner. The color photograph was to appear in the film as a painting: a sixteenth-century miniature of the young bride of the Flying Dutchman. The actual painted portrait was supposed to be a work by the "contemporary" Dutchman—that is, around 1930—and was to represent Ava Gardner, in quasisurrealist style, as the mythical Pandora, accompanied by the box which she bore to earth.

In the letter, Lewin expresses his satisfaction with the most recent version of the (photographic) miniature: "I think it is very beautiful and we shall make good use of it. I like it better than the others because of the expression on Ava's face. She looks quite sweet and innocent, whereas in the other poses she seems a little too sophisticated for the 16th century character, who was supposed to be a nice sweet faithful girl like Desdemona."[22] But Lewin goes on to express some concern about—in fact, to reject—the painted portrait: "It is all my fault—not yours. The result of the pose which I suggested is that Pandora's expression seems to be somewhat furtive and cunning.... That expression should be innocent—perhaps somewhat naive ... if the dialogue is to ring true. This worries me a little bit and it may be that for this reason I shall let someone here take a crack at doing a painting along these lines."

Lewin's tact and his assumption of responsibility belie the fact that Man Ray's painting was appallingly mediocre and lacked not only the proper "innocence" but any surrealist atmosphere whatsoever. Painting was probably not his strongest medium, although he preferred it at this stage of his career, but even so one can only

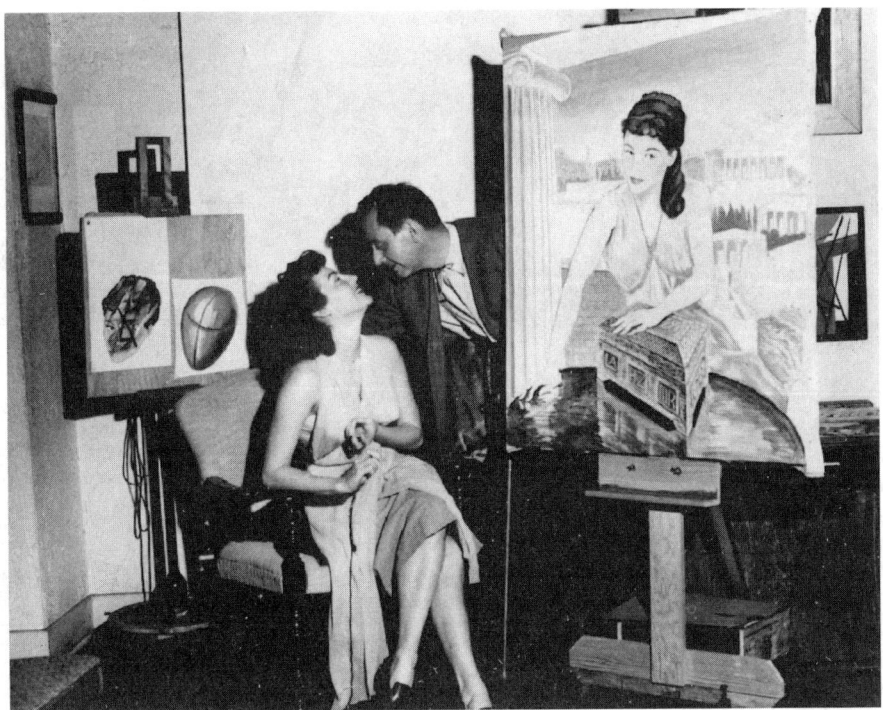

Ava Gardner with Man Ray in his Hollywood studio—probably in late 1949—with his unsuccessful painting of her as Pandora.

marvel at this unlikely image and wonder what on earth Man Ray thought he was doing. Perhaps he was starstruck and looked rather too closely at the model and not closely enough at his likeness of her; or perhaps—although this seems unlikely, given his regard for and gratitude to Lewin—he thought this was the kind of effort appropriate to a commercial film.

Actually, Man Ray seems to have painted another portrait of Ava Gardner in sixteenth-century dress, and this must have been a possible alternative to using the photograph to suggest a Renaissance miniature. This second painting, far superior to the "surrealist" portrait, is a fine likeness of Ava Gardner, painted in a simple, graphic style with heavy black contours that looks like a stained-glass window. There seems to be no documentation of when Man Ray undertook this version of the portrait or whether it was actually undertaken at Lewin's behest. In any case, though, lovely it is, it would have looked even more anachronistic than the photograph that was used, which is closer to the photographic verisimilitude of the northern Renaissance portraitists (such as Hans Holbein). Stained glass was always an essentially ecclesiastical medium and was not used in medieval or Renaissance Europe for so bourgeois and secular a genre as the portrait.

The painting of Pandora that was finally used in the film was by Ferdinand (Ferdie) Bellan, a British artist who was also an art director and scene designer.[23] Bellan's painting more closely achieves Lewin's intention; though hardly uncanny in effect, it is tolerably representative of the strain of surrealism inspired by de Chirico, exemplified by the raked perspectives and strange juxtapositions in the work of painters such as Paul Delvaux and Remedios Varo (both of whom Lewin collected). Although the

Hendrick and the modern Pandora, with Ferdie Bellan's version of Hendrick's painting of the mythical Pandora.

painting and *Pandora* itself have sometimes been described as only fortuitously surrealist ("romantic sensation comes inadvertently near the vision of Delvaux and Ernst"[24]), they are usually considered to have been influenced more directly by surrealism: "The artificial accentuation of colors, violent and contrasting, banishes every trace of realism, and creates an oneiric world, such that the construction of shots evokes a succession of de Chirico paintings (the portrait of Pandora that Mason paints is an almost perfect pastiche)."[25]

That de Chirico's work, along with Delvaux's, was a source of Bellan's portrait cannot be doubted, even without reference to Lewin's frank avowal that the juxtapositions of ancient and modern images in the work of those two artists "especially moved" him and were a major source of inspiration for the film. In the scene in which the painting is introduced—during the first encounter between Pandora and the Flying Dutchman (that is, the first encounter in the lifetime of this Pandora)—after she, in anger and frustration, has literally defaced the portrait, Hendrick's response makes clear both the philosophical and the artistic explanation of the events:

> You haven't hurt my painting; you've helped it [with a palette knife, he begins to scrape at the canvas]. In a moment, I'll show you what I mean. No work of art is complete until the element of chance has entered into it. The unexpected and the surprising are indispensable [he makes some quick brush strokes]. Pandora was the first woman, the Eve of Greek legend, whose curiosity cost us our earthly paradise. I was wrong to portray her as a particular woman—no matter how beautiful. Pandora should appear as Woman in the abstract: bride and mother, the original and generic egghead, from which we can imagine the whole human race to have been hatched. By sheer chance, you have contributed the unexpected element which my painting needed. Now it really is Pandora!

At this point, an insert of the painting reveals that Pandora's head is now a smooth, featureless oval, resembling the mannequins of de Chirico.

It is indisputably de Chirico, and not Man Ray, whose style is evoked in this portrait; and even if Man Ray had executed a more successful painting, it would have testified more to his ability to imitate de Chirico's protosurrealist, dreamlike style than to his own role as a force behind the film. Man Ray's color photograph of Ava Gardner—the portrait that represents a Dutch miniature—is hardly more characteristic of his work than the rejected painting. It is meant, no doubt, to evoke the descriptive style of northern painters such as Holbein. Still, within the film it is anachronistic—in all likelihood intentionally; visual anachronisms (Goutman's disguised Botticelli in *The Moon and Sixpence* and the contemporary paintings that interrupt *Dorian Gray* and *Bel Ami*) are a touchstone of all Lewin's films. Two other works by Man Ray make "cameo" appearances in *Pandora*: a collage in a taverna called Las Dos Tortugas and a chess set in Geoffrey Fielding's study. But these do not constitute significant evidence of Man Ray's real impact on *Pandora and the Flying Dutchman*; for that, one must look beyond his actual collaboration to his influence.

> *Et si tu trouves sur cette terre une femme à l'amour sincère . . .* ("And if you find on this earth a woman who loves sincerely . . ."; Man Ray and Robert Desnos, *L'Étoile du mer*).[26]

Of all the characteristics which separate *Pandora* from Lewin's earlier films—its vivid color, its outdoor settings, its "natural supernaturalism,"[27] its nearly contemporary setting—the most significant is its focus on a woman. Ava Gardner herself is at the center of this newfound focus, as Pandora—a "femme-enfant fatale"—but also as "herself": not as a "real" person, but as icon of a kind of "animal" female sexuality, of a movie goddess, of the ultimate desirable woman. If George Sanders embodied the rather perverse ego ideal around which Lewin's films of the 1940s revolved, Ava Gardner became the specter that haunted all of his films of the 1950s. Although she appeared only in *Pandora,* Lewin was clearly trying to recreate her in his other two films, and he had dearly wished to use her in two of his most cherished but unrealized projects.

Rita Gam, beautiful but rather lifeless and numb in the title role of *Saadia* (1954), is an obvious proxy for Gardner. Lewin was back on the MGM payroll for this production and "had been dished out with a fairly second team of MGM contract actors and actresses."[28] Lewin had an even smaller budget for casting his last film, *The Living Idol* (1957), and the female lead went to Liliane Montevecchi, in one of her earliest (and least successful) roles. Gardner was by then too old for this juvenile part, aside from being beyond the film's financial means, but she was plainly the "type" that Lewin was looking for. Gardner did, of course, star in *The Naked Maja,* but Lewin, finally, had nothing to do with that production; the producers bought but then entirely dispensed with the script he had spent so much time researching and writing with Ava Gardner very much in mind. Lewin's *Diana at Midnight,* an unrealized original script, loosely based on *Faust,* was another project that, for Lewin, depended on Ava Gardner's participation.

The shift from a masculine to a feminine center of gravity that distances Lewin's films of the 1940s from those of the 1950s, then, seems connected to two individual figures: George Sanders and Ava Gardner.[29] Although the films of the 1940s revolved around masculine objects of desire that allowed for what I think are often radical representations of female subjectivity and desire, the female characters in those films—and the actresses who played them—were always secondary. In relocating the center, Lewin not only reorients the axes of gender, of desire, of subject and object, but undermines the essential cultural and moral emphases of his previous films. Now, under the aegis of the feminine, the moral dimension—which always colored the films of the 1940s, though never didactically—is subsumed in a supramoral scenario of love. Culture, too, the framework of the earlier films, is transcended in *Pandora,* which revels in the natural in order to go, as the narrator, Geoffrey Fielding, himself says, "beyond nature."

The surrealist details and allusions in the films of the 1940s testified to Lewin's familiarity and a fascination with the iconography of surrealism, but it is not until *Pandora* that the full impact of surrealism is felt. The decadent, a dominant theme of his films of the 1940s—and a theme that always has a moral dimension—is now supplanted by the marvelous, which is not only beyond nature but also beyond reason and morality.

> Surrealism offers us a hope of existing and projects existence in something beyond natural life; an immanent beyond, however—not posterior to life—a beyond seeming to reveal itself to the one who will seize the World under the aspect of the marvelous.[30]

The immanent "beyond" that *Pandora* aspires to make tangible is the experience of love—mystical, marvelous, convulsive—that is, "mad love" *(l'amour fou).* And this love is a possibility contained by the image of woman. André Breton was the author of *L'Amour fou,* but Man Ray was its primary illustrator, not only in his photographs accompanying the text but, beyond that, through his vast body of work on the female form, eroticism, and sex.

Pandora and the Flying Dutchman derives a good deal of its imagery, general and specific, from Man Ray's many images of women, of eroticism, and of love, as well as from his illustrations for *L'Amour fou.* In fact, in the early, preproduction stages, when *Pandora* was expected to be black-and-white, Man Ray contributed at Lewin's request a

Gypsy musicians and La Pillina's impassioned flamenco performance at Las Dos Tortugas.

La Belle Dame Sans Merci: *Pandora and the Flying Dutchman* (1951)

"photographic script" with general and specific recommendations for the cinematography.[31] Few of his recommendations, most of which assumed black-and-white film, were usable with color, and most were too experimental for a commercial film, even so avant-garde a film as *Pandora* was meant to be. But Lewin did not need these specific recommendations to instill his film with the atmosphere of Man Ray's surrealism.

An early scene, which constitutes the transition between the framing narration and the narrative proper, starts with Geoffrey's recollection of being distracted and lured out one evening by an erotic and disquieting moon (this itself is possibly an allusion to Luis Buñuel's and Salvador Dalí's *Un chien andalou*), and then moves to the taverna, Las Dos Tortugas (a reference to the Two Turtles, the scene of Dorian's encounter with Sibyl Vane in *The Picture of Dorian Gray*), where a feverish flamenco performance is under way. The erotic violence of the flamenco dancer, La Pillina, evokes *Fixed-explosive*, a Man Ray photograph of a dancer caught in convulsed and blurry motion, which illustrates Breton's assertion in *L'Amour fou* that "Convulsive beauty will be

Man Ray, *Explosante-fixe*, 1934.

veiled-erotic, fixed-explosive, magic-circumstantial, or it will not be."[32] Ironically, the moving picture of the dancer, by achieving motion instead of stopping it, contradicts the meaning of this image in Breton's book: the beauty of a frozen explosion.[33]

The surrealist concept of objective chance *(hasard objectif)* is demonstrated in *Pandora* not only by its rather pedantic exposition in the scene in which Hendrick explains to Pandora how she has improved his painting by defacing it, but in another scene, as well: Señora Montalvo (Marguerite d'Alvarez) reading tarot cards that foretell her son Juan's fate. A passage in *L'Amour fou* in which Breton describes fortune-telling with cards is accompanied by a Man Ray photograph that seems to hover behind this scene with Señora Montalvo—the photograph shows a black, sculptured hand laying cards around a crude, obscure figurine.[34]

The most direct quotation of Man Ray's photographs for *L'Amour fou,* however, is a prop that often recurs in *Pandora:* an hourglass. The hourglass, which functions as a symbol of Hendrick's endless existence, and which until the end of the film is always shown in motion (its sands are never seen to stop), has only two compartments but is otherwise very like the five-compartment hourglass photographed by Man Ray to illustrate Breton's articulation of eternity and desire: "Forever, as on the white sand of time and through the grace of this instrument which is used to measure it, but only fascinates you and leaves you hungry, reduced to a stream of milk endlessly pouring from a glass breast."[35] At the end, when Pandora and Hendrick are finally united and are ready to die together, the sand in the hourglass freezes; Pandora marvels, "It's as though we're under a spell, outside of time, unending . . . "; Hendrick echoes her, "Unending . . . "; and the hourglass cracks, as thunder from a sudden squall explodes around them and the yacht sinks.

Another reference to a photograph by Man Ray occurs during a moonlit scene where Pandora, who has dreamed that Hendrick has been killed, runs to his bunga-

Pandora at the window of Hendrick's bungalow.

low. She peers through the windows of two doors, and reverse shots show her from within. The second of these reverse shots, in which Pandora's hands are held up near her head and against a screen, very closely reproduces *The Net* (1931), a photograph by Man Ray from the same period as his work for *L'Amour fou*.[36] *The Net* is one of several images of women similarly patterned—that is, onto whose faces and bodies images are projected—including a series of Lee Miller at a window, which Man Ray produced in the early 1930s and which suggest another category of beauty in *L'Amour fou*, the "veiled-erotic."

The third category of beauty in Breton's formulation, after "veiled-erotic" and "fixed-explosive," is "magic-circumstantial," and this is the category that contains the quasimystical sense of desire as fate and the perception of objective chance as an aesthetic force. It is beauty in its "magic-circumstantial" sense that pervades much of *Pandora and the Flying Dutchman*—in the plot, and in any number of images and scenes that refer to particular and generalized surrealist imagery. "Magic-circumstantial" beauty is seen, for instance, when the camera regards Ava Gardner's face so intently, doubling and tripling it by photographs and paintings placed in depth, *en abyme;* dwelling on its serene, frozen perfection in the long, elegiac shot that begins Hendrick's flashback to the events of his recitation ("It was her face. It was her face still, though now white and cold as marble"); and contrasting with this the highly colored, animated visage of the second Pandora, who, when she sees the painting Hendrick

Man Ray, *The Net*, 1931.

"It was her face. It was her face still, though now white and cold as marble . . . " With these words, Hendrick begins his recitation of the events that led to his condemnation.

has made of her without ever (so far as she knows) having met her, says, "It's me—not as I am, but as I should like to be." But the painting is indeed of her, as she once was and once again will be. Pandora is a reincarnation in the most literal sense, for until Hendrick offers her the opportunity to love and therefore to die, she is only a heartless, anaesthetized body (a point that Janet, her rival for Stephen's affections, is wont to make[37]), a simulacrum of the woman she has been and will become again only at the moment of death.

The impossible beauty of all this is the beauty of the "magic-circumstantial" a surrealist twist on the uncanny. It is represented in the film by metamorphic and mysterious images, as in a single shot from an early scene in which Pandora, having induced Stephen to push his racing car into the sea, leans over the edge of the cliff, throws her head back, and revels in the spectacle of its violent descent into the water. This shot is a transition: it follows a high-angle close-up of her ecstatic face thrown back—which is reminiscent of photographs by Man Ray (*Head,* 1923) and Jacques-André Boiffard (an untitled photograph of a foreshortened nude, 1930)—and it precedes a strange composition, in which Pandora's head, in profile, fills the entire foreground as she lies on the ground, vowing to marry Stephen, who stands in the middle ground behind her, static and rigid as a nearby Celtic monolith.

In the transitional image, as described by Sylvie Trosa, the "camera frames in a tilt-shot the angle of the rocks which overlook the sea. One distinguishes a form which seems to be the silhouette of Pandora's body. But the shadow moves and, by a striking effect of trompe l'oeil, reveals not her body, but Gardner's face in profile, in extreme close-up, which stands out against the background of the sea below her."[38] The ambiguous, silhouetted curves suggest, too, the rolling hills of a landscape, a permutation which intensifies one's impression that these images are related to the mutations of form characteristic of so many surrealist photographs—for instance, Brassaï's *Ciel postiche* (*False Sky*, 1932–1934). The multiple rotations, ambiguities, and metamorphoses in this series of shots suggest the manipulation and mutation of the human body to effect what Rosalind Krauss has called "the process of seeing *as if* . . . that propels the image into the realm of the vertiginous," and realizes the "dissident" surrealist Georges Bataille's notion of the *informe* ("formless").[39]

Another image—a painting—although it is not directly referred to in the film, is emblematic of Lewin's tribute to *l'amour fou*, to the surrealist iconography of the early 1930s, and specifically to Man Ray's inventory of images of erotic love. Man Ray's most ambitious painting of that period—and his favorite among his own paintings—*The Lovers, or Observatory Time* (1932–1934), "hung for some months over [the artist's] bed," according to Roland Penrose, who then continues with a quotation from Man Ray, "like an open window into space. The red lips floated in a bluish grey sky over a twilit landscape. . . . The lips, because of their scale, no doubt, suggested two closely joined bodies."[40]

Lewin would have been introduced to this painting in 1948, while he was writing his script for *Pandora*. At that time, Man Ray rescued it from his studio in Paris, where it had spent the war, brought it to Los Angeles, and exhibited it in his one-man show at the Copley Gallery there.[41] William Copley later wrote about his move to Los Angeles and the establishment of his gallery: "Southern California in 1946 was a most unlikely and certainly a most unnecessary place to proselytize Surrealism. As Man Ray once said, there was more Surrealism rampant in Hollywood than all the Surrealists could invent in a lifetime. The natives didn't know this. . . . Being the dedicated Surrealists that we were, we were sharply aware of the necessity to demonstrate that popular and primitive art were by nature surreal."[42]

The two lips, liberated from the body, literally elevated to the status of an icon of mad love, come to stand for more than two figures locked in an embrace; they are a sign, too, of the unexamined but—according to Man Ray, Copley, Lewin, and their friends—inevitable embrace between surrealism and popular culture. The lips floating in the sky are a totem of the domain in which Hollywood and surrealism cohabit and which they rule together. The law of this land is love. "Mainstream cinema comes ethically closest to Surrealism in the expression of love," Paul Hammond observes[43] (if anything, understating the case) by way of introducing André Breton's assertion that "what is most specific of the means of the camera is obviously the power to make concrete the forces of love which, despite everything, remain deficient in books. . . . The radical powerlessness of the plastic arts in this domain goes without saying (one imagines that it has not been given to the painter to show us the radiant image of a kiss). The cinema is alone in extending its empire there, and this alone would be enough for its consecration."[44] The "radiant image of a kiss," is, of course, exactly what Man Ray aspired to create in *The Lovers, or Observatory Time*,[45] in which the lips light up the evening sky like a celestial body.

Ava Gardner's lips, painted a deep blood-red, hover in the dark-blue "day-for-night" vistas of the Mediterannean sea and sky, almost like the phantom lips in Man Ray's painting. From the beginning of the film, when a remarkable reverse tracking shot begins with a swinging bell inscribed with the name "Alberto" tolling for the dead,[46] to the end, when the story has come full circle, the film is concerned with conveying surrealist content. This is as true of the approach to the narrative as it is of the imagery. As Lewin himself indicated,[47] the legend of the Flying Dutchman itself has a surrealist aspect in its refusal to be bound by temporal limits; and in *Pandora* the use of the legend conveys a "liquidation of time"[48] when, simultaneously, the hourglass freezes and the word "unending . . . " is uttered. The film aspires to the irrational beauty which Ferdinand Alquié says "can only be grasped in the heat of an excitement we would call existential if the word did not evoke now a completely different climate. We may call it 'vital,' if we remember that Breton's goal is to attain 'real life'—keeping always in mind that the word life is not used here as biologists use it but in the philosophic sense of existence. Living is not necessarily existing. . . . Living and ceasing to live are imaginary solutions. Existence is everywhere."[49] This is close to Lewin's own philosophy:

> Eternity, indeed, might be defined as the life span of that substance which has the least consciousness of its own activity. In this sense, though we may none of us be immortal, we are all eternal.
>
> The artist perhaps intuitively perceives this, since when he is most successful he creates a sense of breathlessness, of suspended animation, of action under the aspect of eternity. This is the true aesthetic emotion, which has nothing whatsoever to do with pity or terror, but has more to do with what James Joyce, using a term out of Thomas Aquinas, called "radiance." It is the artist's intuitive apprehension that subjective time is the only constant in a relative world.[50]

The "action under the aspect of eternity" that Lewin tried to convey in this letter (to a popular science magazine) was what he attempted to effect aesthetically in *Pandora*. It is achieved most poignantly in the image that he said had inspired the film, "the racing car on the beach—a modern machine being driven at great speed past the statue of a Greek goddess standing on the sands"—not only because of the Chiri-

Pandora, intrigued by the shining white yacht in the harbor, spontaneously quits the company of Geoffrey and Stephen, to whom she has just become engaged; runs to the shore, past the monumental, serene gaze of a goddess; disrobes; and then plunges into the sea.

coesque juxtaposition of ancient and modern but because of the camera movement: the camera, tracking with the racing car, pivots around the goddess and takes her point of view.[51] The poignancy of this viewpoint is also paradoxical, since the goddess has no head—she is *acéphale* ("headless")—an image and a term favored by surrealists generally and adopted as the name of a "secret society" and a short-lived review (1936–1939) by the circle around Georges Bataille.[52] Headless, and made of stone, the Hellenistic goddess has no consciousness of her own activity, but she conveys the ineffable regard of the ages, as does the monumental female head that "watches" Pandora run to the sea, strip (just out of view of the camera), and swim out to the yacht in the bay where her destiny awaits her.

When, later in this scene, Pandora emerges from the sea and climbs onto the deck of Hendrick's ghost ship, as Raphaël Bassan puts it, "Lewin, the aesthete, plays an admirable game of hide-and-seek with the censor."[53] The moonlit water having just sufficiently obscured her body as she swam, Pandora is then shown in erotic fragments: first her dripping hair and glistening shoulders and then, when she climbs aboard, her bare feet, as she walks on tiptoes toward a hatch; when she removes the cover in order to see into the cabin, it also, conveniently, shields her nakedness.[54] The odd, almost fetishistic close-up of her tiptoeing feet echoes the pose of a statue she has passed on the beach, which is also on tiptoe. She will later cavort with this statue—a prop department pastiche based on incompatible types, part Apollo or Adonis (it has the long, loose youthful tresses associated with those gods), part Dionysian reveler or satyr. Its stance, on tiptoes, reproduces that of dancers like the bronze satyr from the House of the Faun in Pompeii and also recalls another image from Pompeii: a naked female dancer with cymbals, from the dionysiac frieze in the Villa of the Mysteries, who spins on tiptoes in a bacchic frenzy, a golden scarf—not unlike the one Pandora will drape around the sculpture on the beach—billowing off her shoulders.

The use of the various antiquities is most prominent in these two scenes. In the first, the ancient objects loom large and portentous, from Pandora's and Stephen's midnight drive past the goddess, to the Celtic monolith standing on the precipice from which Stephen pushes his car, to the sculptures that occupy the waterfront archaeological site to which Geoffrey brings the two, and from which Pandora embarks upon her swim. In the second—the beach party held to celebrate Stephen's world record, a scene that Lewin singled out for its surrealist character—"men in full dress suits dance with girls in bathing suits to the music of 'You're Driving Me Crazy' played by a jazz combination erotically disposed among fragments of ancient statues with the sea in the background."[55]

Initially, the beach party scene uses the antiquities to much lighter and more absurdist effect. The people who are shown dancing and frolicking are minor characters and extras; they do not include the film's two protagonists, who are in a sense obliged, by virtue of their mythic nature, to feel the weight of the ages and the eyes of the gods upon them. Wonderfully strange, distorted shots characterize this scene: a close-up shows a saxophone being played above a monumental, fallen head of Neptune; a trombonist lies supine in the sand, his head cushioned by the hip of a sleeping hermaphrodite; a fragment of an Ionic column supports a glass and a bottle of champagne; a bas-relief of an equestrian lies flat in the sand amidst the feet of the dancers; a drunken girl in fancy dress deflects an ardent suitor, breaks out laughing in hysterical glee, then walks on her hands, so that her skirt falls down over her head and arms, leaving only her kicking, upside-down legs exposed.

The levity of this passage is in sharp contrast to the languorous gravity of the next part of the scene, in which Pandora and Hendrick escape the party and go to a quiet part of the beach, where, wrapping her yellow silk scarf, luminous in the phosphorescent moonlight, around the pastiche sculpture, Pandora asks Hendrick, who gazes out to sea, "What do you see out there? The past or the future? Or some fabulous land beyond the map?" This is one of the wordiest scenes in the film: Hendrick recites passages from Matthew Arnold's "Dover Beach;"[56] Pandora, at great length, confesses her love for Hendrick and her willingness to die for him (though she does not yet know that he requires this of her); and when she asks him what he would sacrifice for her, he gazes out to sea, and slowly but definitely responds, "My salvation."

The contrast in this scene between Hendrick's ominous, brooding silences and Pandora's euphoric, irrepressible pronouncements reflects an overall tension in the film between ineffable silence and expository noise. This same tension is felt even more markedly in the contrast between Hendrick and the narrator, Geoffrey. Hendrick is, after all, not only a legendary seaman but also a contemporary painter—a surrealist. Visually, *Pandora* is Hendrick's film; it is full of mystery, melancholy, and desire. But its aural register (with the exception of the moody, elegiac score) belongs to Geoffrey, the scholar; it is analytical, literary, academic.

Geoffrey often puts a lens—a magnifying glass or a telescope—between himself and the objects of his scrutiny, and this reflects his emotional distance as a character; it facilitates his role as narrator, but it disables him artistically and impairs his capacity for empathy. Geoffrey's role as a kind of hinge between the objective narration and the subjective characters is established at the outset, through a distinctly auteurist flourish. "Production designer John Bryan has made several changes in the local landscape," Catherine O'Brien wrote in a feature article about the production of *Pandora*. "Into the old Moorish town wall which dominates the bay and encloses the old town of Tossa, he has built an arch of local stones of the same period in which swings a massive bell (named Alberto after the director).... It is through this bell tower that the opening shot in 'Pandora and the Flying Dutchman' is filmed from a tracking ramp at an incline of 30 degrees, perched precariously on a pinnacle of rocks over the clear, blue sea. As the bell clangs to and fro, the camera tracks backwards to frame an exciting scene on the beach far below.... Higher still, on a rostrum with a similar sloping tracking ramp, has been built the balcony from which Geoffrey ... and his niece, Janet, ... watch the drama on the beach through a telescope."[57]

Gilles Deleuze has used this elaborate sequence to indicate how problematic subjective and objective perception can be in cinema. He writes that *Pandora* "opens with the long shot of a beach where groups are running towards a point; the beach is seen from a distance and from a height, through a telescope on the promontory of a house. But very quickly we learn that the house is inhabited, the telescope used, by people who are very much part of the set under consideration: the beach, the point which attracts the groups, the event taking place there, the people mixed up in it.... Has the image not become subjective?"[58] Both descriptions—O'Brien's and Deleuze's—are mistaken, however, in referring to this as the opening scene of the film.

The credits at the beginning of *Pandora* are followed by a shot of the surf with expository titles superimposed: "According to the legend, the Flying Dutchman was condemned to wander the seas eternally, unless he could find a woman who loved him enough to die for him...." "The seaport of Esperanza, on the Mediterannean coast of Spain, about twenty years ago...." Then comes a picturesque, almost documentary-style scene of the crew of a local fishing boat (who are plainly local people, not professional actors) chatting and joking in untranslated Catalan as they pull in their nets. This rather remarkable although generally unremarked scene ends with an expression of horror on the face of one fisherman, as he looks down at his catch. Only later do we learn that he has caught the bodies of the protagonists.

In this way, *Pandora* registers one further shift between the objective and the subjective. The scene recalls the robust romanticism of Lewin's good friend, the documentary filmmaker Robert Flaherty (who died the year *Pandora* was released). And its use of untranslated foreign dialogue recalls Albert Lewin's assertion that "foreign pictures often seem artistic to us because we do not understand the dialogue and consequently are still regarding them as silent pictures,"[59] and his quest for "that 'counterpoint,' that non-synchronous co-ordination of visual and auditory images" that he imagined would liberate the sound film from the prosaic effects of synchronous speech.[60] This quest would continue with sad, if inconclusive, results for the rest of the decade.

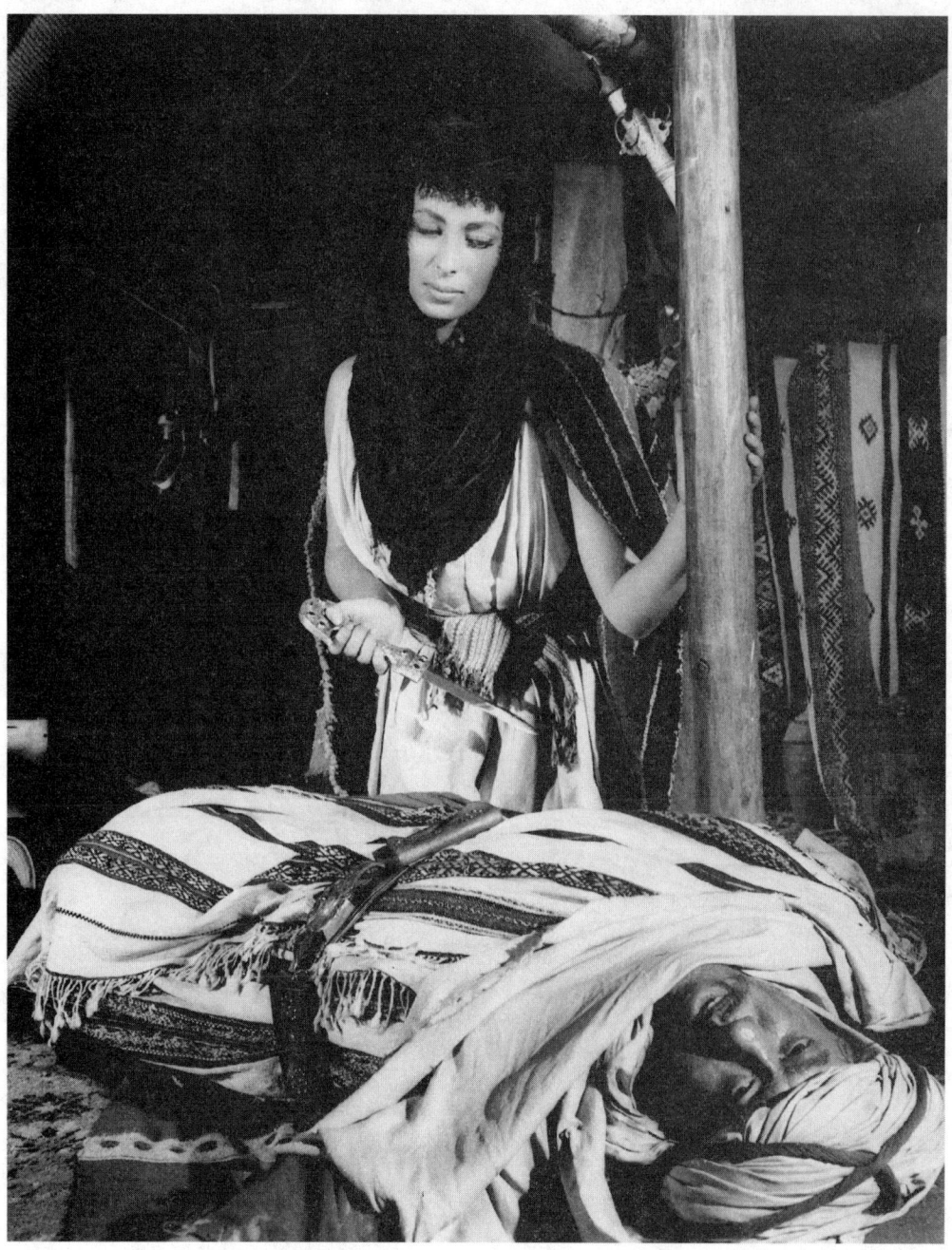

Saadia (1954). Rita Gam, as the title character, in a scene reminiscent of the biblical account of Judith and Holofernes, kills the bandit Bou Rezza (Michel Simon) to save her village from plague.

CHAPTER 5

Blessed Benightedness:
Saadia (1954) and *The Living Idol* (1957)

The so-called primitive peoples don't know they are poor, illiterate, and superstitious until we tell them. We take their blessed benightedness away from them, and what we give them in return is of doubtful value.

Albert Lewin[1]

You know, I got along well with the bullfighters in Spain. They carry amulets. I carry amulets. Bullfighting is hazardous. Filmmaking is hazardous. You need to make expiatory gestures to the gods. Maybe that's what my films are all about.

Albert Lewin[2]

Pandora and the Flying Dutchman was Albert Lewin's most ambitious film, and in many ways his most beautiful. Yet it lacked the overall coherence, or balance, that its two predecessors, despite their inherent problems, just barely managed to achieve. In discussing *Pandora,* its admirers and its critics often resort to the term "vertiginous" to characterize its unsettling and puzzling contrasts—not only those "intentional" contrasts meant to achieve a surrealist effect, but its embarrassing swings between clumsiness and grace, pedantry and poetry, travesty and tragedy. Its failings and virtues suggest that in writing an original screenplay, Lewin lacked the restraint and sensibility that characterized his interpretations of existing material.

This same problem is seen in the unhappy results of his last two films. *Saadia,* taken from an obscure minor novel, and *The Living Idol,* an original script, rely heavily on Lewin's talent as a writer, and they do not attest well to it. Neither does the novel that Lewin published near the end of his life, *The Unaltered Cat* (1967), which is nominally about an anthropologist who learns that his young wife is a cat-person (a premise that had been used far more excitingly by Jacques Tourneur in 1942, in the film *Cat People*). In this novel, Lewin seems to reveal an overeducated, somewhat dilettantish desire to expound upon the most diverse philosophical, aesthetic, and academic points: the characters in the story certainly expound and argue and pontificate ad nauseam.[3] Such a story can have interest only so far as it evokes a sense of horror, if not through the literal claims of the narrative, at least through its metaphorical power. But the only

Saadia

Morocco, about 1953. A young French-educated prince, the Caid, Si Lahssen (Cornel Wilde), has brought to his principality western innovations, and a medical friend, Henrik (Mel Ferrer). Henrik serves as a doctor for the ancient walled village of Aïn el Oued—a settlement on the edge of the Sahara—and for a nearby military post. One day, Si Lahssen accompanies Henrik on a medical call where he assists his friend with an emergency appendectomy on a motherless, superstitious young Berber woman, Saadia (Rita Gam), despite the protests of Saadia's mentor, the sorceress Fatima (Wanda Rotha), whose attachment to Saadia has an unhealthy air. While Henrik operates, Fatima employs her own, more magical healing methods: in a voodoo-like ritual, she substitutes a figurine for the patient and invokes spirits.

Henrik and Fatima clash at Saadia's sickbed as the girl recovers. Fatima's promise that the devil will strike Henrik at the next full moon seems to be fulfilled when an outbreak of bubonic plague occurs then. Henrik's powers, those of western medicine, can fight the plague, but only with a vaccine, and the vaccine is captured and held for ransom by bandits when the airplane transporting it crashes in the mountains. Saadia, an expert horsewoman, rides to the bandits' camp and boldly recovers the medicine by pretending to be seduced by their chief, Bou Rezza (Michel Simon), whom she then murders, escaping, just barely, with her life—and with the vaccine. The epidemic is stopped; the loss of life is relatively small and contained.

The village and the fort celebrate. Saadia, who since her recovery has been unable to hide her deep feelings of gratitude and admiration for Henrik, has endeared herself not only to him, but also (it is later revealed) to Si Lahssen, the Caid. Si Lahssen has confided his feelings only to his advisor, Khadir (Cyril Cusack), after the latter's discovery of a cache of drawings that Si Lahssen has made of Saadia's face. Henrik, too, whose disposition has been melancholic and reserved, seems drawn to Saadia's beauty and spiritual strength. But Fatima is not done with this romantically troubled trio. She steals a portrait of Henrik by Si Lahssen and uses it to invoke further evil. The possible result of her mischief is a vengeful assault on Saadia by the Berber bandits, when she is riding in the company of Henrik, Si Lahssen, and his princely entourage. In the ensuing shooting, Si Lahssen is gravely wounded and, in delirium, reveals his love for Saadia. The film ends with love and prayer overwhelming the forces of evil, Si Lahssen's swift (almost miraculous) recovery, and finally his marriage to Saadia.

horror in *The Unaltered Cat* is its author's evident intellectual *horror vacui,* or "fear of the void"; and whatever power the plot might have had is diluted by the deluge of ideas flowing across its rather flimsy premise. The novel, finally, reads like a dinner-table conversation at a faculty club—sometimes erudite, informative, and provocative, but too often tedious, didactic, and tendentious.

The same adjectives are applicable to *The Living Idol,* Lewin's last film, from his own preposterous story of reincarnation and human sacrifice, set among Mayan ruins in Mexico—a critical and commercial disaster. *Saadia*—a tale of a confrontation between western medicine (and metaphysics) and Moroccan sorcery, and the fate of a beautiful young Berber woman, a local Caid, a French doctor, and their village—was only marginally more successful. These two films have been described by Philip Kemp as symptomatic of problems in Lewin's entire oeuvre, problems that were incipient in the earlier works: "Both films were disappointing, marred by weak casting, and overwhelmed by the preciousness which had always threatened Lewin's work."[4]

Saadia and *The Living Idol* are most similar to Lewin's earlier films in Lewin's evident attempts to balance his intellectual and aesthetic preoccupations with what he deemed marketable. But by the 1950s, Lewin's intellectual interests were shifting, and so were the methods of, and the market for, the commercial film industry, in ways that would prove incompatible and thus boded ill for his subsequent career. In the immediate postwar period, Lewin's interests had, geographically, shifted away from Europe and toward the Americas and nonwestern cultures;[5] and he, along with many surrealists, had become increasingly attracted by the ineffable, the occult, and the supernatural. But his interest in these phenomena, or metaphenomena, exceeded that of most of his surrealist peers and was more academic. By the late 1950s, he was corresponding with Robert Graves and Cyrus Gordon, among others, on arcane and esoteric matters relating to mythology, comparative religion, archaeology, and anthropology.[6]

Meanwhile, the Hollywood film industry was undergoing major changes, caused by a variety of forces. Among these were the "Paramount decree" by the Supreme Court in 1949, which was the result of a successful antitrust suit first brought about a decade earlier against the vertical integration of the five major film studios;[7] the meteoric rise of television, which was posing an increasing threat to the vitality of the already financially troubled film industry;[8] the postwar return of foreign markets for American pictures, and a simultaneous threat of protectionism on the part of many countries which wanted to boost their own film industries;[9] technological and organizational innovations which, in combination with economic advantages, encouraged location shooting abroad;[10] and the pernicious interference of the House Committee on Un-American Activities (HUAC), whose two infamous Hollywood hearings (1947 and 1951), and the blacklisting of over 200 film workers, intimidated and depleted the industry, leaving it scarred and divided into the 1960s and well beyond.[11]

These forces had some positive effects, evident in *Saadia* and *The Living Idol,* but also had negative effects on several ambitious projects that Lewin was unable to realize in the 1950s, despite his supposed influence at MGM, to which he had returned as a production executive after the second demise of Loew-Lewin in 1948. These unrealized projects, which Lewin had thoroughly researched and for which he had either written the scripts or developed elaborate treatments, were closer in spirit and theme to his earlier films. They included, in the earlier years of the decade, two literary adaptations: one of Henrik Ibsen's *Peer Gynt,* with Edvard Grieg's *Peer Gynt Suite* as its score; and the second of a minor French novel of the 1920s, Albert Adès's *Un roi nu (A Naked King),* about artists in turn-of-the-century Paris.

Two cherished projects from the later 1950s were original scripts and were (like the two proposed adaptations) much more literary and eurocentric than *Saadia* and *The Living Idol*—the films he was able to produce. The first of these proposed original scripts was a life of Goya. This was sold, after Lewin failed to find support for it, to the producers of *The Naked Maja* (1958), who discarded it. The second was an ornate script that combined thematic elements from *The Picture of Dorian Gray* and *Pandora and the Flying Dutchman*. It was called *Diana at Midnight* and was inspired by the Faust legend, which was itself to appear as the theme of a modern ballet within the story line.[12] Both of these later projects were conceived as vehicles for Ava Gardner, whom Lewin very much wanted to use again in a film.[13]

These unrealized films are more recognizable as Lewin products than the two he did make in those years. Lewin himself might have agreed with this assessment. His correspondence of the 1950s reveals a distinct (though tempered) frustration with his inability to launch these projects, into which he had poured so much time, money, and energy—much more, evidently, than was given to the scriptwriting or preproduction research of *Saadia* and *The Living Idol*. In fact, when Lewin was honored with a retrospective at the Cinémathèque Française in 1958, *The Living Idol*—his most recent film—was not even included in the program, and this suggests that he himself probably considered it unsuccessful,[14] although the decision to exclude it may have been made by Henri Langlois and Mary Meerson, who conceived the retrospective. In any case, though, Lewin was strangely silent, during the last decade of his life, about both *Saadia* and *The Living Idol,* devoting much less discussion to these late films than to the four earlier ones in interviews and in his own statements about his career. It was in this period that Lewin was first quoted as saying that "in each film he makes . . . an hour and a quarter is for the producers, the censors, and the lousy public, and only one quarter of an hour for his own pleasure and that of the good public."[15]

Nonetheless, these two less than successful films represent a full third of Albert Lewin's total directorial product and cannot be neglected. Despite their contrast with his several unrealized films of the 1950s, the two narratives do represent one principal direction of Lewin's ideas in his later years; they have a great deal in common with his novel *The Unaltered Cat*. And there is some continuity between his earlier films and *Saadia* and *The Living Idol*. In fact, in one significant respect they perpetuate a focus of Lewin's oeuvre—that is, in their heightened use of art. In the use of art objects within these two films, an enduring proposition of Lewin's entire body of work becomes manifest.

> In spite of years of racial, if not religious admonition, I find myself irresistibly attracted to graven images, and am quite sure that Moses descending from the mountain with the tablets of divine law found my prototype among those worshipping the golden calf (Albert Lewin).[16]

In *The Moon and Sixpence,* there is something of the ineffable in Charles Strickland's "nostalgia" for a primitive place he has never yet seen, as embodied in a Tahitian idol that haunts this film. The uncanny aura of art is emphasized by the revelation in color of the "visionary" pictures he has made while blind and in the last stages of leprosy. This same technique was used to enhance the power of art in *The Picture of Dorian Gray* and *The Private Affairs of Bel Ami*. In *Dorian Gray,* there is a magical equivalence between the portrait and its subject—the man portrayed—and supernatural power is attributed to an Egyptian figurine of a cat; in *Bel Ami,* the horrible image of the temptation of Saint Anthony seems a hallucination, or projection, of

Georges Duroy's inner conflicts. In *Pandora and the Flying Dutchman,* the uncanny encounter which is the theme of the film is brought about around a portrait. To a greater or lesser extent, each of these narratives accords art a magical quality that it is assumed, in the modern world, not to have. At one level this is a metaphor of the "magic" of movies, but at another level it points to an interest in a more "savage" view of representation that became increasingly prominent in Lewin's work, his art collecton, and his correspondence in the 1950s.

In *Saadia,* "civilized" and "primitive" art forms are contrasted only to be fused in terms of their uses. The film's basic theme and two of its main characters are introduced, after the credits, by a rather pedantic expository voice-over narration:

> Morocco is a land of strange and haunting contrasts. Here, the primitive camel and the gasoline truck take on fuel side-by-side for the long haul over mountain and plain and desert. The mingling of old and new creates dramatic patterns in the lives of the people and in the character of the young prince, the Caid, Si Lahssen. Educated in France, he has brought his western knowledge to the service of his country. Through crowded streets and noisy marketplaces, he drives his modern motor car to the ancient gate of the walled town and where the new, paved road parallels the time-worn camel trail, he moves swiftly to the military post, which guards the village of Aïn el Oued, one of the age-old settlements on the edge of the Sahara. Inside the post, he drives to the hospital of his friend Henrik, the doctor, whose greatest struggle is to overcome witchcraft and sorcery in the remote villages of the district.[17]

Saadia. The sorceress Fatima (Wanda Rotha) uses a doll as a surrogate in a ritual of black magic, invoking the aid of demons to cure her disciple Saadia.

These two male characters, Si Lahssen (played by Cornel Wilde) and Henrik (Mel Ferrer), soon encounter the two main female characters: Saadia (Rita Gam), who is a motherless Berber girl; and the sorceress Fatima (Wanda Rotha), who has been a sort of mentor to her. The circumstances are dramatic—Saadia is suffering from what turns out to be appendicitis, and Henrik performs an emergency appendectomy on the spot, with his friend Si Lahssen assisting, while barnyard animals look on. Meanwhile, however, Fatima is invoking her own powers of healing. According to the narration: "In her hut above the village the sorceress Fatima prepared to use the statuette which in her witchcraft symbolized Saadia, in a ritual of black magic." She implores the "demon she had invoked": "The maiden, Saadia, do not let her die. Save her. Save Saadia and send her back to me." Fatima is then "possessed with devils" and is shown supine and semiconscious, clutching the statuette to her breast and fondling it passionately. There is a narcissistic and homoerotic overtone to Fatima's interest in Saadia that is portrayed as unhealthy. When Saadia is recovering and Henrik, the doctor, encounters Fatima at the girl's bedside, he suggests as much to her:

> I'm told that when you're in the mood you can conjure up an elegant devil that gives you more delight than any mortal man.... But this devil who delights you has given you no children. I understand you, Fatima, and I have compassion for you. You are a lonely woman—lonely and childless. You wanted Saadia near you. Saadia could be your child. You would make her a witch like yourself—shunned by everyone else, cursed with the evil eye so that no one would have anything to do with her and you would have her all to yourself. There would be no others to take her from you—no husband, no father, no friends. She would belong to you and to you alone, and you would not have to be lonely anymore.

Then Henrik, in response to Fatima's assertion that he must not believe in her powers, continues:

> You're mistaken. I do believe in them. I believe that human thought is a powerful force that can be used for evil if it's concentrated on one object with sufficient intensity—and for good, also, fortunately. That is what prayers are for. You have a statuette of Saadia, I suppose?

Here the basic conflict of the narrative is set up. Beyond this point, Fatima's powers, which are considerable, are pitted against the propositions of enlightenment.

Saadia is a flawed film, a film of contrasts which are almost as strange as those it attributes to Morocco, and which derive from the same quasisurrealist aesthetic Lewin cultivated in *Pandora,* when he consciously juxtaposed ancient and modern, animate and inanimate in evocative tableaux. The three romantic leads—Wilde, Ferrer, and Gam—give leaden, almost embarrassed performances; Lewin was evidently not an expert drama coach and probably contributed to this stiffness by urging the kind of restraint that had worked more effectively for Hurd Hatfield in *Dorian Gray.* As a result, the leading roles are overpowered by the character parts, played with much greater zest and irony by Wanda Rotha, Michel Simon, Marcel Poncin (as Moha, Saadia's father) and Jacques Dufhilo (as a bandit leader), although it appears that these parts too, particularly Rotha's, lost a good deal of their strength when Lewin lost control of the editing. "It was the theme in *Saadia* that intrigued me, not the story: the conflict between medicine and witchcraft," stated Lewin:

Saadia. Si Lahssen (Cornel Wilde), Henrik (Mel Ferrer), and Khadir (Cyril Cusack) surrounded by authentic North African trappings.

My arrangement with Dore Schary [then MGM's head of production] was that I would shoot it in Morocco, which I did, and edit and score it in England. I was supposed to bring back a complete picture. But TV had thrown Hollywood into a panic. I began getting frantic notes about the budget and finally I had to come back and cut it at the studio in Hollywood.

I showed it to Dore. Now, the character of the sorceress was tremendously important, because she illustrated the theme. Wanda Rotha was impressive in the part, stole the picture in its first form. Dore objected to the emphasis on her. He pointed to her elaborate fiery death scene and said, "That dame goes down like the Titanic! She's only a character woman, Al." He reduced her part—her death is now merely indicated—in favor of the love story, which I had thrown in merely as a sop to the public.[18]

In the editing, the alternately pedantic and sensationalistic script also seems to have lost any sense of balance it may initially have had; after a certain point, Fatima's story fades away, and the conclusion feels abrupt. The authentic and often beautiful locations, settings, costumes, and other "native" details come almost to seem the raison d'être of the film.[19]

Saadia does have some scenes of cinematic and scenic splendor and choreographic verve, including two consecutive scenes during a full moon. In one, Saadia is standing outdoors in the moonlight, secretly watching and listening as Henrik, at his piano, plays a Chopin prelude (the same prelude, of course, that was the leitmotif in *Dorian Gray*), when some merry French soldiers come by singing and draw her attention to the full moon, about which Fatima has made such ominous predictions. The next scene is a birthday celebration for the captain of the fort, at which Moroccan women perform native songs and dances for the French company.

But the most relevant thematic elements in *Saadia* are those that connect this film to Lewin's earlier work: its interest in the uses (and abuses) of art and its cultivation of one of the more primordial aspects of representation—magic. Repeatedly in his

One of Si Lahssen's many fantasy portraits of Saadia.

work, Albert Lewin contrives to reanimate the representational image with magic, uncanniness, and power. In his films, representations are the locus of a desire that distorts. In *Saadia,* Fatima lavishes on the statuette of Saadia a concentrated desire that is made to seem evil, quite apart from its homoerotic nature. But we later discover that Si Lahssen, the French-educated, "civilized" prince, is just as passionately focused on representations of Saadia. The walls of his private room are covered with drawings of her that reveal a desire no less obsessive than Fatima's.

Si Lahssen's representations may be more mimetic—a presumed measure of distance from magical thinking—but they no less firmly establish the object of his wishes.[20] And Fatima does not insist on abstraction in the representations she will employ. She finds Si Lahssen's very naturalistic portrait drawing of his friend Henrik as effective as a figurine, or more effective, for her magical purposes. If Si Lahssen is less effective than Fatima in influencing the object of his desire, that is not because mimetic representation is less powerful, but rather because the artist, who no longer has faith in the magic of his representation, has less power.

Saadia's father, Moha (Marcel Poncin), leads the bride to her nuptials with the Caid, Si Lahssen, in the film's splendid concluding spectacle.

The Living Idol

The Yucatan, about 1956. At the site of an ancient Mayan pyramid, Professor Alfred Stoner (James Robertson-Justice) and his Mexican friend and colleague, Manuel Acosta (Eduardo Noriega), are involved in an archaeological excavation. Juanita (Liliane Montevecchi), Manuel's teenage daughter, and Terry Matthews (Steve Forrest), a young roving correspondent for *Time* magazine, accompany Stoner to a buried temple chamber within a pyramid, where the sight of a fantastic red stone jaguar frightens Juanita. Her father speculates that her fear is related to her Mayan ancestry and the terrible excitement that the age-old sacrificial Jaguar cult still inspires in their people.

Juanita visits Terry one night and confesses her love for him. Terry tells her he has been assigned to Korea, but that he hopes to return to her. A few days later Manuel is crushed and dies beneath a great stone slab bearing the image of a jaguar devouring a human heart. Professor Stoner and his wife Elena (Sara Garcia) adopt Juanita and leave for their home in Mexico City. When Terry returns from Korea and visits the Stoners, he learns from Elena that Juanita has been suffering from inexplicable attacks of melancholy. The Professor, meanwhile, has been preoccupied with his study of human sacrifice, as well as daily visits to a jaguar in the Chapultepec Zoo. When Terry and Juanita find him at the zoo, the jaguar—Balam—becomes frenzied at the sight of Juanita.

At his lecture at University City on human sacrifice through the ages, Stoner entreats Juanita to don Mayan sacrificial garb, which she does reluctantly, fainting at the climax of Stoner's vivid description of the ritual sacrifice. Terry accuses Stoner of deliberately frightening Juanita, but Stoner maintains that there are more ancient and atavistic reasons for her terror. Late that night Stoner leaves for the zoo, where he frees Balam, the jaguar, who mauls his liberator before stealing off through the deserted grounds of the university. Stoner staggers to his car and follows the stealthy cat. Back at Stoner's house, Juanita and Elena have been aroused and notice lights in Stoner's museum. Elena, anxious, telephones Terry, while Juanita starts downstairs, where she encounters the jaguar. Terry arrives in the nick of time and after a mighty struggle, impales the jaguar on an ancient sacrificial knife that the professor has left nearby. As Juanita, seemingly transformed by the mythic conflict, calmly contemplates the dead jaguar, Terry goes to the museum, where he finds Stoner dying from his wounds amidst a shambles that suggests that the ancient jaguar idol, like his living counterpart, had magically escaped his stone bonds.

In an epilogue, Terry and Juanita are married after Juanita is cured of her "loss of soul" sickness by a reenactment of the ancient ritual to which, it is implied, she was subjected in an earlier incarnation.

The conflation in *Saadia* of two initially contrasted attitudes toward art—the "modern" and the "primitive"—is repeated in Lewin's last film, *The Living Idol,* which he called a "highbrow horror film."[21] Here, the identity between the thing depicted and the depiction initially seems to be a delusion but is finally left as a disturbing possibility. In *The Living Idol,* an archaeologist, Alfred Stoner, a kind of mad genius (played by James Robertson-Justice), becomes convinced that his adopted daughter, Juanita Acosta (Liliane Montevecchi), is a reincarnation of—or in some manner retains the soul of—a Mayan virgin sacrificed to a Mexican god, represented by a fierce red jaguar in a pyramid he has been excavating.[22] Stoner sees in Juanita's "pure Indian" features an uncanny resemblance to the sculptured visages of Mayan maidens.

Professor Stoner's conviction that there is some identity between Juanita and an ancient sculpture is very like Norbert Hanold's belief in the "reality" of Gradiva, a young woman depicted on a bas-relief, in Wilhelm Jensen's novel *Gradiva: A Pompeiian Fancy* (1903), which Freud analyzed in his *Delusion and Dream* (1906–1907). But when Lewin moves away from the possibility of delusion, he also moves away from any possible psychosexual explanations for the phenomenon.[23] Stoner's conviction is coupled with another—its complement: he also believes that a jaguar in the Chapultepec Zoo is somehow the living counterpart of the stone idol to which the virgin, Juanita's counterpart, was sacrificed. Professor Stoner describes Juanita's "inexplicable attacks of melancholy" as "loss-of-soul-sickness" and is delighted by her terror at both the ancient and the living jaguar, and by the caged animal's apparent frenzy upon seeing her.[24] He contrives to prove his theory conclusively by releasing the animal from the zoo to pursue its destiny, and Juanita's destiny. The cat indeed makes its way to

The Living Idol (1957). Alfred Stoner (James Robertson-Justice), a professor of archaeology, points out to a reporter, Terry Matthews (Steve Forrest), the uncanny resemblance between Juanita Acosta (Liliane Montevecchi), the professor's adopted daughter, and an ancient bust of a Mayan maiden.

The Living Idol. Terry wrestling with Balam, the jaguar, in the film's mythic conclusion.

Juanita, after seriously injuring Stoner, but she is saved, of course, by a lover, Terry Matthews (Steve Forrest), an American journalist who has come to Mexico to write about Stoner's excavations. When Matthews goes to the museum to which Stoner has removed the jaguar idol and other excavated objects, he "finds the Professor there, bleeding badly from his wounds. The museum is a shambles, the walls battered, the floor covered with fragments of ceramic pieces, as if the stone sculpture of the jaguar had come to life at the moment when the real one was liberated from his cage, and had wrecked the museum trying to escape."[25]

The most unusual aspect of *The Living Idol* is also its most academic aspect: a scene in which Professor Stoner lectures on the history of human sacrifice, using as illustrations lantern slides of a series of watercolors by Carlos Mérida that were made expressly for the film. Mérida, who was born in Guatemala in 1893, was active in Mexico for most of his long career. He was an early advocate of the revival of indigenous styles and motifs. His best-known works, public murals and paintings, combine these "native" qualities with a distinctly cubist system. The pictures he made for *The Living Idol* are bold and colorful illustrations in which his usually rather abstract, geometric primitivism is subordinated to the expository demands of the lecture. Instead of the cubistic stylization common in his other work of that period, Mérida gives these a more "primitive" effect. Unmodulated, graphically delineated figures are organized hieratically on flat ground. These figures manage to appear rather naive and at the same time to suggest, subtly, the known representational style of each culture whose sacrificial methods are represented.

The eighteen images represent: (1) a Carthaginian sacrifice to the idol Moloch; (2) the Cretan Minotaur; (3) Andromeda and Perseus; (4) the sacrifice of Iphigenia; (5) an ancient Mesopotamian sacrifice on a ziggurat; (6) Abraham and Isaac; (7) a gladiatorial contest in an arena in imperial Rome; (8) a Dravidian Hindu sacrifice; (9) a druid sac-

Carlos Mérida, *An Ancient Mesopotamian Sacrifice upon a Ziggurat,* one of eighteen watercolors he created in 1956 to be used in *The Living Idol* for Professor Stoner's slide lecture on the history of human sacrifice.

rifice; (10) a prehistoric cave drawing believed to record a human sacrifice (but this is a dubious interpretation); (11) Hitler, reviewing a goose-stepping parade of German troops (an even more dubious example of the theme); (12) a Renaissance painting of the crucifixion; (13) a classic Mexican sacrifice—immolation on the platform of a pyramid—copied from the Florentine Codex, prepared in the sixteenth century by Fra Bernardino de Sahagun; (14) an illustration in the Codex of a sacrifice to Xipe-Totec; (15) an illustration in the Codex of a sacrifice of the youth to Tezcatlipoca; (16) an illustration in the Codex of the "sacrifice of the new fire," in which the light is kindled in the breast of the victim; (17) the skull-rack in front of the pyramid in the central square of Tenochtitlan; (18) a Mayan maiden in sacrificial robes, her arms and legs stretched out and bound to crossed posts (the Professor has Juanita costumed and posed to duplicate this image).

An art historian would no doubt be interested in this eccentric pedantry, but this scene weighs heavily on the ultimate effect, weakening whatever visceral thrills this "highbrow horror film" might offer. A slide lecture is usually soporific even to an academic audience, and despite several superficial similarities to cinema (projection of photographic material, accompanying "sound," etc.), it is a medium whose entertainment value must be reckoned considerably less. James Robertson-Justice, the Scottish-born actor who plays Stoner, was, incidentally, well qualified for the role of a savant, and working with him was evidently Lewin's greatest pleasure during production. Robertson-Justice had been educated at Marlborough College and the University of Bonn, had earned a doctorate, and may thus have been the only person Lewin worked with in film whose academic credentials outstripped his own; "formerly a journalist and a naturalist, he became an expert in falconry and trained Prince Charles in that ancient hunting art. He held the honorary post of rector of the University of Edinburgh."[26]

The Living Idol. Juanita fantasizes—or perhaps remembers—being sacrificed as a maiden of the ancient Maya.

However, neither Robertson-Justice's own talents as a wit and raconteur in private life, nor those of the character he was called on to play, are able to lend plausibility to the awkward and badly acted story of *The Living Idol* or to make it very diverting. Like *Saadia, The Living Idol* does include some beautiful filmic moments. A spectacular carnival scene, an odd silhouetted dance, and a scene on a train are among its intriguing eccentricities. But, even more plainly than in *Saadia,* these are merely odd visual conceits wasted on the ponderous unfolding of a preposterous tale.

In the final analysis, *Saadia* and *The Living Idol* cannot be said to have done much more for Lewin personally than to have afforded him an opportunity to broaden his travels and his art collection and to have prepared him, by their failure, for the mandatory retirement that followed the heart attack he suffered in 1959.[27]

Why Albert Lewin, as he gained experience and autonomy, lost his grip on what "works" in the movies is a thorny question. Although his last films, no less than the earlier ones, aspire to an equilibristic navigation between his own aesthetic and intellectual preoccupations and the tastes of the moviegoing public, there is little doubt that with each successive film, Lewin tended to move further away from his ideal. Perhaps in departing from the literary sources and western cultural milieus that constituted his real expertise and drew his true affections as a scholar and an amateur, Lewin let go of the reins that had given his stories—even such extravagent stories as *Pandora*—a modicum of aesthetic control. *Pandora* represented a radical break from a really very consistent project upon which Lewin had been embarked in his work of the 1940s: *The Moon and Sixpence, Dorian Gray,* and *Bel Ami*. Those three films, all black-and-white, were all derived from strong literary sources and centered on different versions of a single fascinating and sexually enthralling male type—dandy, artist, cad—in fin-de-siècle Europe. With *Pandora,* although Pandora shares the cinematic foreground with the Flying Dutchman, Lewin's focus shifted to a female object—and in his work this shift was seismic. In *Pandora,* the filmic universe, as the environment for the mythic, eternal, fatal woman, opens up in Technicolor onto nature, ancient, ineffable, and sublime—a shift that was clearly determined not only by Lewin's own internal artistic development but also by certain economic and technical conditions of the film industry that encouraged foreign and location shooting and allowed freer use of color.

The supernatural was a motif in the earlier films, but in the films of the 1950s, beginning with *Pandora,* it is the driving force of the narrative and is associated with femininity. Women's destiny, in Lewin's later work (including his novel *The Unaltered Cat*), involves reincarnation, voodoo, and metamorphosis, and this primitive fantasy of women's immanent yet ineffable mystery, although certainly not without strong literary precedent, is one, it seems, with which Lewin achieved at best ambivalent results.

Money, no doubt, also played a significant part in the decline of his career. Lewin was a canny production supervisor for MGM, and he may later have been an auteur, but he was neither a technician nor an acting coach. Neither was he rich enough to finance his own movies. No matter how uniquely his own the strong, idiosyncratic style—or styles—in which his finest films were rendered, the vision they represent was achieved on the strength of cinematographers like Harry Stradling, Russell Metty, and Jack Cardiff; designers like Gordon Wiles and John Bryan; composers like Herbert Stothart, Darius Milhaud, and Alan Rawsthorne; actors like George Sanders, Angela Lansbury, Hurd Hatfield, and James Mason; and at least one goddess, Ava Gardner. While some auteurs could make do with smaller budgets and lesser talents, Lewin evidently could not.

The massive heart attack Lewin suffered in 1959 put an end to his film career at a time when he knew it, in any case, to have waned. In a letter to Man Ray, Lewin remarked of his convalescence: "Since producing and directing are out of the question (and would be even without my invalidism, since the Hollywood parade has passed me by), I have kept busy by writing a play."[28] A few months later, in a letter responding to one from Man Ray, he said, "I think your idea of invisible paintings is brilliant, though we're glad to have some of the visible ones. I'm engaged in making invisible movies—I thought perhaps I could raise the money for them since nobody seemed to want to put up funds for anything visible and audible. So far no takers."[29]

Early in his career, Albert Lewin was a shrewd advisor to Irving Thalberg and had a reputation for almost infallible instincts as a producer at MGM. But of his six films as a director, only his first, *The Moon and Sixpence,* made a considerable profit. His second, *The Picture of Dorian Gray,* was at least as popular, and it has been his most critically acclaimed work, but it was also a phenomenally expensive production. Beyond this point, Lewin's films became not only less commercially viable and more and more eccentric but also, by almost any standards, progressively more uneven and flawed. What Lewin remarked sadly about the history of cinema—that it has a happy ending if told backwards—is, ironically but indisputably, more true of his own career.[30]

The Private Affairs of Bel Ami (1947). Outside Notre Dame Cathedral, Georges Duroy (George Sanders) bears down on Marie de Varenne (Frances Dee), to the mournful strains of her husband's organ music.

CHAPTER 6

The Mystery and Melancholy of a Scene: Albert Lewin as Auteur

> I, too, am not a mystic. I am a materialist, but I believe that words, even spoken words, are matter, that thoughts are matter, and that emotions are matter, and since matter, we have been told, is indestructible, they continue to exist, passionately seeking a living utterance out of their gray Elysium. The poet's ancestors have chosen him to speak for them. . . . They inhabit the billions of cells in his mind and celebrate ancient festivals in his sleep when the guards are off duty.
>
> Albert Lewin[1]

The sense of representational objects as potent effigies—images with a heightened relationship to that which they represent—is one of the most consistent attributes of Albert Lewin's small but distinctive body of work as a director. When he said, in a letter to Robert Graves, "I . . . am quite sure that Moses descending from the mountain with the tablets of divine law found my prototype among those worshipping the golden calf,"[2] he was expressing—albeit somewhat whimsically—a deeply personal, lifelong visceral excitement about art that is evident in his literary, dramatic, musical, and, especially, visual passions. Art was to Albert Lewin a creed and an ideology unto itself. "The only religions that interest me," he wrote in the same letter to Graves, "are those which have as little preceptual morality as possible and which use elaborate ceremony and ritual, combining all the arts for a moving theatrical effect. This goes back, I suppose, to the magic which my corpuscles remember from the arcane caves where the bull was painted on the wall to be assaulted by symbolic javelins thrown by dancing and chanting priests." In his life and in history Lewin had seen little other than art to inspire his confidence. "How . . . you can maintain your optimism is a mystery to me," Lewin wrote to the author John Howard Lawson, Hollywood's most steadfast Marxist, in 1938 about their differences over communism and the coming war. "I know you are deeply sincere, and so I must conclude that you are the dupe of your own humanitarianism. All your thoughts are fathered by wishes. You have withdrawn from a too frightful world into a land of chimeras.

"As for me, I am a profound pessimist. I think nothing can stop the march of fascism. . . . Fascism will wax and flourish over an unhappy world for a couple of hundred years until a new, young culture will rise phoenix-like out our embers, as the

Albert Lewin with some of the pre-Columbian, Asian, and African works in his extensive art collection. On the wall behind him is *Zebra Family* (1942), by the self-taught American painter Morris Hirshfield (photo by A. P. Raisbeck).

Egypt of Thebes rose out of the Egypt of Cairo, the Greece of Athens out of the Greece of Mycenae, Rome out of Etruria, and Christian Europe out of Rome. These births and deaths involve changes without necessarily involving improvements—at least to the naked eye."[3]

In his allusions to "ancient festivals" and "arcane caves," Lewin articulated, as he often did, a view similar to that which Philip Rieff attributes to Sigmund Freud—that the "artist is gifted in a rare manner for which Freud demands respect and attention. Lacking the kind of knowledge scientists and men of affairs use, nevertheless the artist has something better: 'psychic knowledge.' Being endowed in a way superior to the ordinary neurotic with atavistic capacities, the artist can 'draw from sources that have not been made accessible to science.'"[4] This idea, that artists are rather like mediums of their ancestors—vessels of atavistic human actions, aspirations, and beliefs—is accompanied in Lewin's aesthetics by a profound interest in the various "childhoods" of art.

In his musings about the history of art and literature, and in his art collecting, Lewin dwelled on images and objects that, to him, represented beginnings—art of an individual or collective naiveté or youth. Until he became friendly with Man Ray, Lewin's art collection had consisted mainly of "naive" paintings and "primitive" sculpture. "This might be a reaction against his own sophistication, I suggested," Man Ray later recollected; "although young, the movies were certainly not primitive art. My statement could have influenced him, for he soon began to acquire works of a more cerebral nature, like those of some of the Surrealists."[5] However, Lewin was also interested in artistic decadence, as is abundantly evident in his first three films: *The Moon and Sixpence, The Picture of Dorian Gray,* and *The Private Affairs of Bel Ami.* This is less incongruous than it might at first appear, for not only does the decadence of a culture stand in a complementary relationship to its own infancy, but the decadence of one culture is inevitably linked—through its demise—to the infancy of another. (In fact, two such cultures may coincide, as with late Roman and early Christian civilization.) And decadence often cultivates a taste for "otherness": the exotic, the ancient, the esoteric, the primitive. Lewin's view of the "primitive other," though, is as a part of oneself: an ancestor, a memory, a seed. His strange cinema, born of a youthful enthusiasm, evolves from this peculiar variant of primitivism, from his romance with the individual and the collective past.

In the early 1920s, when Lewin became so irresistably captivated by cinema that he abandoned forever his careers as scholar and critic, moving pictures were, after all, still a very young art, although certainly no longer "naive" or "primitive," if they ever had been naive or primitive at all. Within the modern western paradigm, the other arts—particularly literature, which was Lewin's first love—seemed already past the point of decadence. To him this tradition was becoming tiresome:

> I don't blame [Gertrude] Stein for being bored with the frozen forms of English syntax. Poetry is alive when languages themselves are in a formative state. Shakespeare beat soft steel to shoe the stallion Pegasus. The same was true of Homer's Greek and the French of the Roland. Writing now is playing cribbage with polished bones. (Some people are good players.) English is a dead language and writing a process of exhumation. Stein thinks she can revivify the corpse by an autopsical excision of nouns, adjectives and punctuation marks. A literary Pollyanna putting cold cream on a chancre. Joyce, meeting the problem with genius, goes down to a dazzling defeat. There is only one hope—let the Japs settle England, and the Russians follow them, and a new language may be born, as living English came out of the mingled blood, groans, shrieks, cries, and the ecstasy of raped Celts, Romans, Saxons, and Normans. The price of creation is chaos.[6]

Lewin's seeming indifference to the fate of individual souls and his cynicism about the fate of particular cultures was the complement of his genuine faith in the phoenixlike persistence and power of art. Charlie Chaplin, Buster Keaton, and *The Cabinet of Doctor Caligari* were an epiphany to Lewin, and his response reveals a sense of the magical possibilities of a visual medium in a formative stage. At this stage, an entirely new, silent "language," born of a fortunate mating of history and technology, is combined with the aspects of the eternal, the universal, to which he was attracted in western art forms: from Mycenaean jewelry and Homer's *Iliad* to Botticelli's *Primavera* and François Villon's *Ballade des dames du temps jadis*,[7] to de Chirico's *Mystery and Melancholy of a Street* and Franz Kafka's *The Castle*. This is reflected in the seriousness with which he contemplated the silliness of Buster Keaton's *The Playhouse* (1921), a short comedy about a stagehand's fantasy of playing every role at a variety show—conductor, musicians, dancers, and audience:

> It is both as film artist and as art collector that Lewin views the Keaton *oeuvre*. Lewin finds more in *The Playhouse* than the admitted technical originality and virtuosity, startling as these are.
>
> A few years ago, on location in Mexico, Lewin was recalling the picture, which he had not seen again since 1921. With a memory like Buster's own he went over the sequences. Then, however, he dwelt on "atmosphere." "An altogether extraordinary emotional

effect," he observed, "came from the dreamlike, obsessive, hallucinatory repetition of that strange frozen face. It was almost nightmarish—a phantasmagoria of masks.

"There is no question," Lewin concluded, "that Buster Keaton, among other things, was a surrealist even before surrealism. Such fantasy! Not even Pirandello ever conjured up such extraordinary visions."[8]

Albert Lewin responded above all to visual fantasy and stylization in silent cinema and often decried the trend toward a formulaic and banal dramatic realism that he observed early in the development of narrative cinema and believed was exacerbated by the introduction of synchronous sound, which he felt tended to root the camera in a shallow and predictable field of vision in front of figures who were static except for their moving lips.

Lewin's deliberate and stylized movement of figures in space, which often invokes, by means of patterned floors, the metaphor of chess pieces being moved about on a board; his repeated use of dolls, puppets, and mannequins; the studied, often quite affectless circumscription of speech and movement characteristic of his direction of actors; and the copious visual symbolism placed within carefully and densely composed frames—these are effects of a view of men and women as at the mercy of forces, internal and external, much greater than they can control or even imagine. His characters suffer from the delusion that they are autonomous, while the audience is given to understand that they are pawns.

Lewin dwelt on this tragic view of humanity in an unpublished essay, "The Marionette." He described a marionette as "the ultimate irony": "And how are we, aware of the string and the voice, to contemplate him without pity and terror, feeling the strings upon our own members—the strings of immediate and remote circumstance—the economic, psychological, biological, and geological determinisms that move our feet into the patterns of biography? 'I am that I am!' asserts the marionette. 'Tat tvam asi!' The affirmation reverberates through the labyrinth of evolution, up by star and star to the silence of those holes in the sky which awe even the astronomers."[9] The distinctive style of Lewin's films, particularly the three in black-and-white, derives not only from this esoteric and tragic view of the world but also from a romance with silent cinema, a romance based on philosophical considerations and on nostalgia for its charm. Lewin's slightly recondite sensibility was, in fact, touted in a Paramount press release about him during his term there: "So far he hasn't inflicted poetry on the trustful movie fans. But one of his delusions is that rolling melodrama, with primitive impulses and simple types, is folk art. If you agree with him and say that folk art is nothing if not anonymous, he will agree with you half way and remark that the names won't mean anything a hundred years from now, but that the films, if the gelatine doesn't gum up, will be both amusing and hallowed by age."[10]

For Lewin, the major problem of talking cinema was its tendency, by virtue of its focus on synchronized speech—and its correlative tendency to show speech by predictable, frontal, fairly close shots, and dialogue by simple cross-cutting—to relegate staging, music, and visual complexity to lesser roles. "Action and dialogue should be coordinated with the original musical score," Lewin stated to an interviewer in 1947. "The actors would say their lines and make their movements corresponding with the rhythm of music."[11] Late in his life, he elaborated on this theory to John Russell Taylor, who described Lewin's sense "that to show people talking on screen while you hear what they are saying is nearly always enfeebling." Taylor then quotes Lewin as saying, "I really only caught on to the implication of what I'd been doing at the end of my career, when it was too late. But I think I now have the answer.... Nowadays so much filming is post-synchronised: the film and the sound are separately conceived and artificially combined afterwards. But these separate creations are done in the wrong order. The thing to do is to record a perfect track first, and then get the actors to perform to a playback for the cameras.... The difference this makes to the sharpness and rhythm of the playing is fantastic. I've done it in bits and pieces in all my films.... I would have liked so much to try it throughout in just one film."[12]

If one reflects on Lewin's directorial works with this statement in mind, the "bits and pieces" in which he attempted to set dialogue and action to music become evident. That attempt explains the self-sufficiency and the almost balletic aura of a few very special scenes in his films. These scenes feature complex mise-en-scène and distinctly uneconomical shots.[13]

In one such scene, from *The Picture of Dorian Gray*, the intensity of Dorian's sins and the degradation of his hidden life are given form in an almost operatic way. This follows a scene in which Dorian wishes Gladys good-night at her door. As Gladys shuts the door, the voice-over narrator explicates Dorian's dark thoughts, as he wonders whether his role in Alan Campbell's suicide will be marked in blood on the portrait which registers his evil deeds. The narrator explains that for Dorian "there were other paths to forgetfulness beside the one Alan Campbell had chosen," as Dorian instructs a cab driver to take him to Blue Gate Field—where Albert Lewin will experiment with a musically motivated mise-en-scène.

The scene at Blue Gate Field (which has already been established as a setting for Dorian's infamy) begins with what I would call a "prelude": this introduction starts without music and ends when Chopin's Prelude (No. 24 in D minor, Op. 28) is stopped. The scene then progresses to a full "movement," which corresponds to the duration of Beethoven's "Moonlight" Sonata. At the start—that is, during the "prelude"—James Vane, who has been listening to the fire and brimstone of a street preacher, is lured into the den of iniquity at Blue Gate Field by the strains of the Chopin, which is the same piece that he heard eighteen years ago, shortly before setting sail on a merchant ship, when "Sir Tristan" played it for Sibyl—James's sister.[14] The "prelude" gives a semiaerial view of the wretched, solitary house in the dark quiet night, with Vane's silhouette and his shadow as he runs—a rare outdoor scene (though it was probably not shot outdoors) in this film of exquisite and artificial interiors. It recalls the expressionism of the moodiest of film noir and, more directly, the uncanny vistas of de Chirico's paintings, such as *The Mystery and Melancholy of a Street* (1914). Lewin greatly admired de Chirico, and in his films he often evoked de Chirico's style—its manifold symbolism (clocks and phallic forms, for instance), its classical allusions, its deep perspectives, its graphic shadows, and its often static, puppetlike figures arranged as if in tableaux. Most of all, though, it was the atmosphere of de Chirico's paintings of 1913 and 1914—uncanny, mysterious, nostalgic—that Lewin aspired to reproduce.

The part of this scene at Blue Gate Field that I call the full "movement" is played to the melancholic strains of Beethoven's "Moonlight" Sonata and is characterized by a heavy atmosphere of sexual and moral depravity; it stands out from the balance of the film by virtue of its almost operatically integrated music, staging, dialogue, and imagery. In the rest of the film, there are, of course, complex layers of narrative, music, and detail, but these generally work on the principle of counterpoint: dense, sophisticated dialogue is "interpreted" by symbolic imagery; an almost Brechtian distance is established, and the exquisite artificiality of the treatment at once mimics and comments on Dorian's aestheticism and his masklike demeanor.

Giorgio de Chirico, *Mystery and Melancholy of a Street,* 1914.

In the scene at Blue Gate Field, by contrast, the seemingly more integrated and "realistic" decor and dialogue suggest intoxication, prostitution, and despair. It has as its major leitmotif a hangman's noose, which has been prefigured in the previous scene: when Dorian leaves Gladys, the coachman's whip frames Dorian's head like a noose. Now, James Vane continually fingers a bit of rope tied into a noose; and Adrian Singleton—one of the many implied victims of Dorian's seductive evil—bitter and dissolute (and played very effectively by Morton Lowry), twice draws a gallows and noose, and he also recites three lines from a quatrain in Oscar Wilde's "Ballad of Reading Gaol" describing the hanging of a prisoner:

> But grim to see is the gallows-tree,
>   [With its adder-bitten root,]
> And, green or dry, a man must die
>   before it bears its fruit![15]

The grim, almost narcotic tempo of the scene at Blue Gate Field, especially in contrast to the sparkling banter of the social gatherings shown elsewhere in the film, and its pervasive sense of moral exhaustion and indifference manage to effect the spirit of Wilde's "opium dens, where one could buy oblivion, dens of horror where the memory of old sins could be destroyed by the madness of sins that were new,"[16] even though the Production Code forbade any explicit representations. In Wilde's story, it is a "fallen woman" who betrays Dorian to Vane by addressing him as "Prince Charming"; in Lewin's version, this function carried out by a talented, literate (though ruined) young gentleman—Adrian—who can thus realistically add to the pathos of the scene by quoting Wilde's own (later) morbid verse.

The Picture of Dorian Gray (1945). Dorian (Hurd Hatfield) is confronted by James Vane (Richard Fraser) at the end of the scene at Blue Gate Field.

In a scene in *The Private Affairs of Bel Ami,* similarly, although much more sparingly, the action leads to a musical piece which Lewin has made part of the story line and in which the actors' movements and lines are carefully and meaningfully choreographed and uttered. Georges Duroy, the title character, comes up against a woman—the only one among all the many women in this film—who is unmoved and unmovable by his charms and who, in the course of their dialogue, will express the sharpest reproof of him. This scene takes place outside the Cathedral of Notre Dame, where Georges has gone for an illicit tryst with a devout Roman Catholic married woman, Virginie Walter; unable to find her, he has escaped from the misty, oppressive atmosphere of the faithful (among whom stands an inexplicable frozen, white figure in a cruciform posture) into the portal, where he encounters an acquaintance, the intransigently virtuous Marie de Varenne. Georges bears down on Marie while the camera moves back and forth to the mournful chords of an organ and a luminous rose window shines like a beacon (this too is inexplicable, since the scene takes place in daylight). "I think you're probably the only really good woman I've ever known," confesses Georges, in a last attempt to seduce Marie. "I'm sorry for you, Monsieur," she responds, as she mounts the stairs to the organ loft where her husband awaits her; "there are millions of us."

Another powerfully choreographed scene, also in *Bel Ami,* is the one at Charles Forestier's deathbed. A thrilling and morbid effect is created, both thematically and visually, by the tension between the deep-focus mise-en-scène and the graphic shadows cast upon Georges and Madeleine as they move about the space to the mournful strains of Darius Milhaud's score.

Both the technical and the expressive aspects of such scenes can also be found in a few other passages in these two films, and occasionally in Lewin's films of the 1950s—usually in scenes which are circumscribed by music and in which the mood is in part created by the music; for instance, there are two earlier scenes in *Dorian Gray* in which Dorian plays a Chopin prelude for Sibyl Vane. The strength of the music (by Beethoven, Milhaud, and Chopin) gives such scenes a sense of completeness and atmospheric depth.

These "experimental" scenes are almost like films within a film, though not in a reflexive sense. Rather, Lewin appears to be constructing passages to meet the challenge of cinematically expressing deeply moving affect by means other than the sentimental and predictable conventions usually adopted in Hollywood. It is not the characters who are moved; nor is it they who are moving. These scenes are moving as a whole because of the effect of their coherent fusion of pictorial, musical, poetic, balletic, and compositional elements. They are miniature, cinematic *Gesamtkunstwerke*.

In each of these scenes, music imbues the scenario with a lamentful and moral tone that suggests the almost tragic insufficiency of the characters, as though a force behind the music were compelling their movements. This sense of characters moved about as puppets or as chessmen on a board occurs often in Lewin's films, although it is often conveyed with less affect than in these scenes. Not coincidentally, puppets, dolls, and marionettes are constant leitmotifs in *Dorian Gray* and *Bel Ami;* and not only do chessboards appear in several of Lewin's films, but in all three of his black-and-white films there is prolific use of checkerboard-like floors on which his characters move (or are moved) deliberately about.

The invocation of the game of chess clearly suggests an existential view of the narrative events, but it also must be seen in light of the surrealists' fascination with the game. Man Ray and Marcel Duchamp, who were both friends of Lewin's, were two of the most ardent chess players among the avant-garde, and Lewin used one of Man Ray's chess sets in *Pandora*. Hans Richter later collaborated with Lewin's friends Duchamp, Max Ernst, and Dorothea Tanning, among others, in bringing a chessboard to life in his surrealist anthology film, *8 X 8* (1957). Lewin's awareness of the surrealists' absorption with chess is reflected in a line from his novel *The Unaltered Cat* (1967): "Suddenly these vociferous nonconformists are in undeviating agreement on the literary and philosophical significance of the Marquis de Sade, on the sublimity of 'Maldoror' by Lautréamont, and on the unparalleled virtues of the game of chess."[17]

Of the three scenes described above—Blue Gate Field, Notre Dame, and Charles Forestier's deathbed—one is introduced by death and the other two by the mystery and melancholy of Christian faith: the scene in Blue Gate Field opens with the street preacher's gloomy admonitions; the scene in *Bel Ami* opens with Georges Duroy's uneasy stroll through the cathedral. The moral intensity of these scenes, however, precludes a strictly Christian interpretation. The scenes are morbid and claustrophobic and offer no sense of possible redemption for the vengeful James Vane, the utterly sinful Dorian, or the ambitious, adulterous Georges.

These scenes, too, exploit melancholic methods to evoke a high-pitched sexual tension. Although the scene in Blue Gate Field (unlike the two scenes from *Bel Ami*) is not "about" an encounter between a man and a woman, it has at its center a rather enigmatic passage between James Vane and a sultry Frenchwoman, in which their conversation is diverted momentarily from revenge to sex, when Vane observes that she is not English and she responds, "What is English? There are men . . . and there are women." This line, which does not explicitly advance the plot, adds sexuality—specifically, sexual difference—to the web of tension that has already been spun around the scene. And implicitly, of course—that is, as a palpable subtext—homosexual tension is a possibility in the relationship between Dorian Gray and the embittered, ruined Adrian Singleton.

In the two scenes in *Bel Ami,* sexual difference is the scaffolding of the drama. George Sanders, as Duroy, expressing the contempt for women that he brandishes in all three of his roles in Lewin's films, circles around Marie de Varenne like a predator. She, meanwhile, articulates a "feminine" view of love—of grace—that is less about desire than about faith. This is the film's only hint that its world is not bound entirely by ambition, greed, vanity, pride, hypocrisy, and lust. In the deathbed scene, Madeleine and Georges negotiate their contract—a matter of sexual and economic convenience—in voices subdued by the company of death. In syncopation with the music, these mutually incomprehending dialogues between men and women acquire a lyrical sadness.

However, because of the tension that I have already noted between what I call (for want of better terms) Lewin's academic or critical penchant and his artistic penchant, such lyrical passages can become lost in the overall sense of density and irony of his films. This is one problem for such ambivalent fans as Jean-Pierre Coursodon and Bertrand Tavernier, who describe Lewin as having been "a rare and precious auteur, but he remained always a dilettante, who played with cinema as with a marvelous toy and whose talent always took refuge behind irony. It is even permissible to ask if this attitude does not correspond to an avowal of impotence on the part of an artist incapable of realizing the plenitude of his gifts."[18] Coursodon and Tavernier imply Lewin's ability to effect an unusual, lyrical, and elegiac synthesis of filmic elements in passages such as these three scenes, and they take it as a loss for cinema that Lewin lacked the will (perhaps even the virility) to devote his gifts to films that might have been wholly sincere. I think these critics fail to appreciate how rich (and in a sense avant-garde) Lewin's films were in terms of their multilayered content and visual elements. Each one is like an archaeological site, in which the well preserved remains of some strange outpost of a recognizable civilization—classical Hollywood cinema—stand on the residue of many others: modern literature, classical art, Asian philosophy, medieval legend, ancient mythology, and so on. Beneath the narrative, with its obvious appeals (sexual allure, glamorous wealth, shameless ambition, moral corruption, unforseen horror), can be glimpsed a wealth of symbols, metaphors, and allusions, while beneath all this rubble, more or less sensibly (depending upon the knowledge and determination of the archaeologist), the site is supported by the buried walls of disparate cities of erudition, buttressed by irony, perversity, and play.

That may sound grandiose, but a great deal of art works this way. If commercial cinema, more than other art forms, relies on formulas—which is debatable—it is certainly not the case that it must do so. "Archaeological,"[19] often ironic, works have a varied history in the modern period, particularly in literature, from Gustave Flaubert's *Salammbo* (1863) and *The Temptation of Saint Anthony* (1874) to James Joyce's *Ulysses* (1914–1921) to Salman Rushdie's *Satanic Verses* (1988), but also in visual art and cinema, from Edouard Manet's *Déjeuner sur l'herbe* (1863) to Duchamp's *Large Glass* (1915–1923) to Jean-Luc Godard's *Contempt* (1963). According to Susan Sontag, such works are manifestly "constructed," as opposed to "secreted":

"Stylization" in a work of art, as distinct from style, reflects an ambivalence (affection contradicted by contempt, obsession contradicted by irony) toward the subject-matter. This ambivalence is handled by maintaining, through the rhetorical overlay that is stylization, a special distance from the subject. But the common result is that either the work of art is excessively narrow and repetitive, or else the different parts seem unhinged, dissociated.[20]

Although one might hesitate to group Albert Lewin with figures such as Flaubert, Joyce, Manet, and Duchamp, that does not alter the fact that his work shares many features with theirs—particularly with respect to stylization and pastiche. And unlike Coursodon and Tavernier, I am loath to dismiss any work on the basis of pastiche, which can be a vehicle for irony and humor and in that sense, at least, has a very important place in the history of the arts—especially in the modern period, when, for the first time, this element was successfully introduced into the "higher" forms of visual art.

If Lewin had a "fatal flaw" as an auteur, perhaps it was what he referred to as his "indurated contrariness"—what I have described as his perversity. Like his own characters, Lewin tempted fate. He was drawn to extremes, and his art was undermined by his irreverent wish to see how far one could go in transgressing and defying the canon that genuinely represented a Hollywood creed. As Claude Arnaud observed of Dorian Gray's and Pandora Reynolds's attacks on their own portraits: "Their attempts to efface these traces of subjugation to myth are paid for in kind: one cannot attack with impunity a work of art, that spark of sacred fire that the gods have entrusted to men."[21] Moving pictures, too, are art. And like idols and icons, they are imbued with myth, power, and magic. Albert Lewin was in a better position than most to understand this. Nonetheless, in his own directorial career, he progressively distanced himself from the formulas which constituted the mythic elements of Hollywood movies. Ironically, it was by using mythic themes that he did this. His films denatured cinema by exploring its ancestral forms.

NOTES

INTRODUCTION

1. Quoted in Bernard Rosenberg and Harry Silverstein, eds., *The Real Tinsel* (Macmillan, New York, 1970), p. 123.
2. Albert Lewin, letter of resignation to Eddie Mannix of MGM, March 11, 1944. Albert Lewin Papers, Cinema-Television Library and Archives of Performing Arts, University of Southern California (hereafter referred to as Lewin Papers, USC).
3. Lawrence Levine, *Highbrow/Lowbrow: The Emergence of Cultural Hierarchy in America* (Harvard University Press, Cambridge, Mass., 1988), pp. 221–222. Levine's source for the etymology of these terms is the O.E.D. Supplement. See also Joan Shelly Rubin, *The Making of Middlebrow Culture* (University of North Carolina Press, Chapel Hill, 1988), especially the introduction.
4. *Harper's Magazine,* vol. 198, no. 1185 (February 1949), p. 25.
5. Lynes, quoting Greenberg, p. 21. The passage is from Greenberg's contribution to "The State of American Writing, 1948: A Symposium," *Partisan Review* (August 1948), reproduced in Clement Greenberg, *Collected Essays and Criticism,* vol. 2: *Arrogant Purpose, 1945–1949* (University of Chicago Press, Chicago, Ill., 1986), pp. 257–258.
6. See, for instance, Adolf Hitler's remarks about "degenerate" art in his "Speech Inaugurating the *Great Exhibition of German Art, 1937*" in Herschel B. Chipp, ed., *Theories of Modern Art* (University of California Press, Berkeley, 1971), pp. 474–483.
7. Lynes, p. 21.
8. From a letter to Will and Ariel Durant, January 14, 1952 (Lewin Papers, USC). It is perhaps ironic that this particular complaint was registered with the Durants, who were noted popularizers and mediators of philosophy—as some would say, "middlebrow" translators of great ideas. See Rubin, chap. 5.
9. James Agee, Review of *The Picture of Dorian Gray, The Nation,* (March 10, 1945), reprinted in *Agee on Film* (Beacon, Boston, Mass., 1967), p. 147.
10. Herb Sterne, Review, *Rob Wagner's Script,* vol. 31, no. 701 (March 31, 1945), p. 14.
11. From an unpublished letter quoted in Joel E. Siegel, letter to the editors, *Velvet Light Trap,* no. 11 (Winter 1974).
12. The eloquent four-and-a-half page letter (Lewin Papers, USC), evidently never sent, defends *The Picture of Dorian Gray,* charge by charge, against Agee's criticisms.
13. Andrew Sarris, *The American Cinema* (Dutton, New York, 1968), p. 189. Lewin's company in this category includes Richard Brooks, John Frankenheimer, Stanley Kubrick, Richard Lester, Sidney Lumet, Tony Richardson, John Schlesinger, and Robert Wise. These directors appear to be damned, to have committed a "mortal sin"—in contrast to those in the category "lightly likable," who have the dubious distinction of being described as "talented but uneven ... with the saving grace of unpretentiousness" (p. 171). (It should be noted that many of these "American" directors are actually British.)
14. For example, Sarris speaks of Lewin's "naive conception of refinement" in *Film Culture,* no. 28 (Spring 1963), p. 40; David Thomson writes in *A Biographical Dictionary of Film* (Morrow, New York, 1976), that Lewin's "arty aspiration showed like a teenage slip," and "he cultivated a garish sophistication ... and sometimes achieved real vulgarity" (p. 322); and Ephraim Katz, in *The Film Encyclopedia* (Putnam, New York, 1979), although he is more generous,

resorts to similar terms: "a curious but interesting mixture of the naive and the sophisticated, the dilettantish and the fascinating, the vulgar and the refined" (p. 717).

15. John Russell Taylor, *Strangers in Paradise: The Hollywood Émigrés, 1933–1950* (Holt, Rinehart, and Winston, New York, 1983), p.236.

16. Richard Hofstadter, *Anti-Intellectualism in American Life* (Vintage, New York, 1963), p. 19.

17. Arkadin [John Russell Taylor], "Film Clips," *Sight and Sound*, vol. 37, no. 1 (Winter 1967–1968), p. 47.

18. Rosenberg and Silverstein, p. 118.

19. Letter to Charles Reznikoff, January 26, 1942 (Lewin Papers, USC).

20. This is Lewin's own characterization of his style, from his unsent letter to Agee (see above, note 12).

21. See Chapter 2. See also Réda Bensmaïa, "La figure d'inconnu ou l'inconscient épinglé: Le Portrait de Dorian Gray d'Albert Lewin," *Iris*, no. 14–15 (Autumn 1992), pp. 177–186.

22. According to the *New York Times*, as quoted in Robert Sitton, "Albert Lewin: Director and Innovator," *Park East*, vol. 3, no. 11 (March 24, 1966), p. 8. For a discussion of sexual themes in *The Private Affairs of Bel Ami*, see Chapter 3. See also Douglas McVay, "The Private Affairs of Bel Ami (1947)," *Movietone News*, no. 66–67 (March 13, 1981), pp. 62–64.

23. Jesse Zunser in *Cue*, excerpted in Irving Hoffman, "'Affairs of Bel Ami' Draws Both Praise and Censure," *Hollywood Reporter*, June 18, 1947, p. 8.

24. Bosley Crowther in the *New York Times*, in Hoffman.

25. "You Are a Professor, Of Course," *Monthly Film Bulletin*, vol. 52, no. 622 (November 1985), p. 357. Other critics, including John Russell Taylor and several French critics, have seen a relationship between Lewin and these two directors, Godard in particular.

26. F. Scott Fitzgerald, "Pat Hobby and Orson Welles," *The Pat Hobby Stories* (Scribner, New York, 1962), p. 41.

27. Arthur Knight, *The Liveliest Art: A Panoramic History of the Movies* (Macmillan, New York, 1957; Mentor, New York, 1979), p. 189.

28. Rosenberg and Silverstein, p. 118.

29. Georges Sadoul, *Dictionary of Films*, translated, edited, and updated by Peter Morris (University of California Press, Berkeley, 1972), p. 317.

30. Erwin Panofsky, "Style and Medium in the Motion Pictures." *Critique*, vol. 1, no. 3 (January–February 1947), p. 16.

31. Letter to Dwight MacDonald, March 18, 1958 (Lewin Papers, USC).

32. Philip T. Hartung, *Commonweal*, vol. 55 (December 14, 1951), p. 254.

33. Herman G. Weinberg, "Lettre de New York (February 1952)," *Cahiers du Cinéma*, vol. 2, no. 10 (March 1952), p. 45.

34. Milne reviewed the film when it was shown as part of the series "Visual Cinema" at the Institute of Contemporary Arts in London in August 1985. *Monthly Film Bulletin*, vol. 52, no. 619 (August 1985), pp. 261–262.

35. François Truffaut et al. "F comme femme," *Cahiers du Cinéma*, vol. 5, no. 30 (Christmas 1953), p. 33. My translation.

36. *Amour-érotisme et cinéma* (Le Terrain Vague, Paris, 1957), p. 406. My translation.

37. London *Observer*, August 4, 1985.

38. Letter to Yves Kovacs, July 1, 1964 (Lewin Papers, USC). The substantive portions of this letter, written in response to a request for a statement for a special double number ("Surréalisme et cinéma") of *Études cinématographiques*, appeared in French translation in the journal's second volume on this subject, no. 40–42 (1965), pp. 167–169.

39. André Breton, "Second Manifesto of Surrealism," *Manifestoes of Surrealism*, Richard Seaver and Helen R. Lane, trans. (University of Michigan Press, Ann Arbor, 1972), p. 123.

40. Among those who consider it a "masterpiece" are: François Truffaut et al. (1953), Ado Kyrou (1957), Jean-Paul Török (1980), Vincent Amiel (1982), Raphaël Bassan (1982), Jacqueline Nacache (1982), and Tom Milne (1985). The harshest voices on the opposing side include C. A. Lejeune (1951), Richard Winnington (1951), Russell Davies (1985), and John Coleman (1985), who deemed *Pandora* a "supreme folly." See the Bibliography for these references.

41. Kingsley Canham, "Henry Hathaway," in *World Film Directors,* vol. I, *1890–1945,* John Wakeman, ed. (Wilson, New York, 1987), pp. 442–443.

42. Unpublished, unfinished, undated typescript, c. 1941 (Lewin Papers, USC).

43. *New York Times* "Television" section, in a capsule review of *Peter Ibbetson* (May 2–8, 1993, p. 29), describes it as a "heavy, musty antique. It creaked even then."

44. Sylvie Trosa, "Pandora: Albert Lewin." *Cinématographe,* vol. 73 (December 1981), p. 59. My translation.

45. Richard Combs, "Retrospective: The Picture of Dorian Gray," *Monthly Film Bulletin,* vol. 52, no. 622 (November 1985) pp. 355–356.

46. Judith Mayne, *Cinema and Spectatorship* (Routledge, London, 1993), pp. 105–122.

47. Bensmaïa, "La figure d'inconnu . . . "

48. Statement in Cinémathèque Française, *Hommage à Albert Lewin* (Paris, c. 1958). My translation.

CHAPTER 1

1. Albert Lewin, letter to Ernestine Evans, October 9, 1941 (Lewin Papers, USC).

2. Albert Lewin, quoted in Bernard Rosenberg and Harry Silverstein, eds. *The Real Tinsel* (Macmillan, New York, 1970), p. 123.

3. In thirty-two days, at a cost of $401,000, according to Lewin. Rosenberg and Silverstein, p. 115.

4. In a letter to Lewin dated February 9 (1940?), Maugham responded to the scenario: "I consider it a brilliant piece of work. Your treatment seems to me not only ingenious but highly original and if it results in a successful picture I believe you will achieve something very like a revolution in the picture industry. You have produced a highly adult piece of work and adhered very honestly to the theme of the story. I cannot imagine that a movie could be adapted in a better way." Gallery of Modern Art, *A Tribute to Albert Lewin* (New York, 1966), p. 5.

5. Sarah Kozloff, *Invisible Storytellers: Voice-Over Narration in American Fiction Film* (University of California Press, Berkeley, 1988), pp. 32–33.

6. Albert Lewin, unpublished screenplay of *The Moon and Sixpence,* first draft, dated January 16, 1942, introductory note to scene 1 (Lewin Papers, USC).

7. See David Bordwell, Janet Staiger, and Kristin Thompson, *The Classical Hollywood Cinema* (Columbia University Press, New York, 1985), pp. 36–37.

8. Philip T. Hartung, review of *The Moon and Sixpence,* in *Commonweal,* vol. 36 (October 2, 1942), pp. 566–567.

9. Albert Lewin, audiotape recorded on the occasion of the Gallery of Modern Art's retrospective in 1966.

10. Albert Lewin, unsent letter to Rev. Patrick J. Masterson, National Legion of Decency, October 20, 1942 (Lewin Papers, USC).

11. On censorship, see: Richard Randall, "Censorship: From *The Miracle* to *Deep Throat,* in *The American Film Industry,* Tino Balio, ed. (University of Wisconsin Press, Madison, 1976), pp. 432–457; Olga J. Martin, *Hollywood's Movie Commandments* (Wilson, New York, 1937; Arno Reprints, New York, 1970), which includes as an appendix "The Motion Picture Production Code of 1930."

12. Rosenberg and Silverstein, pp. 120–121.

13. Albert Lewin, audiotape (see note 9 above).

14. From the same passage in Somerset Maugham, *The Moon and Sixpence* (Doran, New York, 1919), pp. 299–300.

15. Abigail Solomon-Godeau, "Going Native: Paul Gauguin and the Invention of Primitivist Modernism," in *The Expanding Discourse: Feminism and Art History,* Norma Broude and Mary D. Garrard, eds. (HarperCollins, New York, 1992), pp. 314–315.

16. "Movie of the Week: *The Moon and Sixpence,*" in *Life,* vol. 13 (September 14, 1942), p. 50. This article relates that Loew-Lewin and United Artists (who released the picture)

"received a stern letter from the painter's eldest son, Émile Gauguin, who now lives in Philadelphia. Émile threatened to sue if any Gauguin art was used in the movie, as this would conclusively identify Maugham's disreputable hero with his father."

17. Albert Lewin, audiotape (see note 9 above).
18. Hartung, p. 567.
19. Gallery of Modern Art tribute, 1966.
20. Solomon-Godeau calls this "bricolage" and cites Camille Pisarro as having disparaged it as, "All in all . . . the art of a sailor, picked up here and there" (p. 328).
21. Albert Lewin, letter to Pegeen Sullivan, 16 November, 1945 (Lewin Papers, USC).
22. "Botticelli in Hollywood," in the magazine of his college fraternity (Pi Lambda Phi), *The Frater,* vol. 5, no. 1 (March 1925), pp. 36.
23. Ibid., p. 5.
24. Ibid., pp. 4, 6.
25. Ibid., p. 6.
26. Ibid.
27. Lewin's propensity toward travesty is suggested by an episode during the production of *The Picture of Dorian Gray,* when he leaped at what seemed to be an opportunity to have Greta Garbo as Dorian (ultimately, this proved impossible). See my discussion of that film in Chapter 2.

CHAPTER 2

1. Oscar Wilde, from "The Decay of Lying," *The Works of Oscar Wilde* (Galley, Leicester, England, 1987), pp. 912, 930.
2. Albert Lewin, Memo to Mr. Block, n.d. (c. 1924; Lewin Papers, USC).
3. Barbara Charlesworth, *Dark Passages: The Decadent Consciousness in Victorian Literature* (University of Wisconsin Press, Madison, 1965), p. 54.
4. Max Tessier, "Albert Lewin," *Dossiers du cinéma: Cinéastes,* vol. III (Casterman, Paris and Tournai, 1974), p. 133.
5. There was some pressure on Wilde from friends and potential publishers to modify certain elements in the novel, which had originally appeared in the July issue of *Lippincott's Monthly Magazine;* and the book was turned down by one publisher, Macmillan, "on the ground that it contained unpleasant elements," before being accepted by a smaller firm, Ward, Lock, and Company. Richard Ellmann, *Oscar Wilde* (Knopf, New York, 1988), pp. 314–322.
6. Cinematic realism has been the subject of a great deal of contemporary theory. See, for instance, Colin MacCabe, "Theory and Film: Principles of Realism and Pleasure"; and Jean-Louis Baudry, "The Apparatus: Metapsychological Approaches to the Impression of Reality in Cinema," both in *Narrative, Apparatus, Ideology,* Philip Rosen, ed. (Columbia University Press, New York, 1986), pp. 179–197 and 299–318, respectively.
7. For discussions of the tensions and ambiguities in Wilde's novel, see Jan B. Gordon, "'Decadent Spaces': Notes for a Phenomenology of the Fin de Siècle," in *Decadence and the 1890s,* Ian Fletcher, ed. (Holmes and Meier, New York, 1979), pp. 31–58; and Charlesworth, pp. 53–80 (chapter on Wilde).
8. On "excess," see Kristin Thompson, "The Concept of Cinematic Excess," in *Narrative, Apparatus, Ideology,* pp. 130–142; and Stephen Heath, "Film and System, Terms of Analysis," parts I and II, *Screen,* vol. 16, no. 1 and 2 (1975), pp. 7–77, and 91–113, respectively.
9. Oscar Wilde, "The Picture of Dorian Gray," in *The Picture of Dorian Gray and Other Writings by Oscar Wilde,* Richard Ellmann, ed. (Bantam, New York, 1982), p. 3.
10. Motion Picture Production Code (guidelines for self-censorship of the Motion Picture Producers and Distributors Administration), cited by Gilbert Seldes in "S-e-x," in *Film: An Anthology,* Daniel Talbot, ed. (University of California Press, Berkeley, 1966), p. 179.
11. Michel Foucault considers this painting emblematic of a baroque worldview and descriptive of the epistemology of seeing. See Foucault, *The Order of Things: An Archaeology of the Animal Sciences,* translation of *Les mots et les choses* (Random House, New York, 1973), chap. 1.

12. As described in David Bordwell, Janet Staiger, and Kristin Thompson, *The Classical Hollywood Cinema* (Columbia University Press, New York, 1985), p. 76, in a summary by Bordwell of the best work done on noir. He cites the following: Alain Silver and Elizabeth Ward, *Film Noir: An Encyclopedia Reference to the American Style* (Overlook, Woodstock, N.Y., 1979); E. Ann Kaplan, ed., *Women in Film Noir* (British Film Institute, London, 1978); R. Borde and E. Chaumeton, *Panorama du film noir américain* (Éditions d'Aujourdhui, Paris, 1953/1976); Paul Schrader, "Notes on Film Noir," *Film Comment,* vol. 8, no. 1 (Spring 1972), pp. 11–13; and Janey Place and L. S. Peterson, "Some Visual Motifs of Film Noir," *Film Comment,* vol. 10, no. 1 (January 1974), p. 31.

13. Parker Tyler, "Dorian Gray: Last of the Movie Draculas," *View,* vol. 7, no. 1 (October 1946), p. 21.

14. Ibid.

15. Albert Lewin, quoted in Arkadin [John Russell Taylor], "Film Clips," *Sight and Sound,* vol. 37, no. 1 (Winter 1967–1968), p. 47.

16. Cable from Ben Goetz to Eddie Mannix, 1943 (Lewin Papers, USC).

17. I. I. Altman, letter to Lewin, September 29, 1943 (Lewin Papers, USC).

18. Joseph I. Breen, in charge of the Hays office, recommended a number of script changes in order that "there will be no possibility of any inference of sex perversion, anywhere in this story." Letter of September 13, 1943 (Lewin Papers, USC).

19. My discussion of Bensmaïa's paper, *Le portrait peint au cinéma,* which he delivered in 1991 at a conference at the Louvre Musum in Paris, is based on a typescript that he was kind enough to give me. It has since appeared in print (with the other proceedings of that conference): "La figure d'inconnu ou l'inconscient épinglé: Le Portrait de Dorian Gray d'Albert Lewin," *Iris,* no. 14–15 (Autumn 1992), pp. 177–186.

20. The scene in the club, which in the finished film is a rather short series of shots with voice-over exposition, was evidently much longer originally. It was one of two scenes over which Lewin, who wanted to keep them in the final cut, fought a losing battle with Pandro S. Berman. One can assume, therefore, that Donatello's *David* was meant to play a more significant role than it now does. Albert Lewin, letter to Pandro S. Berman, October 7, 1944 (Lewin Papers, USC).

21. Raymond Bellour, "Ideal Hadaly," *Camera Obscura,* 15 (Fall 1986) p. 119.

22. Jacqueline Rose, *Sexuality in the Field of Vision* (Verso, London, 1986), p. 53.

23. Mladen Dolar, "'I Shall Be with You on Your Wedding-Night': Lacan and the Uncanny," *October,* no. 58 (Fall 1991), p. 11; Dolar also points out in a footnote (n. 14, p. 11) that "the heroes of these stories are always male.... The double is also a device to avoid a relationship to femininity and sexuality in general." The first psychoanalytic study of the theme of the double was Otto Rank's article "Der Doppelgänger" (1914), and Rank later explored the theme again in "The Double as Immortal Self," reprinted in *Beyond Psychology* (1939; reissued by Dover, New York, 1958), pp. 62–101. Freud took up the problem, partly in response to Rank, in his essay "The Uncanny" (1919), reprinted in in *Studies in Parapsychology* (Macmillan/Collier, New York, 1963), pp. 19–60.

24. Ellmann (pp. 20–21) cites no authority for this interpretation earlier than 1972, so it seems that Lewin, although his scholarship was unpublished, might claim to have originated this possibility. Meinhold's story dates from 1847.

25. Oscar Wilde, "Some Literary Ladies" (a review of *Three Generations of English Women: Memoirs and Correspondence of Susannah Taylor, Sarah Austin, and Lady Duff Gordon,* by Janet Ross), *Woman's World* (January 1889), reprinted in *A Critic in Pall Mall* (in the Ravenna edition of the *Works of Oscar Wilde;* Putnam, New York, n.d.), p. 190. Lewin's discovery is recounted in detail in a letter to Oliver St. John Gogarty, April 23, 1954 (Lewin Papers, USC).

26. Leo Braudy, *The World in a Frame* (Doubleday, Garden City, N.Y., 1976), p. 227. The theme of the double in horror films is also discussed, with reference to *The Picture of Dorian Gray,* by S. S. Prawer, *Caligari's Children: The Film as Tale of Terror* (Da Capo, New York, 1980), pp. 55–57.

27. The screenplay for *The Picture of Dorian Gray* indicates that Lewin originally intended to contrast Baudelaire's *Les fleurs du mal* (which Lord Henry reads) to the coachman's reading

matter, a luridly illustrated "penny dreadful," such as *The Dark Woman* or *Plot and Passion*. Screenplay, dated November 5 and 29, 1943 (Lewin Papers, USC).

28. See Lewin's comments in the interview with Bernard Rosenberg and Harry Silverstein, eds. *The Real Tinsel* (Macmillan, New York, 1970), pp. 118–119.

29. The cat is a custom-made copy of one in the collection of the City Art Museum of Saint Louis, according to Lewin's correspondance during the summer of 1943 with Charles Nagel, then the museum's acting director, and Walter Simon, who cast the copy (Lewin Papers, USC).

30. Piedro, of the Devi Dja company, letter to Lewin, January 16, 1944 (Lewin Papers, USC).

31. Doug McClelland, *The Unkindest Cuts: The Scissors and the Cinema* (Barnes, Cranbury, N.J., 1972), p. 189.

32. On the symbolism in this scene, see James Bueselink, "Albert Lewin's Dorian Gray," *Films in Review,* vol. 37, no. 2 (February 1986), pp. 100–106.

33. He had read and loved the Old French version of Beroul in graduate school (see Chapter 1).

34. From Eugène Vinaver's foreword to Norman B. Spector's translation from the Old French of the so-called *version commune* (on which the Beroul poem was based) of *The Romance of Tristan and Isolt* (Northwestern University Press, Evanston, Ill., 1973), p. xv. Vinaver, as it happens, was an associate of Lewin's good friends Barbara and Hugh Gray; and Hugh Gray, with Vinaver, had founded an Arthurian Society at Oxford. When Lewin was planning a research trip to England for *Knights of the Round Table,* Robert Flaherty had given him an introduction to the Grays, with whom he and his wife Millie then toured Arthurian locations (see the Chronology).

35. For a detailed list, see Susan Felleman, "On the Boundaries of the Hollywood Cinema: Art and the Films of Albert Lewin," dissertation, City University of New York (1993), p. 80.

36. Man Ray, one of the surrealists who were fond of disembodying the eye, had been close to Lewin for about four years by the time the film was shot and had encouraged Lewin to collect surrealist art. See Man Ray, *Self-Portrait* (Andre Deutsch, London, 1963), p. 350.

37. This is the scene over which Lewin had the confrontation with Pandro Berman described earlier.

38. "Mortal Sight" is the title—and theme—of a chapter on Jacques-Louis David's *Oath of the Horatii* in Norman Bryson, *Tradition and Desire* (Cambridge University Press, England, 1984), pp. 63–84. Bryson's psychology of vision is borrowed from Lacan.

39. This is a quotation from Cicero. It is almost impossible to read the words; they appear on a few occasions, but only fleetingly. The quotation appears again in Lewin's novel *The Unaltered Cat* (Scribner, New York, 1967), p. 172.

40. See Susan Felleman, "The Moving Picture Gallery," *Iris,* no. 14–15 (Autumn 1992), pp. 191–200, and other articles in this special issue on "Le portrait peint au cinéma/The Painted Portrait in Film."

41. Technicolor, which had refused Lewin permission to use the process for *The Moon and Sixpence,* again was reluctant to produce an insert for *Dorian Gray* and tried to persuade MGM to give up the idea. Letter from George A. Cave of Technicolor, March 23, 1944 (Lewin Papers, USC). This time, however, Lewin prevailed.

42. The corpse is a dummy that the Albright brothers had made as a model for Ivan's transformed version of the portrait.

43. This skepticism was shared by Lewin's contemporaries and friends among and around the surrealists, not only André Breton, quoted below, but also Marcel Duchamp, who decried and dismissed the purely "retinal" in art.

44. André Breton, "Genesis and Perspective of Surrealism" in *Art of This Century,* Peggy Guggenheim, ed. (Art of This Century, New York, 1942), p. 13.

45. Adolf Hitler, in a speech of July 18, 1937, in Munich; quoted in Guggenheim, p. 7.

46. Charles Reznikoff, letter to Albert Lewin, May 5, 1945 (Lewin Papers, USC).

CHAPTER 3

1. Letter to Pegeen Sullivan, November 16, 1945 (Lewin Papers, USC).
2. Guy de Maupassant, *Bel-Ami* (Éditions Garnier Frères, Paris, 1968), p. 238. Gérard Delaisement, the editor of this annotated edition of the novel, notes (pp. 304–305) that Marcowitch is based on a Hungarian academic painter, Mihaly Von Munkacsy, whose paintings *Milton Dictating Paradise Lost to his Daughters* (now in the New York Public Library) and *Christ Before Pilate* were the unlikely toast of Paris in the early 1880s. *Christ Before Pilate* even inspired a private exhibition similar to M. Walter's in the novel.
3. Quoted in Irving Hoffman, "'Affairs of Bel Ami' Draws Both Praise and Censure," *Hollywood Reporter,* June 18, 1947, p. 8.
4. Albert Lewin, "Fine Art and the Films," *The Temptation of St. Anthony: Bel Ami International Competition and Exhibition of New Paintings by Eleven American and European Artists* (American Federation of Arts, Washington, D. C., 1946), p. 5.
5. According to Harriet Janis, the "idea for this competition was worked out at an enthusiastic conference between Albert Lewin and myself in Hollywood." Harriet Janis, "Artists in Competition: Eleven Distinguished Artists Compete in a Struggle with the Temptation of St. Anthony," *California Arts and Architecture* (April 1946), p. 32.
6. Statements from each of the jurors are included in the *Bel Ami* catalogue, p. 3.
7. All entrants were awarded $500, agreed to allow their work to be included in the traveling exhibition, and retained ownership of their paintings.
8. Virginia Wright, drama column, New York *Daily News,* December 2, 1946 (Lewin Papers, USC).
9. Douglas McVay, "The Private Affairs of Bel Ami (1947)," *Movietone News,* no. 66–67 (March 13, 1981), p. 64, comments on the film's chess-like compositions and movements and, quite accurately, relates these to the Guignol references (to which I shall return) and the metaphorical use of "the marionette at the mercy of its master," which he sees as "connected to the spiritual condition of Man in a godless society."
10. Ibid., p. 62.
11. Kitty Mrosovsky, introduction to her translation of Flaubert's *The Temptation of Saint Antony* (Cornell University Press, Ithaca, N.Y., 1981).
12. Ibid., p. 5.
13. Lewin's long, angry (unsent) letter to James Agee (Lewin Papers, USC), in response to Agee's negative review of *The Picture of Dorian Gray,* composed when Lewin was already deeply engaged in adapting *Bel-Ami,* begins and ends with quotations from Flaubert. A number of Lewin's unrealized film projects were adaptations of French sources, including *Manon Lescaut, Mademoiselle de Maupin,* and *Un roi nu.*
14. McVay, p. 62.
15. Mrosovsky, p. 22.
16. Mrosovsky (p. 10) describes Flaubert's style in *Temptation:* "shifting tableaux and a passive protagonist to dramatise insistent questions about good and evil, illusion and reality, spirit and matter."
17. See Mrosovsky, citing Michel Butor ("genealogy of desire," p. 30) and Flaubert ("metaphysical howl," p. 11).
18. It is now thought to be by Jan Mandyn; see Mrosovsky, p. 7.
19. Linda Nochlin, *Mathis at Colmar: A Visual Confrontation* (Red Dust, New York, 1963), p. 31.
20. Flaubert, Mrosovsky's translation, pp. 224–230.
21. Decalcomania is a surrealist pictorial technique, used first by Oscar Domínguez and often by Ernst, in which a viscous medium—usually ink or paint—is blotted, revealing a topologically distorted image, rather like Rorschach's inkblots, though rarely symmetrical.
22. *Bel-Ami* catalogue, p. 9.
23. Ibid.
24. Sigmund Freud. *Delusion and Dream* (Beacon, Boston, 1956), p. 56.

25. Maupassant, p. 4.
26. Mrosovsky, p. 28.
27. Claude Arnaud, "Les statues meurent aussi," *Cinématographe,* no. 74 (January 1982), p. 60.
28. Cecilia Ager, "Women Only" *Mademoiselle* (April 1947), p. 234.
29. Letter to Lowell E. Redelings, "The Hollywood Scene," *Hollywood Citizen-News* (May 3, 1946), p. 4.
30. *Decision,* vol. 1, no. 3 (March 1941), p. 64. The other respondents were Paul Muni, Walter Wanger, George Cukor, Sylvia Sidney, Howard Dietz, Iris Barry, Howard Clurman, Harry Brand, and Richard Plant. Lewin's implicit umbrage at the notion of the "masses," from which he distances himself with the quotation marks, was stated explicitly by Iris Barry, of the Museum of Modern Art's film department. Her response began: "The use of that expression, 'the masses,' seems to me an unfortunate one since it usually implies the moral or social inferiority of either the higher or the lower income groups" (p. 65).
31. In an interview with Joseph Wechsberg published during the publicity campaign for *Bel Ami,* Lewin discussed his problems with *Madame Curie,* from which he had been removed after ten days of shooting. "Only years later would Lewin tell his friends the reason," Wechsberg wrote; he quoted Lewin as saying, "I couldn't stand it any longer. I just can't get interested in virtuous people. That woman was so damned noble!" Joseph Wechsberg, "Sins That Pay Their Way," *47: The Magazine of the Year,* vol. 1, no. 1 (March 1947), p. 150.
32. The name is Lewin's innovation. The café on Georges DuRoy's mind at the beginning of Guy de Maupassant's novel is the Café Américaine (p. 7).
33. See Laura Mulvey, "Visual Pleasure and Narrative Cinema," *Screen,* vol. 16, no. 3 (Autumn 1975), which is reprinted in several anthologies, including *Women and the Cinema, A Critical Anthology,* Karyn Kay and Gerald Peary, eds. (Dutton, New York, 1977), pp. 412–428. *See also* the many writings by Mary Ann Doane, including her most famous article, "Film and the Masquerade—Theorizing the Female Spectator," *Screen,* vol. 23, no. 3–4 (September–October 1982), pp. 74–88. An entire tradition of analysis stems from and depends on these two writers' tenets.
34. McVay, p. 64.
35. Maupassant, p. 285.
36. See especially Sigmund Freud, "Representation by Symbols," in *The Interpretation of Dreams,* James Strachey, trans. (Avon, New York, 1965), pp. 385 ff.

CHAPTER 4

1. Kitty Mrosovsky, introduction to her translation of Gustave Flaubert, *The Temptation of Saint Antony* (Cornell University Press, Ithaca, N.Y., 1981) p. 23, quoting Flaubert's letter to Louise Colet (1850s), from *Correspondence,* vol. 2, p. 77.
2. Giorgio de Chirico, "Mystery and Creation," *London Bulletin,* no. 6 (October 1938), p. 14, reprinted in *Art in Theory, 1900–1990,* Charles Harrison and Paul Wood, eds. (Blackwell, Cambridge, Mass., 1993), p. 60.
3. André Breton, *Mad Love (L'Amour fou),* Mary Ann Caws, trans. (University of Nebraska Press, Lincoln, 1987), p. 7.
4. Albert Lewin, letter to Helen (Freeman?), May 30, 1951 (Lewin Papers, USC).
5. There are rough notes for *The Flying Dutchman,* dating from 1946 and 1947, among Lewin's papers at USC.
6. The interiors were shot at the Shepperton studios in London; the scene of the speed record was shot in south Wales.
7. Dora Panofsky and Erwin Panofsky, in *Pandora's Box: The Changing Aspects of a Mythical Symbol* (Pantheon, New York 1956), pp. 60 ff, discuss the vicissitudes of meaning behind the somewhat enigmatic painting, *Eva Prima Pandora,* by Jean Cousin, in the Louvre.

8. The poem by Keats (which provided the title for this chapter), was a favorite theme of Lewin's. Research files (Lewin Papers, USC) indicate that Keats's poem, Arnold's "Dover Beach" (which is quoted in the film) and "The Forsaken Merman," and Baudelaire's "The Harbour" were all background for *Pandora*.

9. A highly atmospheric illumination of this "tradition" is Mario Praz, *The Romantic Agony* (Oxford University Press, New York, 1951), which includes a chapter, "La Belle Dame Sans Merci," that enumerates the incarnations of the "fatal woman" in European art and literature from the late eighteenth to the early twentieth century. Praz's book (originally in Italian, 1930) first appeared in English in 1933; Lewin would certainly have known it. The second, heavily revised edition (published in Italian, 1950), coincidentally, appeared in English the same year that *Pandora* was released—1951—and included a few added references to surrealism.

10. Heinrich Heine, *Aus den Memoiren des Herren von Schnabelewopski, Heines Werke,* vol. 2 (Aufbau-Verlag, East Berlin, 1981), p. 310.

11. "On the way from its Wagnerian mists to the plain light of day, the nordic legend is allied with Greek fable, and the Dutchman, septentrional Ulysses, sets foot in the land of the gods," Jean-Paul Török wrote in "Eva Prima Pandora," *L'Avant-Scène du Cinéma,* no. 245 (April 1980), p. 4. In choosing the obscure term *septentrional* for "northern," rather than *nord* or *boréal,* Török is probably playing on its similarity to *septennal* ("septennial"), which can refer to the duration of the Dutchman's endless terms at sea. Lewin, a lover not only of Homeric epic but also of James Joyce, could not have been unaware of the affinity between the odysseys of the Dutchman and Ulysses.

12. Heine, p. 311. Lewin's screenplay follows these aspects of Heine's version of the legend faithfully, and this line from Heine is repeated almost verbatim in the Dutchman's recitation.

13. According to Panofsky and Panofsky, the Greek word for the vessel in the classical versions of the Pandora myth is *pithos,* and the Latin is *dolium.* They find Erasmus responsible for the substitution of the word *pyxis* for *pithos,* for exegetical reasons not particularly relevant here.

14. Ferdinand Alquié, *The Philosophy of Surrealism,* Bernard Waldrop, trans. (University of Michigan Press, Ann Arbor, 1969), pp. 5–16.

15. Letter to Yves Kovacs, July 1, 1964 (Lewin Papers, USC). The substantive portions of this letter, written in response to a request for a statement for a special double number, "Surréalisme et cinéma," of *Études Cinématographiques,* appeared in French translation in the journal's second volume on this subject, no. 40–42 (1965), pp. 167–169.

16. Mason was interviewed by Rui Nogueira in *Focus on Film,* no. 2 (March–April 1970), p. 25.

17. Claude Arnaud, "Albert Lewin: Les statues meurent aussi," *Cinématographe,* 74 (January 1982), p. 58.

18. Raphaël Bassan, *La Revue du Cinéma,* vol. 368 (January 1982), p. 64.

19. André Breton, *Manifestoes of Surrealism,* Richard Seaver and Helen R. Lane, trans. (University of Michigan Press, Ann Arbor, 1972), p. 123.

20. Jane Livingston, "Man Ray and Surrealist Photography," *L'Amour fou: Photography and Surrealism* (Abbeville, New York, 1985), p. 120.

21. Letter to Man Ray, February 16, 1950 (Lewin Papers, USC).

22. The reference to Desdemona confirms the suggestion by Vincent Amiel and Sylvie Trosa that *Othello* is a third layer in Lewin's sandwiching of Greek myth and medieval legend in *Pandora.* See Amiel, "Le cinéma retrouvé . . . (Pandora)," *Positif,* no. 251 (February 1982), p. 65 and Trosa, "Pandora: Albert Lewin," *Cinématographe,* vol. 73 (December 1981), p. 58.

23. See Edward Carrick, *Art and Design in the British Film* (Dennis Dobson/Arno Reprint, London, 1972), pp. 35–36.

24. David Thomson, *A Biographical Dictionary of Film* (Morrow, New York, 1976), p. 322.

25. Trosa, p. 58.

26. Intertitle from Man Ray's film, from a scenario based on poetry by Robert Desnos, *L'Étoile de mer* (1928). See Inez Hedges, "Constellated Visions: Robert Desnos's and Man Ray's

L'Étoile de mer," in *Dada and Surrealist Film,* Rudolf Kuenzli, ed. (Willis, Locker, and Owens, New York, 1987), p. 103.

27. This term is adopted from M. H. Abrams's title for his study of romantic literature *Natural Supernaturalism* (Norton, New York, 1971), in which he argues that romantic writers aspired "to save traditional concepts, schemes, and values which had been based on the relation of the Creator to his creature and creation, but to reformulate them within the prevailing two-term system of subject and object, ego and non-ego, the human mind and consciousness and its transactions with nature" (p. 13). The term is appropriate for Lewin's esoteric, intellectual version of surrealism—a movement which André Breton, it should be remembered, characterized as the "prehensile tail" of romanticism in his lecture "What Is Surrealism?" (1934), reprinted in Franklin Rosemont, ed., *What Is Surrealism? Selected Writings* (Monad, New York, 1978), book 2, p. 132.

28. Letter to the author from John Hawkesworth, the film's art director, May 18, 1991.

29. This was the explanation of a close friend of Lewin's, Betty Silverstein, who met Lewin and his wife Millie during the production of *The Living Idol* in Mexico. Betty Silverstein's husband, Maurice Silverstein, was MGM's representative in Latin America at the time (he was later a major MGM producer). Interview with Betty and Maurice Silverstein, New York, November 6, 1991.

30. Alquié, p. 6.

31. Man Ray, "Pandora and the Flying Dutchman—A Photographic Script," dated June 18, 1949 (Lewin Papers, USC).

32. Breton, *L'Amour fou* (French ed., Gallimard, Paris, 1939), p. 21 (the photograph is reproduced on p. 17); in Mary Ann Caws's translation, the text and the photograph are on pp. 19 and 20, respectively.

33. Flamenco is a Gypsy art. For an account of the casting and participation of Gypsies in *Pandora,* see Halsey Raines, "Hollywood: Ava Gardner, Bulls, Gypsies and a 'Dutchman' in Spain," *Compass* (November 25, 1951), p. 27.

34. Breton, *L'Amour fou* (French ed.), pp. 20 (text) and 28 (photo); Caws translation, pp. 16 (text) and 17 (photo).

35. Ibid. (French ed.), pp. 134 (text) and 132 (photo); Caws translation, pp. 114 (text) and 115 (photo).

36. The relationship between Man Ray's photograph and Lewin's framing shot has been noted also by Jean-Paul Török in the *Pandora* scenario he prepared for *L'Avant Scène* (p. 64, n. 14); this is cited above, in note 11.

37. At the celebration of the speed record, Janet, in a drunken rage, yells at Pandora, "You haven't got an honest emotion in your body. You're interested only in sensation, not in sentiment."

38. Trosa, p. 59.

39. Rosalind Krauss, "Corpus Delicti," *October,* no. 33 (Summer 1985), p. 33. See also Georges Bataille, "Formless," in *Visions of Excess: Selected Writings, 1927–1939,* Allan Stoekl, ed. and trans. (University of Minnesota Press, Minneapolis, 1985), p. 31.

40. Roland Penrose, *Man Ray* (Thames and Hudson, London, 1975/1989), p. 104. The quotation is from Man Ray, *Self Portrait* (Andre Deutsch, London, 1963), p. 255. May Ray also produced a solarized photograph of disembodied lips in the same period for his album *The Age of Light* (1934).

41. See Penrose, pp. 161 ff; and William Copley, "Portrait of the Artist as a Young Art Dealer," unpublished manuscript, Archives of American Art (roll 2709, frames 414 ff).

42. Copley, pp. 2, 6. Of Man Ray's friendship with Lewin, Copley writes (p. 10): "He had too few friends of the kind he needed. There was Allie Lewin, . . . a tiny white-headed aging imp, along in years and quite deaf, but with a sense of humor one could live on. He was always turning his hearing aid off at the slightest threat of boredom. He loved Man and his work and the Surrealists. Those of them who knew him, loved him back."

43. Paul Hammond, ed., "Available Light," introduction to *The Shadow and Its Shadow* (British Film Institute, London, 1978), p. 43.

44. André Breton, "As in a Wood," in Hammond, pp. 82–83. This essay originally appeared the same year as *Pandora,* in *L'Age du cinéma,* no. 4–5 (August–November 1951), pp. 26–30.

45. Penrose, pp. 100–101.

46. Catherine O'Brien, "Pandora's Unit Got the Thrill of a Real Bullfight," *Cinema Studio,* vol. 5, no. 116 (May 1950), p. 19.

47. In his letter to Yves Kovacs (see note 15 above).

48. I have borrowed the term "liquidation of time" from Gérard Legrand, "Turkey Broth and Unlabelled Love Potions," in *The Shadow and Its Shadow,* p. 164. This essay originally appeared in *L'Age du cinéma* no. 4–5 (August–November 1951), pp. 17–20.

49. Alquié, p. 6.

50. Letter to Watson Davis, *Science News Letter,* April 30, 1941 (Lewin Papers, USC).

51. This shot sets up tension between the breathless speed of the racing car and the immobility of the ancient, sculptured goddess that recalls, but also calls into question, an assertion by the futurist Filippo Marinetti: "A roaring car that seems to ride on grapeshot is more beautiful than the *Victory of Samothrace."* Martinetti, "The Foundation and Manifesto of Futurism" (originally published 1909), in Harrison and Wood, p. 147.

52. See Bataille, pp. xix–xxiii, 199–200, 262–263. Another headless, or acephalic, sculpture is featured in the closing scene of the film, when the camera pans across Geoffrey's balcony. Detailed location prop lists (Lewin Papers, USC) from the files of the art department for *Pandora* (John Bryan and John Hawkesworth), indicate sculptures which correlate to those seen in the final film, as well as others not seen. Included are specific references to several "headless" figures, as well as, among the antiquities missing from the final film: "a grotesque stone Cyclidean [Cycladic] idol," a bronze Eros, a bronze horse head, a crouching torso, and "hobble-skirted buffoons in arrested dancing postures, one with ivory eyes and another with a great single Cyclopean eye made of a round silver ball which shines in contrast to the dark bronze."

53. Bassan, p. 64. Regarding the relationship of *Pandora* to surrealism, Bassan maintains that "if there is surrealism in *Pandora* it is toward the complex constructions of Raymond Roussel, his 'machines célibataires,' that one must look for it" (p. 64).

54. This shot, the close-up of Pandora's tiptoing feet, is missing from the print from which Kino copied its video (1995).

55. Letter to Yves Kovacs (cited above, note 15).

56. "The sea of faith / Was once, too, at the full / . . . the world, which seems / to lie before us like a land of dreams, Hath really neither joy, nor love, nor light / . . . we are here as on a darkling plain / Swept with confused alarms of struggle and flight, / Where ignorant armies clash by night."

57. O'Brien, p. 19.

58. Gilles Deleuze, *Cinema 1: The Movement-Image,* Hugh Tomlinson and Barbara Habberjam, trans. (University of Minnesota Press, Minneapolis, 1986), p. 71. The tolling bell, of course, also refers to Hemingway's novel of the Spanish Civil War, *For Whom the Bell Tolls* (Scribner, New York, 1940).

59. Albert Lewin, "R.I.P.: Obituary for a Dead Art," unpublished manuscript (Lewin Papers, USC).

60. Letter to Dwight MacDonald, March 18, 1958 (Lewin Papers, USC).

CHAPTER 5

1. Albert Lewin, *The Unaltered Cat* (Scribner, New York, 1966), p. 81. The line is spoken by the protagonist, "Robbie" Roberts.

2. Quoted in Robert Sitton, "Albert Lewin: Director and Innovator," *Park East* (March 24, 1966), p. 8.

3. An important model for Lewin's novel was David Garnett's *Lady into Fox* (1923), a somewhat ironic treatment of the theme, in which a young, perfectly well-bred, newlywed Englishwoman turns into a vixen.

4. Philip Kemp, "Albert Lewin," in *World Film Directors,* vol. I, John Wakeman, ed. (Wilson, New York, 1987), p. 660.

5. On themes related to surrealism during its exile from Paris and its sojourn in the Americas, see the exhibition catalogue, *El surrealismo entre viejo y nuevo mundo* (Centro Atlantico de Arte Moderno, Las Palmas de Gran Canaria), 1989–1990, especially the essays by Edouard Jaguer ("El surrealismo por encima del viejo y del nuevo continente"); Martica Sawin ("El surrealismo etnográfico y la América indígena"); and Lourdes Andrade, "De amores y desamores: Relaciones de México con el surrealismo"). English translations of these articles can be found in the back of the catalogue, pp. 319–332.

6. Lewin and Graves met in 1957, when Lewin was in Spain doing research for his script on Goya. Subsequently, they had an active correspondence for several years. Lewin was introduced to Gordon, a prominent scholar of ancient Mediterranean and near eastern cultures, religions, and languages, through Marie Syrkin (wife of the poet Charles Reznikoff), who was Gordon's colleague at Brandeis University. That friendship, which also began in the late 1950s, lasted until Lewin's death.

7. RKO, Paramount, Loew's (MGM), Twentieth-Century-Fox, and Warner each controlled production, distribution, and exhibition of their films. MGM, Lewin's studio, was the last of the major five to sign its consent decree, and its divorcement of its holdings took most of the rest of the decade to achieve. See Ernest Borneman, "United States versus Hollywood: The Case of an Antitrust Suit"; and Michael Conant, "The Impact of the Paramount Decrees," both in *The American Film Industry,* Tino Balio, ed. (University of Wisconsin Press, Madison, 1976), pp. 332–345 and pp. 346–370, respectively. See also Robert Sklar, *Movie Made America: A Cultural History of American Movies* (Vintage/Random House, New York, 1975), pp. 272–274.

8. According to Balio (p. 321), "The industry decided to differentiate its product and make the most of its natural advantages over its rival. It would exploit wide screens, color, and 3-D," among other strategies. See also Freeman Lincoln, "The Comeback of the Movies," in Balio, pp. 371–386; and Sklar, pp. 269–271 and 276–279.

9. See Thomas H. Guback, "Hollywood's International Market," in Balio, pp. 387–409; and Sklar, pp. 274–276.

10. See David Bordwell, Janet Staiger, and Kristin Thompson, *The Classical Hollywood Cinema* (Columbia University Press, New York, 1985), on the package-unit system, "runaway" productions, location shooting, and Technicolor (pp. 332–333; 349–357).

11. See John Cogley, "The Mass Hearings," in Balio, pp. 410–431; Sklar, pp. 260–267ff; and Victor S. Navasky, *Naming Names* (Viking, New York, 1980).

12. Albert Lewin, letter to Jerome Robbins, February 3, 1958 (Lewin Papers, USC). The letter sought Robbins's participation as choreographer.

13. She did appear as the Duchess of Alba in *The Naked Maja.*

14. Cinémathèque Française, Musée du Cinéma, *Hommage à Albert Lewin,* essays by Jean Renoir and Henri Langlois (Paris, c. 1958). Brochure.

15. Ado Kyrou, *Amour-érotisme et cinéma* (Le Terrain Vague, Paris, 1957), p. 405. This claim—or, perhaps, excuse—is repeated elsewhere, but its source is never indicated.

16. Letter to Robert Graves, May 20, 1959 (Lewin Papers, USC). The letter continues: "The Jews disparagingly called it a calf, but it was obviously a noble Sumerian bull with a heavenly blue beard, blue bands, blue eyes, and blue-tipped golden horns, the legacy of Hathor and, I suppose, Artemis, enclosing a countenance of soft yellow gold. I confess that I still prefer the bull to the Mosaic ukase, and suspect that the Jews proscribed graven images and preferred eloquence because they had no gift for the plastic arts and a big talent for words."

17. In the film, the name of the village is only spoken (and never by native actors); it is not shown in writing and does not appear in the credits. I have transcribed it with the advice of Abdallah Kahil, on the basis of other North African place names and Arabic meanings. Aïn el Oued would mean "source of the river," or "riverhead."

18. Lewin, quoted in Doug McClelland, *The Unkindest Cuts: The Scissors and the Cinema* (Barnes, Cranbury, N.J., 1972), p. 188.

19. As J.-A. Fieschi remarked of Lewin's films, "He seemed more concerned with their gloss than with their depth, with visual ritual than with universality. At worst, he gave us that unbelievable *Saadia,* purely a set decorator's film, in which the textiles and objects fail to endow the parodic anecdote with the least gravity." Albert Lewin entry, "Directed By: 60 + 60 (+1) Cinéastes," *Cahiers du Cinéma,* vol. 25, no. 150–151 (December 1963–January 1964), "Situation II du cinéma américaine," p. 141.

20. "The more firmly the belief in the 'magical identity of the picture' prevails, the less attention we need to pay to its external attributes. Likeness is the tie which links picture and depicted when the belief in their identity has vanished." Ernst Kris, *Psychoanalytic Explorations in Art* (Schocken, New York, 1964), p. 77.

21. Ross, Don. "Horror with Archeology: Lewin and the Jaguar Cult," *New York Herald-Tribune* (December 3, 1956), sec. 4, p. 4.

22. The famous postclassical Mayan red jaguar was filmed in situ inside the "Castillo" at Chichén Itzá. "It is a throne, a stone seat, in the form of a jaguar, painted red and inlaid with jade; on its back was a mosaic disc composed of precious materials." Justino Fernández, *A Guide to Mexican Art,* Joshua C. Taylor, trans. (University of Chicago Press, Chicago, Ill., 1969), p. 22.

23. Sigmund Freud, *Delusion and Dream* (Beacon, Boston, 1956).

24. William Lewin, "A Guide to the Discussion of the MGM Photoplay *The Living Idol,*" *Photoplay Studies,* vol. 23, no. 5 (1956–1957), p. 6.

25. Ibid., p. 7.

26. Ephraim Katz, *The Film Encyclopedia* (Putnam, New York, 1979), p. 981.

27. While in Mexico he acquired works by a number of artists more or less loosely associated with surrealism, including Leonora Carrington, Remedios Varo, Wolfgang Paalen, and Alice Rahon, as well as works by Mérida and Hurtado, and a good deal of pre- and post-Columbian pottery, sculpture, and Spanish colonial folk art. For more information, see Susan Felleman, "On the Boundaries of the Hollywood Cinema: Art and the Films of Albert Lewin," dissertation, City University of New York (1993), appendix C: "The Art Collection of Mr. and Mrs. Albert Lewin," pp. 283–297.

28. Letter to Man Ray, October 5, 1960 (Lewin Papers, USC).

29. Letter to Man Ray, January 23, 1961 (Lewin Papers, USC).

30. Letter to Dwight MacDonald, March 18, 1958 (Lewin Papers, USC).

CHAPTER 6

1. Letter to Robert Graves, March 5, 1958 (Lewin Papers, USC).

2. Letter to Robert Graves, May 20, 1959 (Lewin Papers, USC).

3. Letter to John Howard Lawson, March 29, 1938 (Lewin Papers, USC).

4. Philip Rieff, introduction to Sigmund Freud, *Delusion and Dream* (Beacon, Boston, 1956), p. 11.

5. Man Ray, *Self Portrait* (Andre Deutsch, London, 1963), p. 350.

6. Letter to Jim Tully, November 28, 1934 (Lewin Papers, USC).

7. Villon's phrase *"les neiges d'antan,"* from the refrain *"Mais où sont les neiges d'antan?"* ("But where are the snows of yesteryear?"), is quoted in Lewin's letter to Pegeen Sullivan, November 16, 1945 (Lewin Papers, USC).

8. Rudi Blesh, *Keaton* (Collier, New York, 1966), p. 168.

9. "The Marionette," unpublished typescript, n.d. (Lewin Papers, USC).

10. Paramount press release, dated March 24, 1939, Margaret Herrick Library, Academy of Motion Picture Arts and Sciences.

11. Joseph Wechsberg, "Sins That Pay Their Way," *47: The Magazine of the Year,* vol. 1, no. 1 (March 1947), p. 149.

12. Arkadin [John Russell Taylor], "Film Clips," *Sight and Sound,* vol. 37, no. 1 (Winter 1967–1968), pp. 47–48.

13. The scene at Notre Dame in *Bel Ami,* for instance, is 3 minutes 24 seconds long and has 34 shots (thus averaging one shot every 6 seconds). I compared this with a randomly selected passage in a contemporary film of the same genre and "class," *Madame Bovary,* directed by Vincente Minnelli (who was not renowned for filmic economy); that passage had 19 shots in the same period of time.

14. James Beuselink, "Albert Lewin's Dorian Gray," *Films in Review,* vol. 37, no. 2 (February 1986), p. 101, misidentifies the prelude as No. 22 in G Minor.

15. From Oscar Wilde, "The Ballad of Reading Gaol," *The Works of Oscar Wilde* (Galley, Leicester, England, 1987), p. 825. The second line (in brackets) of the quatrain is not spoken in this scene.

16. Oscar Wilde, *The Picture of Dorian Gray and Other Writings,* Richard Ellmann, ed. (Bantam, New York, 1982), p. 159.

17. Albert Lewin, *The Unaltered Cat* (Scribner, New York, 1967), p. 102.

18. Jean-Pierre Coursodon and Bertrand Tavernier, *Trente ans de cinéma américaine* (Éditions CIB, Paris, 1970).

19. In using this metaphor I am influenced, undoubtedly, both by Freud's use of archaeology as a metaphor for psychoanalysis—especially in "Construction in Analysis," in Philip Rieff, ed., *Therapy and Technique* (Collier, New York, 1963), pp. 275–276—and by Michel Foucault's use of it as a model for epistemology in *Archaeology of Knowledge,* A. M. Sheridan Smith, trans. (Pantheon, New York, 1972). However, I am not drawing directly on either theory, nor am I proposing one of such magnitude.

20. Susan Sontag, "On Style," in *Against Interpretation* (Farrar, Straus, and Giroux, New York, 1966), p. 20; the reference to "the greatest art seem[ing] secreted, not constructed" is on p. 33.

21. "Les statues meurent aussi." *Cinématographe,* no. 74 (January 1982), p. 59.

BIBLIOGRAPHY

Note: This bibliography is arranged in four parts: (1) writings by Albert Lewin, (2) general writings about Lewin, (3) writings about Lewin's directorial films, and (4) general works. A major source is: University of California Cinema-Television Library and Archives of Performing Arts, Albert Lewin Papers; cited as Lewin Papers, USC.

I. WRITINGS BY ALBERT LEWIN

Albert Lewin was a prolific writer. There are dozens of unpublished essays, prose pieces, and poems among his papers at USC. Included here are all his published works and any unpublished writings referred to in my text.

"Botticelli in Hollywood," *The Frater* (Pi Lambda Phi Fraternity), vol. 5, no. 1 (March 1925), pp. 3–6.
"Dynamic Motion Pictures," unpublished typescript (Lewin Papers, USC).
"Feet of the Wind" and "Twilight," *Poetry Journal,* vol. 6, no. 4 (February 1917), p. 146. Poems.
"Fine Art and the Films," *The Temptation of Saint Anthony: Bel Ami International Art Competition* (American Federation of Arts, Washington, D.C., 1946), pp. 5–6.
"The Gremlins in Hollywood," *Hollywood Reporter,* vol. 80, no. 37 (October 23, 1944), sec. 2 (Fourteenth Anniversary special issue), n.p.
"The Hollywood Scene," *Hollywood Citizen-News* (May 3, 1946), p. 4. Letter to Lowell E. Redelings.
"How to Do It Yourself in Old Chichen-Itza," *New York Times* (December 16, 1956).
Interview in Bernard Rosenberg and Harry Silverstein, eds., *The Real Tinsel,* (Macmillan, London, 1970), pp. 100–124.
"The Living Idol," unpublished synopsis (Lewin Papers, USC).
"The Marionette," unpublished typescript (Lewin Papers, USC).
"'Peccavi!' The True Confession of a Movie Producer," in Richard Koszarski, ed., *Hollywood Directors, 1941–1976* (Oxford University Press, New York, 1977), pp. 26–34. Originally published in *Theatre Arts* (September 1941).
"Platonic Movies," *Los Angeles Record* (February 16, 1924), p. 1.
"Play Things," *Jewish Tribune* (New York), vol. 37, no. 25 (June 10, 1921), to vol. 39, no. 12 (March 24, 1922). Weekly reviews of drama and film.
"R. I. P.," unpublished typescript (Lewin Papers, USC).
"Surréalisme et cinéma," *Études Cinématographiques,* no. 40–42 (1965), 2e trimestre, pp. 167–169. Statement.
"Symposium: Do You Think That the Films Have a Pedagogical Mission for the Masses? If So, Has Hollywood Production Over the Last Decade Lived Up to It?" *Decision,* vol. 1, no. 3 (March 1941), pp. 61–67. Statement.
"Tiger, Tiger, Burning Bright," unpublished story (Lewin Papers, USC).
The Unaltered Cat (Scribner, New York, 1967). Novel.

2. WRITINGS ABOUT ALBERT LEWIN

"Albert Lewin," *Film Dope,* no. 35 (September 1986), pp. 14–16, entry 974. Filmography.

"Albert Lewin Bequest," *Bulletin of the Society for the Libraries of New York University,* no. 74 (Summer 1968), n.p.

"Albert Lewin, 73, a Filmmaker, Dies," *New York Times* (May 11, 1968), p. 44. Obituary.

"Albert Lewin's Art Yields Fund 149G," *Variety* (December 25, 1968), p. 2.

"Albert Parsons Lewin," *Pi Lambda Phi* (Newsletter), vol. 1, no. 2 (June 1915), p. 3.

Arkadin [John Russell Taylor]. "Film Clips," *Sight and Sound,* vol. 37, no. 1 (Winter 1967–1968), pp. 47–48.

Arnaud, Claude. "Les statues meurent aussi," *Cinématographe,* no. 74 (January 1982), pp. 58–60.

Boussinot, Roger, ed. *L'Encyclopedie du cinéma,* vol. 2 (Bordas, Paris, 1980), p. 788.

Cinémathèque Française, Musée du Cinéma. *Hommage à Albert Lewin* (Paris, c. 1958), essays by Jean Renoir and Henri Langlois.

"Collection of Mr. and Mrs. Albert Lewin," unpublished list of artworks seen on tour (May 12, 1954) sponsored by the Museum of Modern Art (MOMA), New York (Museum of Modern Art Library, New York).

Crisler, B. R. "Gossip of the Films," *New York Times* (November 15, 1936), sec. 11, p. 4.

Crowther, Bosley. "Trademarked Loewin: David H. Loew and Albert Lewin Embark on a New Productive Venture," *New York Times* (March 17, 1940), sec. 10, p. 5.

"Ex-Newarker Big Movie Producer," *Sunday Call* (Newark, N. J.; January 19, 1941), p. 10.

Felleman, Susan. "Albert Lewin," *International Dictionary of Film and Filmmakers,* vol. 2, *Directors,* 3d ed. (St. James, Detroit, Mich.). Forthcoming.

———. "Dr. Look: The Films of Albert Lewin," *Quarterly Guide to Exhibitions and Programs* (July–September, 1994). Published by American Museum of the Moving Image, New York.

———. "How High Was His Brow? Albert Lewin, His Critics and the Problem of Pretension," *Film History,* vol. 7, no. 4 (Winter 1995–1996).

F[ieschi], J[acques]-A[ndré]. "Directed By: 60 + 60 (+1) Cinéastes," *Cahiers du Cinéma,* vol. 25, no. 150–151 (December 1963–January 1964), "Situation II du Cinéma Américaine," pp. 141–142.

Gallery of Modern Art, New York. *A Tribute to Albert Lewin* (1966).

Garsault, Alain. "Albert Lewin: Un créateur à Hollywood," *Positif,* no. 341–342 (July–August 1989), pp. 55–58. This is followed by Garsault's translation of Lewin's "Peccavi," pp. 59–61; and a filmography-biography, pp. 62–64.

"He's Hollywood's Combination Man: Newark's Al Lewin Now Movie Writer, Director and Producer," *Newark Sunday News Magazine* (December 29, 1946), sec. 5, pp. 18–19.

Hines, Thomas S. "Architectural Treasure Renewed: Revitalizing Neutra's Lewin House in Southern California," *Architectural Digest,* vol. 40, no. 10 (October 1983), pp. 176–181, 200.

Jungmeyer, Jack. "Camera's Eye Injures Art: Actuality of Reproduction Makes Exceeding Difficult Task," *Miami Arizona Bulletin* (March 1924, syndicated column). (Lewin Papers, USC.)

Katz, Ephraim. *The Film Encyclopedia* (Putnam, New York, 1979), p. 717.

Kemp, Philip. "Albert Lewin," in John Wakeman, ed., *World Film Directors,* vol. 1, *1890–1945* (Wilson, New York, 1987), pp. 657–661.

Koszarski, Richard, ed. *Hollywood Directors, 1941–1976* (Oxford University Press, New York, 1977), p. 25.

Milne, Tom. "You Are a Professor, Of Course," *Monthly Film Bulletin,* vol. 52, no. 622 (November 1985), pp. 357–359.

"Modern House on the Pacific: The Albert Lewin House at Santa Monica Designed by the Great Architect Richard Neutra Brings the Sea View Inside," *Vogue* (September 15, 1945), pp. 164–165.

Parke-Bernet Galleries, New York. *The Albert Lewin Collection: Primitive and Folk Art, Modern Paintings and Drawings . . . ,* sale no. 2782 (December 17, 1968). Auction catalogue.

———. *Nineteenth and Twentieth Century Paintings and Sculpture . . . Various Other Owners, Including . . . Estate of the Late Albert Lewin, New York,* sale no. 2778 (December 12, 1968). Auction catalogue.

Pfisterer, P. "A House and the Sea: Residence for Mr. and Mrs. Albert Lewin, Santa Monica, Architect, Richard J. Neutra, A.I.A.," *California Arts and Architecture,* vol. 57 (September 1940), pp. 22–23; cover.

Pickard, R. A. E. *Dictionary of 1,000 Best Films* (Association Press, New York, 1971), pp. 299; 332; 343–344.

Ryan, Don. "Night Life in Hollywood," *Los Angeles Record* (May 7, 1923), p. 1.

———. "Tempest-Tossed: First Little Theater Film Production," *Los Angeles Record* (May 29, 1923), p. 1.

Sadoul, Georges. *Dictionary of Film Makers,* translated, edited, and updated by Peter Morris (University of California Press, Berkeley and Los Angeles, 1972), pp. 153–154. The entry on Lewin is written by Morris.

Sarris, Andrew. *The American Cinema: Directors and Directions, 1929–1968* (Dutton, New York, 1968), p. 197.

———. *Film Culture,* no. 28 (Spring 1963), p. 40. Filmographic entry.

———. "Films," *Village Voice* (May 16, 1968), p. 45.

Sennett, Ted. *Great Movie Directors* (Abrams, New York, 1986), pp. 151–153.

Siegel, Joel E. *Velvet Light Trap,* no. 11 (Winter 1974). Letter to the editors.

Sitton, Robert. "Albert Lewin: Director and Innovator," *Park East,* vol. 3, no. 11 (March 24, 1966), p. 8.

Smith, H. Allen. "Fraternity Brothers Make Film without Using a Single Cousin." Syndicated column (Lewin Papers, USC).

Tessier, Max. "Albert Lewin," *Cinéastes III (Dossiers du Cinéma)* (Casterman, Paris and Tournai, 1974), pp. 133–136.

Thirer, Irene. "Screen Views and News: Paramount's Al Lewin Plans 'Knights of the Round Table.'" Column (Lewin Papers, USC).

Thomson, David. *A Biographical Dictionary of Film* (Morrow, New York, 1976), p. 322.

V[ernhes], M[onique], in Raymond Bellour, Jean-Jacques Brochier, et al., eds., *Dictionnaire du cinéma* (Éditions Universitaires, 1966), pp. 438–439.

Wechsberg, Joseph. "Sins That Pay Their Way," *'47: The Magazine of the Year,* vol. 1, no. 1 (March 1947), pp. 147–150.

3. WRITINGS ABOUT LEWIN'S FILMS

Writings in this section are grouped by film. Of contemporary American newspaper and magazine reviews of the films, only those referred to in the text are included here. Impressive collections of clippings of many contemporary reviews can be found in the University of California Cinema-Television Library and Archives of Performing Arts, Albert Lewin Papers (cited as Lewin Papers, USC), and at the Margaret Herrick Library of the Academy of Motion Picture Arts and Sciences.

The Moon and Sixpence

Agate, James. "Strickland and Women," *Tatler and Bystander* (England; February 17, 1943), p. 196. Review.

Bowers, Ronald. "The Moon and Sixpence," *Magill's Survey of Cinema,* English Language Films, ser. 2, vol. 4 (Salem, Englewood Cliffs, N. J., 1980), pp. 1638–1641.

Hartung, Philip T. *Commonweal,* vol. 36 (October 2, 1942), pp. 566–567. Review.

[H. K.] "The Moon and Sixpence," *Punch, or the London Charivari* (February 17, 1943), p. 134. Review.

"The 'Moon' Comes Over the Mountain: After Twenty-Three Years the Famous W. Somerset Maugham Novel, 'The Moon and Sixpence,' Reaches the Screen," *New York Times* (October 25, 1942), sec. 8, p. 4.

"Movie of the Week: *The Moon and Sixpence,*" *Life,* vol. 13 (September 14, 1942), pp. 50–52.

The Picture of Dorian Gray

Aachen, George. "The Picture of Dorian Gray," *Memorable Films of the Forties* (Rastar, Sydney, Australia, 1987), pp. 219–223.

Agee, James. *Agee on Film*. (Beacon, Boston, Mass., 1958), pp. 147–149. Review.

Bensmaïa, Réda. "La figure d'inconnu ou l'inconscient épinglé: *Le Portrait de Dorian Gray* d'Albert Lewin," *Iris*, no. 14–15, pp. 177–186.

Beuselink, James. "Albert Lewin's Dorian Gray," *Films in Review*, vol. 37, no. 2 (February 1986), pp. 100–106.

Cinémathèque Française, Musée du Cinéma. *Initiation au cinéma Américain, 1893–1961: A Tribute to George Eastman House* (Paris, 1963).

Combs, Richard. "Retrospective: The Picture of Dorian Gray," *Monthly Film Bulletin*, vol. 52, no. 622 (November 1985), pp. 355–356.

Felleman, Susan. "The Picture of Dorian Gray," *International Dictionary of Film and Filmmakers*, vol. 1, *Films*, 3d ed. (St. James, Detroit, Mich.). Forthcoming.

Lejeune, C[aroline] A[lice]. "Tough Luck on the Devil: *The Picture of Dorian Gray*," *Chestnuts in Her Lap* (Phoenix House, London, 1947), pp. 148–150. Review.

"Movie of the Week: *The Picture of Dorian Gray*," *Life*, vol. 18 (19 March 1945), pp. 99–102.

Nacache, Jacqueline. "Le Portrait de Dorian Gray," *Cinéma* (Paris), no. 390 (4–10 March 1987), p. 5.

Parish, James Robert, and Gregory W. Mank. *The Best of MGM: The Golden Years, 1928–1959* (Arlington House, Westport, Conn., 1981), pp. 163–164.

Silver, Alain. "The Picture of Dorian Gray," in Frank N. Magill, ed., *Magill's Survey of Cinema* English Language ed., first series, vol. 3 (Salem, Englewood Cliffs, N.J., 1980), pp. 1335–1338.

Thomas, Tony. *The Films of the Forties* (Citadel, Secaucus, N.J., 1977), pp. 142–144.

Tyler, Parker. "Dorian Gray: Last of the Movie Draculas," *View*, vol. 7, no. 1 (October 1946), pp. 18–23.

The Private Affairs of Bel Ami

Biette, Jean-Claude. "Les fantômes du permanent, 13 inédits," *Cahiers du Cinéma*, no. 309 (March 1980), p. 26.

"Ein Wettbewerb für Hollywood," in Glover Laszlo, ed., *Westkunst: Zeitgenössische Kunst seit 1939* (DuMont, Cologne, 1981), pp. 109–111; 380–181.

"Ernst Wins $3,000 Movie Prize," *Art News*, vol. 45, no. 2 (April 1946), p. 15.

Hoffman, Irving. "'Affairs of Bel Ami' Draws Both Praise and Censure," *Hollywood Reporter* (June 18, 1947), p. 8.

"The Importance of Being Ernst," *Art Digest*, vol. 20, no. 13 (April 1, 1946), p. 14.

Janis, Harriet. "Artists in Competition: Eleven Distinguished Artists Compete in a Struggle with the Temptations of St. Anthony," *California Arts and Architecture*, vol. 63, no. 4 (April 1946), pp. 30–33; 52–55.

Lerman, Leo. "Hollywood: Art," *Harper's Bazaar*, vol. 80, no. 2812 (April 1946), pp. 144–45; 213.

Masson, Alain. "Un passé romanesque, sur huit films américains inédits," *Positif*, no. 228 (March 1980), pp. 26–32.

McVay, Douglas. "The Private Affairs of Bel Ami (1947)," *Movietone News*, no. 66–67 (March 13, 1981), pp. 62–64.

Museum of Modern Art, New York. "The Private Affairs of Bel Ami." Press release, presented as part of series, *Saved! A Decade of Preservation: A Tribute to the UCLA Film and Television Archive* (July 8–September 9, 1988).

Parsons, Louella. "Movie Citations of the Month, *Cosmopolitan*, vol. 122, no. 3 (March 1947), pp. 67, 106.

Soby, James Thrall. "The Temptation of Saint Anthony," *Film and Radio Guide*, vol. 13, no. 5 (February 1947), pp. 17–19.

The Temptation of Saint Anthony: Bel Ami International Art Competition (American Federation of Arts, Washington, D. C., 1946).
"La Tentation de Saint Antoine," *Nuit et Jour* (May 7, 1947), pp. 18–19.
Wright, Virginia, *Daily News* (December 2, 1946). Drama column (Lewin Papers, USC).

Pandora and the Flying Dutchman

Amiel, Vincent. "Le cinéma retrouvé: Et lewin, par curiosité, souleva le couvercle . . . (Pandora)," *Positif*, no. 251 (February 1982), pp. 64–65. Review.
Bassan, Raphaël. "Pandora," *La Revue du Cinéma*, vol. 368 (January 1982), pp. 63–64.
Coleman, John. *New Statesman*, vol. 110, no. 2837 (August 2, 1985), p. 30. Note in column.
Davies, Russell. *London Observer* (August 4, 1985), p. 19. Review.
F[ieschi], J[acques]. *Pandora,* entry in "Television: Les films d'octobre," *Cinématographe*, no. 40 (1978).
Hartung, Philip T. *Commonweal*, vol. 55 (December 14, 1951), pp. 254–255. Review.
Hirschhorn, Clive. *The Films of James Mason* (Citadel, Secaucus, N. J., 1977), pp. 96–97.
Kyrou, Ado. *Amour-érotisme et cinéma* (Le Tellain Vague, Paris, 1957), pp. 405–407.
Mason, James. Interview with Rui Nogueira, *Focus on Film*, no. 2 (March-April 1970), pp. 18–36.
Matthews, J. H. "Albert Lewin: *Pandora and the Flying Dutchman* (1951)," in *Surrealism and American Feature Films* (Twayne, Boston, Mass., 1979), pp. 123–140.
Milne, Tom. "Pandora and the Flying Dutchman," *Monthly Film Bulletin*, vol. 52, no. 619 (August 1985), pp. 261–262.
Nacache, Jacqueline. "Pandora," *Cinéma* (Paris), no. 277 (January 1982), pp. 67–68.
O'Brien, Catherine. "Pandora's Unit Got the Thrill of a Real Bull Fight," *Cinema Studio*, vol. 5, no. 110 (May 1950), pp. 19–20.
"Pandora," *L'Avant-Scène du Cinéma*, vol. 245 (1 April 1980), pp. 3–22; 55–72. Special issue on *Pandora:* Full film credits, p. 3. Jean-Paul Török, "Eva Prima Pandora," pp. 4–5; essay. "Biofilmographie," p. 6. Full scenario, translated into French, with illustrations, pp. 7–71. Excerpts from reviews, p. 72.
Raines, Halsey. "Ava Gardner, Bulls, Gypsies, and a 'Dutchman' in Spain, *Compass* (November 25, 1951), p. 27. Column.
Socci, Stefano. "Lo spettatore critico," *Filmcritica*, vol. 37, no. 368 (October 1986), pp. 502–504.
Trosa, Sylvie. "Pandora: Albert Lewin," *Cinématographe*, vol. 73 (December 1981), pp. 58–59.
Truffaut, François, et al. "F comme femme," *Cahiers du Cinéma*, vol. 5, no. 30 ("La femme et le cinéma, numéro spécial"), pp. 29–41.
Weinberg, Herman G. "Lettre de New York," *Cahiers du Cinéma*, vol. 2, no. 10 (March 1952), pp. 44–46.
Winnington, Richard, *Film Criticism and Caricatures, 1943–1953,* Paul Rotha, ed. (Harper and Row, New York, 1976), pp. 120–122; 135.

The Living Idol

Fieschi, Jacques. "The Living Idol," *Cinématographe*, no. 109 (April 1985), pp. 15–16.
Lewin, William. "A Guide to the Discussion of the MGM Photoplay, *The Living Idol*," *Photoplay Studies*, vol. 23, no. 5 (1956–1957), pp. 3–22.
Ross, Don. "Horror with Archeology: Lewin and the Jaguar Cult," *New York Herald-Tribune* (December 3, 1956), sec. 4, p. 4.

4. GENERAL WORKS

Included here are a number of biographies, memoirs, and general studies of individuals and institutions with whom Albert Lewin was associated. Some of these writings are not specifically referred to in the text but were consulted for Lewin's biography and the Chronology.

Abrams, M. H. *Natural Supernaturalism: Tradition and Revolution in Romantic Literature* (Norton, New York, 1971).
Acosta, Mercedes. *Here Lies the Heart* (Reynal, New York, 1960).
Adès, Albert. *A Naked King,* Joseph T. Shipley, trans. (Boni, New York, 1924).
Ades, Dawn. *Dada and Surrealism Reviewed* (Arts Council of Great Britain, London, 1978).
Ager, Cecelia. "Women Only," *Mademoiselle* (April 1947), pp. 234–235; 321–322.
Alexander, Shana. *Happy Days: My Mother, My Father, My Sister and Me* (Doubleday, New York, 1995).
Alquié, Ferdinand. *The Philosophy of Surrealism,* Bernard Waldrop, trans. (University of Michigan Press, Ann Arbor, 1969).
d'Autheville, Francis. *Checkmate to Destiny: The Story of Saadia,* Moura Budberg, trans. (Harvill, London, 1953).
Baldwin, Neil. *Man Ray: American Artist* (Clarkson Potter, New York, 1988).
Balio, Tino, ed. *The American Film Industry* (University of Wisconsin Press, Madison, 1976).
Barr, Alfred H. *Fantastic Art, Dada, Surrealism* (Museum of Modern Art, New York, 1936).
Bataille, Georges. *Visions of Excess: Selected Writings, 1927–1939,* Allan Stoekl, ed. and trans. (University of Minnesota Press, Minneapolis, 1985).
Baudry, Jean-Louis. "The Apparatus: Metapsychological Approaches to the Impression of Reality in Cinema," in Philip Rosen, ed., *Narrative, Apparatus, Ideology* (Columbia University Press, New York, 1986), pp. 299–318.
Bellour, Raymond. "Ideal Hadaly," *Camera Obscura* no. 15 (Fall 1986), pp. 110–135.
Bertin, Célia. *Jean Renoir: A Life in Pictures,* Mireille Muellner and Leonard Muellner, trans. (Johns Hopkins University Press, Baltimore, Md., 1991).
Blesh, Rudi. *Keaton* (Collier, New York, 1966).
Borde, R., and E. Chaumeton, *Panorama du film noir américain* (Éditions d'Aujourd'hui, Paris, 1976; first published 1953).
Bordwell, David, Janet Staiger, and Kristin Thompson. *The Classical Hollywood Cinema* (Columbia University Press, New York, 1985).
Braudy, Leo. *The World in a Frame: What We See in Films* (Doubleday, Garden City, N.Y., 1976).
Brenman-Gibson, Margaret. *Clifford Odets: American Playwright; The Years from 1906 to 1940* (Atheneum, New York, 1981).
Breton, André. *L'Amour fou* (Gallimard, Paris, 1937; facsimile, 1966).
———. "Genesis and Perspective of Surrealism" in Peggy [Marguerite] Guggenheim, ed., *Art of This Century* (Art of This Century, New York, 1942), pp. 13–27.
———. *Mad Love (L'Amour fou),* Mary Ann Caws, trans. (University of Nebraska Press, Lincoln, 1987).
———. *Surrealism and Painting,* Simon Watson Taylor, trans. (Harper and Row, New York, 1972).
———. *What Is Surrrealism?—Selected Writings,* Franklin Rosement, ed. (Monad, New York, 1978).
Bryson, Norman. *Tradition and Desire* (Cambridge University Press, England, 1984).
Carey, Gary. *Anita Loos: A Biography* (Knopf, New York, 1988).
Carrick, Edward, ed. *Art and Design in the British Film: A Pictorial Directory of British Art Directors and Their Work* (Dobson/Arno Reprint, London, 1972).
Caughie, John, ed. *Theories of Authorship,* British Film Institute Readers in Film Studies (Routlege and Kegan Paul, London, 1981).
Centro Atlantico de Arte Moderno. *El Surrealismo entre viejo y nuevo mundo* (Las Palmas de Gran Canaria, 1989). Exhibition catalogue.
Charlesworth, Barbara. *Dark Passages: The Decadent Consciousness in Victorian Literature* (University of Wisconsin Press, Madison, 1965).
Chipp, Herschel B., ed. *Theories of Modern Art* (University of California Press, Berkeley, 1971).

Clifford, James. *The Predicament of Culture: Twentieth-Century Ethnography, Literature, and Art* (Harvard University Press, Cambridge, Mass., 1988).
Copley, William. "Portrait of the Artist as a Young Dealer," manuscript. Archives of American Art, New York (n.d.).
Coursodon, Jean-Pierre, and Bertrand Tavernier. *Trente ans de cinéma américaine* (Éditions CIB, Paris, 1970).
Crowther, Bosley. *The Hollywood Rajah: The Life and Times of Louis B. Mayer* (Holt, Rinehart, and Winston, New York, 1960).
———. *The Lion's Share: The Story of an Entertainment Empire* (Dutton, New York, 1957).
Curtis, James. *Between Flops: A Biography of Preston Sturges* (Harcourt Brace Jovanovich, New York, 1982).
Deleuze, Gilles. *Cinema I: The Movement-Image,* Hugh Tomlinson and Barbara Habberjam, trans. (University of Minnesota Press, Minneapolis, 1986).
Démoris, René. "L'Héritage de la peinture: Le portrait impossible," *Iris,* no. 14–15, pp. 11–23.
Doane, Mary Ann. *The Desire to Desire: The Woman's Film of the 1940s* (Indiana University Press, Bloomington, 1987).
———. "Film and the Masquerade—Theorising the Female Spectator," *Screen,* vol. 23, no. 3–4 (September–October 1982), pp. 74–88.
Dolar, Mladen. "'I Shall Be with You on Your Wedding-Night': Lacan and the Uncanny," *October* no. 58 (Fall 1991), pp. 5–23.
Durant, Will, and Ariel Durant. *A Dual Autobiography* (Simon and Schuster, New York, 1977).
Durgnat, Raymond. *The Strange Case of Alfred Hitchcock, or, the Plain Man's Hitchcock* (Massachusetts Institute of Technology Press, Cambridge, 1974).
Eames, John Douglas. *The MGM Story: The Complete History of Fifty Roaring Years* (Crown, New York, 1975).
Ellmann, Richard. *Oscar Wilde* (Knopf, New York, 1988).
Elsaesser, Thomas. "Mirror, Muse, Medusa: Experiment Perilous," *Iris,* no. 14–15, pp. 147–159.
Enters, Angna. *Artist's Life* (Coward-McCann, New York, 1958).
Felleman, Susan. "The Moving Picture Gallery," *Iris,* no. 14–15, pp. 191–200.
Fitzgerald, F. Scott. *The Pat Hobby Stories* (Scribner, New York, 1962).
Flaubert, Gustave. *The Temptation of Saint Antony,* trans. with Introduction and Notes by Kitty Mrosovsky (Cornell University Press, Ithaca, N.Y., 1981).
Foresta, Merry, et al. *Perpetual Motif: The Art of Man Ray* (National Museum of American Art, Smithsonian Institution, Washington, D.C.; Abbeville, New York, 1988).
Foucault, Michel. *The Archaeology of Knowledge,* A. M. Sheridan Smith, trans. (Pantheon, New York, 1972).
———. *The Order of Things* (Random House/Vintage, New York, 1973).
Freuchen, Peter. *Vagrant Viking: My Life and Adventures,* Johan Hambro, trans. (Julian Messner, New York, 1953).
Freud, Sigmund. "Delusion and Dream in Jensen's 'Gradiva'" (1906), in Philip Rieff, ed., *Delusion and Dream and Other Essays* (Beacon, Boston, 1956), pp. 25–121.
———. *The Interpretation of Dreams,* James Strachey, trans. (Avon, New York, 1965).
———. "The Uncanny (1919)," in Philip Rieff, ed., *Studies in Parapsychology* (Macmillan/Collier, New York, 1963), pp. 19–60.
Garnett, David. *Lady into Fox* (Knopf, New York, 1924).
Gordon, Jan B. "'Decadent Spaces': Notes for a Phenomenology of the *Fin de Siècle,*" in Ian Fletcher, ed., *Decadence and the 1890s,* Stratford-upon-Avon Studies 17 (Holmes and Meier, New York, 1980), pp. 31–58.
Greenberg, Clement. *Collected Essays and Criticism,* vol. 2, *Arrogant Purpose, 1945–1949* (University of Chicago Press, Chicago, Ill., 1986).
Guggenheim, Peggy [Marguerite], ed. *Art of This Century* (Art of This Century, New York, 1942).
Hammond, Paul, ed. *The Shadow and Its Shadow: Surrealist Writings on Cinema* (British Film Institute, London, 1978).

Hansen, Miriam. "Early Silent Cinema: Whose Public Sphere?" *New German Critique*, no. 29 (Spring–Summer 1983) pp. 147–184.

Harrison, Charles, and Paul Wood, eds. *Art in Theory, 1900–1990: An Anthology of Changing Ideas* (Blackwell, Cambridge, Mass., 1993).

Heath, Stephen. "Film and System, Terms of Analysis," parts 1 and 2, *Screen* vol. 16, no. 1–2 (1975), pp. 7–77 and 91–113, respectively.

Hedges, Inez. "Constellated Visions: Robert Desnos's and Man Ray's *L'Étoile de mer*," in Rudolf E. Kuenzli, ed., *Dada and Surrealist Film* (Willis Locker and Owens, New York, 1987), pp. 99–109.

Heine, Heinrich. *Aus den Memoiren des Herren von Schnabelewopski*, vol. 3 of *Heines Werke* (5 vols.; Aufbau-Verlag, Berlin, 1981), pp. 281–339.

Heisner, Beverly. *Hollywood Art: Art Direction in the Days of the Great Studios* (McFarland, Jefferson, N.C., 1990).

Higgins, Winifred Haines. *Art Collecting in the Los Angeles Area, 1910–1960*, dissertation, University of California, Los Angeles (1963).

Higham, Charles. *The Art of the American Film* (Anchor/Doubleday, Garden City, N.Y., 1974).

———, and Joel Greenberg. *Hollywood in the Forties* (Barnes, New York, 1968).

Hindus, Milton, ed. *Charles Reznikoff: Man and Poet* (National Poetry Foundation, University of Maine, Orono, 1974).

Hines, Thomas S. "Richard Neutra's Hollywood: A Modernist Ethos in the Land of Excess," *Architectural Digest*, vol. 53, no. 4 (April 1996), pp. 64–78.

Iris: Revue de théorie de l'image et du son (A Journal of Theory on Image and Sound), no. 14–15 (Autumn 1992). Dominique Païni and Marc Vernet, eds., "Le portrait peint au cinéma [The Painted Portrait in Film]: Actes du colloque tenu au Musée du Louvre les 5 et 6 Avril 1991]."

Jackman, Jarrell C., and Carla M. Borden, eds. *The Muses Flee Hitler: Cultural Transfer and Adaptation, 1930–1945* (Smithsonian Institution, Washington, D.C., 1983).

Janis, Harriet, and Sidney Janis. "Albright: Compulsive Painter," *View*, no. 1, series 3 (1943), pp. 24–26, 31, 35.

Kaplan, E. Ann, ed. *Women in Film Noir* (British Film Institute, London, 1978).

Knight, Arthur. *The Liveliest Art: A Panoramic History of the Movies* (Macmillan/Mentor, New York, 1979).

Kovacs, Yves. "L'Espirit et la lettre," *Études Cinématographiques*, ("Surréalisme et cinéma II"), no. 40–42 (Summer 1965), pp. 183–198.

Kozloff, Sarah. *Invisible Storytellers: Voice-Over Narration in American Fiction Film* (University of California Press, Berkeley, 1988).

Krauss, Rosalind. "Corpus Delicti," *October*, no. 33 (Summer 1985), pp. 31–72.

———. "The Photographic Conditions of Surrealism," in *The Originality of the Avant-Garde and Other Modernist Myths* (Massachusetts Institute of Technology Press, Cambridge, Mass., 1985), pp. 87–118.

———, and Jane Livingston. *L'Amour fou: Photography and Surrealism* (Abbeville, New York, 1985).

Kris, Ernst. *Psychoanalytic Explorations in Art* (Schocken, New York, 1964).

Kuenzli, Rudolf E., ed. *Dada and Surrealist Film* (Willis Locker and Owens, New York, 1987).

Kyrou, Ado. *Le surréalisme au cinéma*, updated ed. (Le Tellain Vague, Paris, 1963).

Lacan, Jacques. *The Four Fundamental Concepts of Psychoanalysis*, Alan Sheridan, trans. (Norton, New York, 1981).

Lauretis, Teresa de. *Alice Doesn't: Feminism, Semiotics, Cinema* (Indiana University Press, Bloomington, 1984).

Levine, Lawrence. *Highbrow/Lowbrow: The Emergence of Cultural Hierarchy in America* (Harvard University Press, Cambridge, Mass., 1988).

Levy, Julien. *Memoir of an Art Gallery* (Putnam, New York, 1977).

———. *Surrealism* (Black Sparrow, New York, 1936).

Loos, Anita. *Kiss Hollywood Good-By* (Viking, New York, 1974).

Los Angeles County Museum of Art. *Man Ray* (1966). Catalogue.
Lynes, Russell. "Highbrow, Lowbrow, Middlebrow," *Harper's Magazine,* vol. 198, no. 1185 (February 1949), pp. 19–28.
MacCabe, Colin. "Theory and Film: Principles of Realism and Pleasure," in Philip Rosen, ed., *Narrative, Apparatus, Ideology* (Columbia University Press, New York, 1986), pp. 179–197.
McGlelland, Doug. *The Unkindest Cuts: The Scissors and the Cinema* (Barnes, Cranbury, N. J., 1972).
Man Ray. *Self Portrait* (Andre Deutsch, London, 1963).
Mandel, Dorothy. *Uncommon Eloquence: A Biography of Angna Enters* (Arden, Denver, Colo., 1986).
Mandelbaum, Howard, and Eric Myers. *Forties Screen Style: A Celebration of High Pastiche in Hollywood* (St. Martin's, New York, 1989).
Martin, Olga J. *Hollywood's Movie Commandments* (Wilson, New York, 1937; Arno Reprint, New York, 1970).
Marx, Samuel. *Mayer and Thalberg: The Make-Believe Saints* (Doubleday, Garden City, N.Y., 1969).
Matthews, J. H. *Surrealism and American Feature Films* (Twayne, Boston, Mass., 1979).
———. *Surrealism and Film* (University of Michigan Press, Ann Arbor, 1971).
Maugham, W. Somerset. *The Moon and Sixpence* (Doran, New York, 1919).
Maupassant, Guy de. *Bel-Ami* (Éditions Garnier Frères, Paris, 1968; first published 1885).
Maurer, Evan Maclyn. *In Quest of the Myth: An Investigation of the Relationship between Surrealism and Primitivism,* dissertation, University of Pennsylvania (1974).
Mayne, Judith. *Cinema and Spectorship* (Routledge, London, 1993).
Metz, Christian. "Photography and Fetish," *October,* no. 34 (Fall 1985), pp. 81–90.
Milhaud, Darius. "Music for the Films" *Theatre Arts,* vol. 31, no. 9 (September 1947), pp. 27–29.
———. *Notes without Music,* Donald Evans, trans. (Knopf, New York, 1953).
Moure, Nancy Dustin Wall. *Painting and Sculpture in Los Angeles, 1900–1945* (Los Angeles County Museum of Art, California, 1980).
Mrosovsky, Kitty. Introduction to Gustave Flaubert, *The Temptation of Saint Antony* (Cornell University Press, Ithaca, N.Y., 1981), pp. 3–56.
Mulvey, Laura. "Visual Pleasure and Narrative Cinema," *Screen,* vol. 16, no. 3 (Autumn 1975). Reprinted in Karyn Kay and Gerald Peary, eds., *Women and the Cinema: A Critical Anthology* (Dutton, New York, 1977), pp. 412–428.
Musée du Louvre. *Le portrait peint au cinéma* (Paris, 1991).
Nadeau, Maurice. *The History of Surrealism,* Richard Howard, trans. (Macmillan, New York, 1965).
National Museum of American Art, Smithsonian Institution. *Perkins Harnly, from the Index of American Design* (Washington, D.C., 1981).
Navasky, Victor S. *Naming Names* (Viking, New York, 1980).
Nessen, Susan Weil. *Surrealism in Exile: The Early New York Years, 1940–1942,* dissertation, Boston University (1986).
Newhouse Galleries. *New Paintings by Angna Enters* (New York, 1958).
Nochlin, Linda. *Mathis at Colmar: A Visual Confrontation* (Red Dust, New York, 1963).
Odets, Clifford. *The Time Is Ripe: The 1940 Journal of Clifford Odets,* intro. by William Gibson (Grove, New York, 1988).
Païni, Dominique. "A Detour for the Gaze," *Iris,* no. 14–15, pp. 5–6.
———. "How Films See Art: A Case Study," Rachel Stella, trans., *Journal of Art,* vol. 4, no. 8 (October 1991), pp. 28–29.
Panofsky, Dora, and Erwin Panofsky. *Pandora's Box: The Changing Aspects of a Mythical Symbol,* Bollingen Series 52 (Pantheon, New York, 1956).
Panofsky, Erwin. "Style and Medium in the Motion Pictures," *Critique,* vol. 1, no. 3 (January–February 1947), pp. 5–28.
Penrose, Anthony. *The Lives of Lee Miller* (Thames and Hudson, New York, 1989).
Penrose, Roland. *Man Ray.* (Thames and Hudson, New York, 1989; first published 1975).
Place, Janey, and L. S. Peterson. "Some Visual Motifs of Film Noir," *Film Comment* vol. 10, no. 1 (January 1974), p. 31.

Poe, Edgar Allan. "The Oval Portrait," in Arthur Ransome, ed., *Tales of Mystery* (Jack, London, n.d.), pp. 26–30.

Prawer, S. S. *Caligari's Children: The Film as Tale of Terror* (Da Capo, New York, 1980).

Praz, Mario. *The Romantic Agony*, 2nd ed., Angus Davidson, trans. (Oxford University Press, London, 1970; first published 1951).

Rank, Otto. "The Double as Immortal Self," in *Beyond Psychology* (Dover, New York, 1958), pp. 62–101.

Renoir, Jean. *Écrits, 1926–1971* (Pierre Belfond, Paris, 1974).

———. *Lettres d'Amérique,* Dido Renoir and Alexander Sesonske, eds. (Presses de la Renaissance, Paris, 1984).

———. *My Life and My Films,* Norman Denny, trans. (Atheneum, New York, 1974).

Reznikoff, Charles. *By the Well of Living and Seeing: New and Selected Poems, 1918–1973* (Black Sparrow, Los Angeles, 1974).

———. "Early History of a Writer," in Anne Waldman, ed., *Another World: A Second Anthology of Works from the St. Mark's Poetry Project* (Bobbs-Merrill, Indianapolis, Ind., 1971), pp. 159–165.

———. *The Manner Music* (Black Sparrow, Santa Barbara, Calif., 1977).

Rodowick, D.N. *The Difficulty of Difference: Psychoanalysis, Sexual Difference and Film Theory* (Routledge, New York and London, 1991).

Rose, Jacqueline. *Sexuality in the Field of Vision* (Verso, London, 1986).

Rosen, Philip, ed. *Narrative, Apparatus, Ideology* (Columbia University Press, New York, 1986).

Rosten, Leo C. *Hollywood: The Movie Colony* (Harcourt Brace, New York, 1941).

Rotha, Paul. *Robert J. Flaherty: A Biography,* Jay Ruby, ed. (University of Pennsylvania Press, Philadelphia, 1983).

Roud, Richard. *A Passion for Films: Henri Langlois and the Cinématheque Française* (Viking, New York, 1983).

Rubin, Joan Shelley. *The Making of Middlebrow Culture* (University of North Carolina Press, Chapel Hill, 1992).

Sadoul, Georges. *Dictionary of Film Makers,* Peter Morris, ed. and trans. (University of California Press, Berkeley, 1972).

———. *Dictionary of Films,* Peter Morris, ed. and trans. (University of California Press, Berkeley, 1972).

Schary, Dore. *Heyday: An Autobiography* (Little, Brown, Boston, 1979).

Schatz, Thomas. *The Genius of the System: Hollywood Filmmaking in the Studio Era* (Pantheon, New York, 1988).

Schrader, Paul. "Notes on Film Noir" *Film Comment,* vol. 8, no. 1 (Spring 1972), pp. 11–13.

Seldes, Gilbert. "S-e-x," in Daniel Talbot, ed., *Film: An Anthology* (University of California Press, Berkeley, 1966), pp. 175–185.

Silver, Alain, and Elizabeth Ward. *Film Noir: An Encyclopedia Reference to the American Style* (Overlook, Woodstock, N.Y., 1979).

Silverman, Kaja. "Masochism and Male Subjectivity," *Camera Obscura,* no. 17 (May 1988), pp. 31–66.

———. *The Subject of Semiotics* (Oxford University Press, New York and England, 1983).

Sklar, Robert. *Movie Made America: A Cultural History of American Movies* (Random House/Vintage, New York, 1975).

Solomon-Godeau, Abigail. "Going Native: Paul Gauguin and the Invention of Primitivist Modernism," in Norma Broude and Mary D. Garrard, eds., *The Expanding Discourse: Feminism and Art History* (HarperCollins, New York, 1992), pp. 313–329.

Sontag, Susan. *Against Interpretation* (Farrar Straus and Giroux/Delta, New York, 1966).

Spector, Norman B., trans. *The Romance of Tristan and Isolt* (Northwestern University Press, Evanston, Ill., 1973).

Spies, Werner, ed. *Max Ernst Retrospective* (Prestel-Verlag, Munich, 1979).

Stothart, Herbert, Jr. "Herbert Stothart," *Films in Review,* vol. 21, no. 10 (December 1970), pp. 622–642.

"Surréalisme et cinéma I," special issue, *Études Cinématographiques,* no. 38–39 (1965).
"Surréalisme et cinéma II," special issue, *Études Cinématographiques,* no. 40–42 (1965), 2e trimestre.
"A Surrealist Looks at Hollywood," *Look* (September 27, 1938), pp. 11–13.
Syrkin, Marie. "Charles: A Memoir," in Milton Hindus, ed., *Charles Reznikoff: Man and Poet* (National Poetry Foundation, University of Maine, Orono, 1974), pp. 37–67.
Talbot, Daniel, ed. *Film: An Anthology* (University of California Press, Berkeley, 1966).
Tanning, Dorothea. *Birthday* (Lapis, San Francisco, Calif., 1986).
Taylor, John Russell. *Cinema Eye, Cinema Ear: Some Key Film-Makers of the Sixties* (Hill and Wang, New York, 1964).
———. *Strangers in Paradise: The Hollywood Émigrés, 1933–1950* (Holt, Rinehart and Winston, New York, 1983).
Thomas, Bob. *Thalberg: Life and Legend* (Random House, New York, 1975).
Thompson, Kristin. "The Concept of Cinematic Excess" in Philip Rosen, ed., *Narrative, Apparatus, Ideology* (Columbia University Press, New York, 1986), pp. 130–142.
Tyler, Parker. *The Hollywood Hallucination* (Simon and Schuster, New York, 1970).
———. *Magic and Myth of the Movies* (Simon and Schuster, New York, 1947, reprinted 1980).
———. *The Three Faces of the Film* (Barnes, New York, 1967).
Vernet, Marc. "Dictatures du pignoché: Les fictions du portrait," *Iris,* no. 14–15, pp. 45–54.
———. "Irrepressible Gaze," *Iris,* no. 14–15, pp. 9–10.
Viatte, Germain, et.al. *Peinture—cinéma—peinture* (Hazan, Paris, 1989).
Waldman, Diane. "The Childish, the Insane and the Ugly: The Representation of Modern Art in Popular Films and Fiction of the Forties," *Wide Angle,* vol. 5, no. 2 (1982), pp. 52–65.
Walker, John A. *Art and Artists on Screen* (Manchester University Press, England, 1993).
Weales, Gerald. *Clifford Odets: Playwright* (Pegasus, New York, 1971).
Wilde, Oscar. *A Critic in Pall Mall: Reviews and Miscellanies,* Ravenna ed. of the works of Oscar Wilde (Putnam, New York and London, n.d.)
———. *The Picture of Dorian Gray and Other Writings,* Richard Ellmann, ed. and intro. (Bantam, New York, 1982).
———. *The Works of Oscar Wilde* (Galley, Leicester, England, 1987).
Williams, Linda. *Figures of Desire: A Theory and Analysis of Surrealist Film* (University of California Press, Berkeley, 1992).
Woods, Alan. "Moving Pictures and the Knowing Eye: Paintings in the Cinema," *Cambridge Quarterly,* vol. 15, no. 4 (1986), pp. 276–79.
Young, Vernon. "Nostalgia of the Infinite: Notes on Chirico, Antonioni, Resnais," *Arts Magazine,* vol. 37, no. 4 (January 1963), pp. 14–21.
Žižek, Slavoj. "Grimaces of the Real, or When the Phallus Appears," *October* no. 58 (Fall 1991), pp. 45–68.
———. "The Undergrowth of Enjoyment: How Popular Culture Can Serve as an Introduction to Lacan," *New Formations,* vol. 9 (Winter 1989), pp. 7–29.

FILMOGRAPHY

Note: This filmography is organized in two parts: realized projects and unrealized projects. Within each of these categories, the listing is chronological. Lewin's role in each project is indicated in parentheses following the title. For each of Lewin's six directorial projects, the complete cast and credits are given; for other projects, only the director and production company are indicated. The following abbreviations are used: adaptation (a), associate producer (ap), black-and-white (b/w), continuity (c), director (d), producer (p), production supervisor (ps), scenarist (sc), story (s). When Lewin's role was collaborative, that is indicated by the prefix co-; when his participation was uncredited, that is indicated by the notation /u.

REALIZED PROJECTS

1924	*Bread* (c); Victor Schertzinger (d); Metro.
1925	*The Fate of a Flirt* (c); Frank R. Strayer (d); MGM.
1926	*Ladies of Leisure* (s, c); Thomas Buckingham (d); MGM.
	Blarney (co-sc); Marcel De Sano (d); MGM.
	Tin Hats (c); Edward Sedgwick (d); MGM.
1927	*A Little Journey* (sc); Robert Z. Leonard (d); MGM.
	Altars of Desire (c); W. Christy Cabanne (d); MGM.
	Spring Fever (co-sc); Edward Sedgwick (d); MGM.
	Quality Street (co-sc; co-a); Sidney Franklin (d); MGM.
1928	*The Actress* (co-sc); Sidney Franklin (d); MGM.
1929	*The Kiss* (ps/u); Jacques Feyder (d); MGM.
	Devil-May-Care (ps/u); Sidney Franklin (d); MGM.
1931	*The Guardsman* (ps/u); Sidney Franklin (d); MGM.
	The Cuban Love Song (ps/u); W. S. Van Dyke (d); MGM.
1932	*Red-Headed Woman* (ps/u); Jack Conway (d); MGM.
	Smilin' Through (ps/u); Sidney Franklin (d); MGM.
1934	*What Every Woman Knows* (ps/u); Gregory La Cava (d); MGM.
1935	*China Seas* (ap); Tay Garnett (d); MGM.
	Mutiny on the Bounty (ap); Frank Lloyd (d); MGM.
1937	*The Good Earth* (ap); Sidney Franklin (d); MGM.
	True Confession (p); Wesley Ruggles (d); Paramount.
1938	*Spawn of the North* (p); Henry Hathaway (d); Paramount.
1939	*Zaza* (p); George Cukor (d); Paramount.

1940 *So Ends Our Night* (co-p); John Cromwell (d); Loew-Lewin. Adapted from Erich Maria Remarque's novel *Flotsam*.

1942 *The Moon and Sixpence* (d, sc); Loew-Lewin. Adapted from the novel by W. Somerset Maugham; 89 minutes; b/w with sepia and color sequences. *Credits:* Producer, David L. Loew. Production design, Gordon Wiles. Musical score, Dmitri Tiomkin. Associate producer, Stanley Kramer. Director of photography, John F. Seitz. Art director, F. Paul Sylos. Editor, Richard L. Van Enger. Sculpture, Nina Saemundsson. Paintings, Dolya Goutman. Technical advice and dances, Devi Dja and Her Bali-Java Dancers. *Cast:* George Sanders, Herbert Marshall, Steve Geray, Doris Dudley, Eric Blore, Albert Basserman, Molly Lamont, Elena Verdugo, Florence Bates, Heather Thatcher, Robert Grieg, Kenneth Hunter, Irene Tedrow.

1945 *The Picture of Dorian Gray* (d, sc); MGM. Adapted from the novel by Oscar Wilde; 110 minutes; b/w with Technicolor inserts. *Credits:* Producer, Pandro S. Berman. Special assistant to the director (production design), Gordon Wiles. Musical score, Herbert Stothart. Director of photography, Harry Stradling. Art directors, Cedric Gibbons and Hans Peters. Set decorator, Edwin B. Willis. Editor, Ferris Webster. Paintings, Henrique Medina and Ivan Le Lorraine Albright. *Cast:* George Sanders, Hurd Hatfield, Donna Reed, Angela Lansbury, Lowell Gilmore, Peter Lawford, Richard Fraser, Reginald Owen, Lydia Bilbrook, Morton Lowry, Douglas Walton, Mary Forbes, Devi Dja and Her Balinese Dancers, Cedric Hardwicke (narrator).

1947 *The Private Affairs of Bel Ami* (d, sc); Loew-Lewin. Adapted from Guy de Maupassant's novel *Bel-Ami;* 112 minutes; b/w with Technicolor insert. *Credits:* Producer, David Loew. Production design, Gordon Wiles. Musical score, Darius Milhaud. Director of photography, Russell Metty. Art director, Frank Sylos. Set decorator, Edward Boyle. Editor, Albrecht Joseph. Painting, Max Ernst. *Cast:* George Sanders, Angela Lansbury, Ann Dvorak, Warren William, Katherine Emery, Frances Dee, John Carradine, Susan Douglas, Albert Basserman, Hugo Haas, Marie Wilson, David Bond.

1951 *Pandora and the Flying Dutchman* (d, s, sc, p); Dorkay Productions (Albert Lewin and Joseph Kaufman)/Romulus. From an original story suggested by the legend of the Flying Dutchman; 122 minutes; Technicolor. *Credits:* Production design, John Bryan. Musical score and conductor, Alan Rawsthorne. Musical director, Hubert Clifford. Director of photography, Jack Cardiff. Assistant art director, Tim Hopewell-Ash. Set decorator, John Hawkesworth. Editor, Ralph Kemplen. Costume design, Beatrice Dawson. Special effects, W. Percy Day. *Cast:* James Mason, Ava Gardner, Nigel Patrick, Sheila Sim, Harold Warrender, Mario Cabre, Marius Goring, John Laurie, Pamela Kellino, Patricia Raine, Marguerite D'Alvarez, La Pillina (flamenco dancer).

1954 *Saadia* (d, sc, p); MGM. Adapted from Francis d'Autheville's novel *Échec au destin;* 82 minutes; Technicolor. *Credits:* Musical score, Bronislau Kaper. Director of photography, Christopher Challis. Art director, John Hawkesworth. Editor, Harold F. Kress. Photographic effects, Tom Howard. *Cast:* Cornel Wilde, Mel Ferrer, Rita Gam, Michel Simon, Cyril Cusack, Wanda Rotha, Marcel Poncin, Anthony Marlowe, Helene Vallier, Mahjoub ben Brahim, Jacques Dufhilo, Bernard Farrel, Richard Johnson.

1957 *The Living Idol* (d, s, sc, co-p); MGM. From an original story; 100 minutes; Eastman Color; Cinemascope. *Credits:* Coproducer, Gregorio Walerstein. Musical score, Mañuel Esperon and Rudolfo Halffter. Director of photography, Jack Hildyard. Art director, Edward Fitzgerald. Assistant art director, Augustin Ytuarte. Editor, Rafael Ceballos. Costumes, Armando Valdes Peza and Ramon Valdiosera. Still photography, Ted Castle. Paintings, Carlos Mérida. Choreography, Jose Silva and David Campbell. Technical Advisor: Luis Aveleyra. *Cast:* Steve Forrest, Liliane Montevecchi, James Robertson-Justice, Sara Garcia, Eduardo Noriega.

UNREALIZED OR UNFINISHED PROJECTS

1937 *Manon Lescaut.* Lewin as producer and George Cukor as director proposed this project to Paramount along with *Zaza,* (1939) both as vehicles for Isa Miranda; *Manon Lescaut* was thought to be too arty, too expensive, and too risky.

1938 *Knights of the Round Table.* Lewin tried for years to produce this—particularly vigorously during his time at Paramount and immediately thereafter. In 1938 he intended it to be scripted by Talbot Jennings and directed by Henry Hathaway and to star, among others, Fredric March, John Barrymore, and Isa Miranda. In 1939, before Paramount called it off, Douglas Fairbanks Jr. had been signed to play Lancelot and Lewin expected Madeleine Carroll and Olympe Bradna to costar; Benjamin Britten had been signed to score it. Shortly after Lewin returned from a trip to England and Wales for research and location scouting, the mounting hostilities in Europe and anxiety about expenses led Paramount executives to call it off. There is no evidence that Lewin had any connection to the *Knights of the Round Table* that Richard Thorpe directed for MGM (1953), although Lewin was at the studio then and the film did feature his favorite actress, Ava Gardner.

Other projects which Lewin advocated for Paramount and which were not realized (at least under his auspices) were:

Northwest Passage, later produced by MGM in color; King Vidor (d). *Gettysburg,* adapted by Clifford Odets from the book *Long Remember;* Lewin saw this as a vehicle for Gary Cooper.

Two Bad Hats. Rewritten by Preston Sturges from a first script by Talbot Jennings; Sturges later directed it himself as *The Lady Eve* (1941) for Paramount.

1939 *The Red Pony.* Lewin proposed this to David Loew as an independent production to be adapted by John Steinbeck from his story and directed by Robert Flaherty. Steinbeck did later adapt it for a color film, directed by Lewis Milestone and with a score by Aaron Copland (MGM, 1949).

1940 *Landfall.* Lewin wanted to adapt this from Nevil Shute's novel about the RAF and produce it for Loew-Lewin as a contribution to Britain's war effort.

1941 *The Mating Call.* This title is attached to two projects. One was an adaptation of Clifford Odets's *Night Music,* on which Odets worked with Lewin in 1941 (Lewin apparently recommended the change in the title); the second was a draft script by Ben Hecht, which may have been an adaptation of the same play. Neither was produced, for financial reasons and, ultimately, because of the dissolution of Loew-Lewin in 1942. In the late 1940s, Jean Renoir bought the film rights to *Night Music,* hoping to produce it with his and Burgess Meredith's short-lived independent company, the Film Group, which planned to make low-budget features from stage plays but in fact produced none.

Wind, Sand, and Stars. Lewin and Jean Renoir, recently arrived from France, discussed adapting the book by Antoine de Saint-Exupéry for Loew-Lewin. David Loew did, later, produce a Renoir film, *The Southerner* (Production Artists, 1945) with Robert Hakim.

Titles that Loew-Lewin registered reflect some of the other material that Lewin wanted to retain an option to develop; but there were dozens of these, and certainly not all of them can be considered actual projects. They include: *The Aeneid; Ali Baba and the Forty Thieves; Arabian Nights; Don Quixote; Don Juan; Enoch Arden; Fingal's Cave; Gil Blas; Hans Brinker: The Silver Skates; Henry Esmond; The History of Tom Jones, a Foundling; Hypatia; The Iliad; Ivanhoe; Jane Eyre; Johannes Brahms and Clara Schumann; John Brown's Body; The Legend of Sleepy Hollow; The Life of John Keats; Little Dorrit; Lorna Doone; The Marble Faun; Mesmer; The Moonstone; Moby-Dick; Mysteries of Paris; The Odyssey; Paul and Virginia; A Pilgrim's Progress; Pudd'nhead Wilson; Rip van Winkle; The Scarlet Letter; Sinbad the Sailor; Thaddeus of Warsaw;* and *Volpone,* among many others.

1942   *Madame Curie* (d). Lewin was assigned to this when he returned to MGM in 1942 but lasted only ten days before being removed from the production by Sidney Franklin (p) and replaced with Mervyn LeRoy (d).

1949   *Quo Vadis* (ps). Lewin was associated with this production only while John Huston was slated to direct it and Gregory Peck to star in it; when these two left the project; so did Lewin. The film was released in 1951 (MGM); Mervyn LeRoy (d).

1952   *Peer Gynt.* Lewin devoted considerable time and energy to researching and writing an adaptation of Ibsen's play ("combined with the music of Grieg's 'Peer Gynt Suite'"), hoping to undertake a production with a London company after he completed *Saadia.*

1953   *A Naked King* (which Lewin sometimes called *A Quite Naked King*). Lewin had written this adaptation of Albert Adès's novel *Un roi nu* and planned to direct it for an independent production company in Europe, but he never got it off the ground.

Hank. This original script, set in Latin America, made even less progress toward realization.

1954   *Mademoiselle de Maupin* and *Socrates.* Lewin was under contract to Jacques Grinieff to do preproduction research on one or the other of these themes, but nothing appears to have come of either.

1957   *Goya* (sc). Lewin prepared a script, which he envisioned for Yul Brynner as Goya and Ava Gardner as the Duchess of Alba, and it was bought by the producers of *The Naked Maja;* but ultimately they used none of it. The film was an Italian-American coproduction: it did star Ava Gardner, with Anthony Franciosa as Goya, and it was directed by Henry Koster; it was released in 1958 (MGM).

Diana at Midnight (sc). This was another of Lewin's original screenplays, a modernized version of the Faust legend (with a Faust ballet featured in the story), which he planned to produce and direct himself, with Ava Gardner starring. This project was left unrealized when Lewin suffered a heart attack in 1959. In the late 1950s Lewin also researched themes from India for a film he evidently never wrote.

1960   *Bruges la Morte*. An adaptation of the book by Georges Rodenbach that Lewin worked on briefly while recovering from his heart attack.

PHOTO CREDITS

Note: Illustrations not otherwise credited were provided by Susan Felleman.

Front jacket and pages 62, 67, 68, 73, 80, 86, 88, 90, 94, 105, and 111: The Museum of Modern Art Film Stills Archive, New York

Back jacket and pages 3, 7, 9, 50, 53, 66, 84, 87, 113, and 118: University of Southern California, Cinema-Television Library and Archives of Performing Arts, Los Angeles

Frontispiece (page ii): Ann Lewin Diament; © 1997 Artists Rights Society (ARS), New York; ADAGP; Man Ray Trust, Paris

Pages 5, 18, 30, 35, 56, 69, 96, 100, 109, 112, 114: Photofest, New York

Page 33: Richard Koszarski

Page 37: Uffizi Gallery, Florence; photo courtesy of Alinari/Art Resource, New York

Page 59: The Art Institute of Chicago

Page 71: Wilhelm-Lehmbruck-Museum der Stadt Duisburg, Germany

Pages 91, 93: © 1997 Artists Rights Society (ARS), New York; ADAGP; Man Ray Trust, Paris

Page 122: Private Collection; photo courtesy of Aquavella Gallery, New York

INDEX

Actress, The, 2, 153
Adès, Albert, *Roi Nu, Un* (*A Naked King*), 7, 8, 103, 156
Age d'Or, L' (*Age of Gold*), 21
Agee, James, 12–14
Ager, Cecelia, 74
Albright, Ivan (Le Lorraine), 6, 60, 63, 65, 67, 154
Albright, Malvin (Zsissley), 6
Alquié, Ferdinand, 83, 96
Altars of Desire, 153
Alvarez, Marguerite d', 2, 7, 92, 154
American Federation of Arts, 66
American Jewish Relief Committee, 1–2
Amour fou (mad love), in *Pandora,* 83, 90–95. *See also* Breton, André; Man Ray; surrealism/surrealists
anachronism, in Lewin's films, 65, 68, 89
anthropology, Lewin's interest in, 8, 103
anti-intellectualism, 15, 19; as factor in Lewin's reception, 15–19; in Hollywood, 15
Anti-Intellectualism in American Life (Hofstadter), 15
antiquities, use in Lewin's films, 52, 97
Antonioni, Michelangelo, 17
Aquinas, Saint Thomas, 96
archaeology, 8, 103, 110–11, 125
Arensberg, Walter and Louise, 5
Arnaud, Claude, 73, 126
Arnold, Matthew, 98
art/art objects, use in Lewin's films, 33–36, 47, 51–53, 59–60, 63, 68, 86–89, 104, 107, 108, 111–13
Arthurian themes, 54–56; locations, 4. *See also* Knights of the Round Table
Asia, Lewin's travels in, 8. *See also* orientalism
auteurism, 11, 115, 126
Autheville, Francis d', *Échec au Destin,* 154. *See also* Saadia
Aveleyra, Luis, 155

Balinese-Javanese dance, 6, 53, 154
"Ballad of Reading Gaol, The" (Wilde), 122
Balzac, Honoré de, 74
Bar at the Folies-Bergère (Manet), 69
Barefoot Contessa, The, 85
Barnes, Djuna, 2
Barnes, Howard, 14
Barr, Alfred H., 8, 65
Barrie, James M., *Quality Street,* 2
Barrymore, John, 155
Bassan, Raphaël, 85, 97
Basserman, Albert, 28, 63, 64, 77, 154
Bataille, Georges: *acéphale* (headless), 97; *informe* (formless), 95
Bates, Florence, 28, 31, 154

Battleship Potemkin, The, 22
Baudelaire, Charles, 70; *Les Fleurs du mal,* 51
Beardsley, Aubrey, 13, 52, 56, 70, 83; "How Sir Tristram drank of the love drink," from *Morte d'Arthur,* 13, 54, 56
Bed Without Pillows (Lewin), 8
Beethoven, Ludwig van, "Moonlight" sonata, 121, 124
Bel-Ami (Maupassant), 6, 17, 63, 65, 72, 78. *See also Private Affairs of Bel Ami, The*
Bel-Ami Competition, 6, 65–68; exhibition of, 6, 66, 72
Bellan, Ferdinand (Ferdie), 87–88
"Belle Dame Sans Merci, La" (Keats), 83
Bellour, Raymond, 48
Bensmaïa, Réda, 24, 47
Bergman, Bernard, 1
Bergman, Ingmar, 17, 79
Bergman, Ingrid, 8
Berman, Eugene, 65, 67
Berman, Pandro S., 6, 15, 51, 53, 154
Bern, Paul, 2
Béroul, *Tristan et Yseut,* 37
Bilbrook, Lydia, 154
Billikopf, Jacob, 1
Blarney, 153
Blore, Eric, 28, 63, 154
Boiffard, Jacques-André, 94
Bond, David, 64, 69, 77, 79, 154
Botticelli, Sandro, 34–38, 89; *Birth of Venus,* 38; *Spring* (*Primavera*), 34, 37–38, 119
"Botticelli in Hollywood" (Lewin), 38
Boyle, Edward, 154
Bradna, Olympe, 155
Brahim, Mahjoub ben, 154
Brandeis University, 8
Brassaï, *Ciel postiche* (*False Sky*), 95
Braudy, Leo, 50
Bread, 2, 153
Breen, Joseph, 43
Breton, André, 22, 60, 81, 95, 96; *L'Amour fou* (*Mad Love*), 83, 90–95; *Second Manifesto of Surrealism,* 85
Britten, Benjamin, 155
Brown, John Mason, 14
Brueghel, Pieter, the Younger, 70
Bruges la Morte, 157
Bryan, John, 98, 115, 154
Brynner, Yul, 156
Buddha/Buddhism, 53, 70
bullfighting, in *Pandora and the Flying Dutchman,* 82, 83, 101
Buñuel, Luis, 21, 57, 85, 91

161

Cabinet of Dr. Caligari, The, 11, 19, 22, 119
Cabre, Mario, 82, 154
Cahiers du Cinéma, 21; "F comme femme," 21
Callot, Jacques, 70
Cameron, Kate, 14
"camp," 22, 85
Campbell, David, 155
Cardiff, Jack, 21, 83, 84, 115, 154
Carradine, John, 64, 67, 154
Carrington, Leonora, 8, 65, 67
Carroll, Madeleine, 155
Castle, Ted, 155
Castle, The (Kafka), 119
Cat People, 101
Ceballos, Rafael, 155
censorship, 16–17, 31–32, 43. *See also* Hays Office; Legion of Decency; Motion Picture Production Code
Cézanne, Paul, 68
Chabrol, Claude, 21
Challis, Christopher, 154
Chaplin, Charlie, 22, 119
Charlesworth, Barbara, 41
chess: as metaphor and motif in Lewin's films, 120, 124; as surrealist preoccupation, 124
Chien Andalou, Un (Andalusian Dog), 57, 91
China Seas, 3, 153
Chirico, Giorgio de, 22, 37, 57, 81, 85, 87–88, 96–97; *Mystery and Melancholy of a Street,* 119, 121
Chopin, Frédéric, Prelude (No. 24 in D minor, Op. 28), 107, 121, 124
Cinémathèque Française, 9; "Hommage à Albert Lewin," 8, 104
Citizen Kane, 19, 32
Clifford, Hubert, 154
Clift, Montgomery, 45
color inserts in Lewin's black-and-white films, 34–36, 60, 63, 72, 81, 83
Columbia University, 1, 11
Combs, Richard, 24
Comédie Humaine, Le (Balzac), 74
comparative religion, Lewin's interest in, 103
Confessions of a Nazi Spy, 29
Contempt, 17, 21, 125
"convulsive beauty," in *Pandora,* 91–95. *See also* Breton, André; Man Ray; surrealism/surrealists
Conway, Jack, 46
Cook, Alton, 14
Cooper, Gary, 155
Copley, William, 95
Copley Gallery (Los Angeles), 95
Copley Society (Boston), 66
Coursodon, Jean-Pierre, 125–26
Creelman, Eileen, 14
Crime and Punishment (Dostoevsky), 75
Cromwell, John, 154
Crosby, Floyd and Aelis, 7
Crowther, Bosley, 14, 63
Cuban Love Song, 153

Cukor, George, 155
Culver City, 2
Curley, Mayor James M. (Boston), 66
Cusack, Cyril, 102, 154

Dalí, Salvador, 6, 21, 57, 65, 67, 85, 91
D'Annunzio, Gabriele, 70
David (biblical), sculptures in *The Picture of Dorian Gray,* 47–48, 52
Davies, Russell, 21
Davis, Frank, 2
Dawson, Beatrice, 84, 154
Day, W. Percy, 154
Days of Glory, 45
Death Valley, 5
decadence, as theme of Lewin's films, 70, 90, 119
decalcomania, 71
De Chirico, Giorgio. *See* Chirico, Giorgio de
Decision, 75
Dee, Frances, 64, 73, 154
Degas, Edgar, 17, 67, 70; *Bellelli Family,* 67
Deleuze, Gilles, 98
"Delusion and Dream" (Freud), 111
Delvaux, Paul, 22, 65, 68, 87–88
Denmark, German occupation of, 5
depravity, as theme in Lewin's films, 32
desire, in Lewin's films: female, 31–32, 45, 53, 58, 72–73, 75–79; male object of, 45, 76–77, 115
Desnos, Robert, 89
Devi Dja and Her Bali-Java Dancers, 6, 53, 154
Devil-May-Care, 2, 153
Diana at Midnight (Lewin), 8, 20, 89, 104, 157
Dolar, Mladen, 49
dolls, as motives and metaphors in Lewin's films, 67, 69, 76, 120, 124. *See also* Petit Guignol; Punch and Judy; puppets; voodoo
Donatello, 47
Dorkay Productions, 154
Dostoevsky, Fyodor, *Crime and Punishment,* Lewin on, 75
double (theme), 49–50
Double Indemnity, 29
Douglas, Lloyd C., 13
Douglas, Susan, 64, 72, 154
"Dover Beach" (Arnold), 98
Dragon Seed, 46
dreams, in Lewin's films, 77–78
Dr. Jekyll and Mr. Hyde (Stevenson), 49
Duchamp, Marcel, 4, 65, 85, 124, 126; *Large Glass (The Bride Stripped Bare By Her Bachelors, Even),* 125
Dudley, Doris, 28, 30, 154
Dufhilo, Jacques, 106, 154
Durant, Will and Ariel, 6
Dvorak, Ann, 64, 67, 154

Échec au Destin (d'Autheville), 154
Educational and Recreational Guides, Inc., 3
Egyptian cat figurine, in *Dorian Gray,* 51, 53, 104
8 X 8, 124

Eisenstein, Sergei, 20
Ellmann, Richard, 49
Emerson, John, 3
Emery, Katherine, 64, 65, 154
Encyclopaedia Britannica films, 2
England, Lewin's travels to, 4, 7, 8, 9, 155. *See also* London
Ensor, James, 68
Enters, Angna, 5, 7, 8, 9
Ernst, Max, 6, 7, 22, 57, 85, 88, 124, 154; *Temptation of Saint Anthony,* 6, 63, 65, 67–72, 77
Eskimo, 2
Esperon, Mañuel, 155
Europe: émigrés in Hollywood, 14; Lewin's travels in, 2, 4, 8; relation of Lewin's films to films from, 17; as setting for Lewin's films, 8. *See also* England, France, Spain
Evans, Ernestine, 2, 27
Eve (biblical), 83, 88
Eve future, L' (Villiers de l'Isle-Adam), 48
eye, disembodied, as surrealist icon, 57–58

Fairbanks, Douglas, Jr., 155
Farrel, Bernard, 154
Fate of a Flirt, The, 153
Faust, 8, 89, 104, 157
femme-enfant (child-woman), in *Pandora,* 83, 89. *See also* surrealism/surrealists
Ferrer, Mel, 102, 105, 154
Festival Mondial du Film et des Beaux-Arts, Brussels (1947), 6
Festival of the Development of Cinema in the U.S., London (1967), 9
fetish/fetishism, 76–77
Feyder, Jacques, 2, 5
Film Group, 156
film noir, 29, 45, 76
filmography, 153–57
Fini, Leonor, 65
Fitzgerald, Edward, 155
Fitzgerald, F. Scott, "Pat Hobby and Orson Welles," 18
Flaherty, Robert, 2, 3, 6, 18, 99, 155
flamenco, in *Pandora,* 83, 91–92
Flanner, Janet, 2
Flaubert, Gustave, 17, 70, 75, 81, 83, 126; *Salammbo,* 125; *Tentation de Saint Antoine, Le,* 68–71, 125
Fleurs du mal, Les (Baudelaire), 51
Flotsam (Remarque), 5, 154. *See also So Ends Our Night*
Flying Dutchman (legend), 83, 95
Fontanne, Lynn, 2
Forbes, Mary, 154
Ford, John, 18
foreign markets for U.S. films in 1950s, 103
Forrest, Steve, 110, 112, 155
framing, as visual trope in Lewin's films, 51
France: Lewin's travels to, 2, 4, 8; reception of Lewin's films in, 21–23, 83. *See also* Paris

Franklin, Sidney, 156
Fraser, Richard, 42, 63, 64, 79, 154
Freeman, Helen, 7
French Cancan, 70
Freuchen, Peter, 2, 3, 5
Freud, Sigmund: on artists, 118; "Delusion and Dream," 111; on dreams, 78; on "the return of the repressed," 72
Furthman, Jules, 3

Galatea and Pygmalion (legend), 38, 48, 85
Gallery of Modern Art, retrospective tribute to Albert Lewin, 9
Gam, Rita, 89, 102, 105, 154
Garbo, Greta, 2, 45
Garcia, Sara, 110, 155
Gardner, Ava, 8, 21, 82–89, 93–95, 104, 115, 154, 155, 156–57
Gauguin, Paul, 19, 29, 32–34; *Manao tupapau,* 34; *Man with an Ax,* 34; *Nevermore,* 34; *Upaupa,* 34; *Where do we come from? What are we? Where are we going?,* 34
Gautier, Théophile, 83
Geray, Steve, 28, 30, 154
Gettysburg, 3, 155
Gibbons, Cedric, 45, 154
Gilmore, Lowell, 42, 154
Godard, Jean-Luc, 9, 17, 21, 125
Goethe, Johann Wolfgang von. *See also Faust*
Gogarty, Oliver St. John, 3
"Golden Statue, The" (Lewin), 1
Goldfarb, Sarah (née Lewin), 1
Goldwyn, Samuel, 1
Goldwyn Pictures, 1, 11
Good Earth, The, 3, 11, 153
Gordon, Cyrus, 8, 103
Goring, Marius, 82, 154
Goutman, Dolya, 34–36, 89, 154
Goya, Francisco, 8, 20, 104, 156
Gradiva: A Pompeiian Fancy (Jensen), 111
Graves, Robert, 8, 103, 117
Gray, Barbara and Hugh, 2, 4, 6, 7, 8
Greenberg, Clement, 12
Grieg, Edvard, *Peer Gynt Suite,* 103, 156
Grieg, Robert, 154
Griffith, D. W., 18
Grinieff, Jacques, 156
Grossbard, Sol, 3
Grosz, George, 6
Grünewald, Matthias, 70
Guardsman, The, 2, 153
Guggenheim, Peggy, 6
Guglielmi, Louis, 65, 68
Guilbert, Gilles and Claire, 5
Guitry, Sacha, 19

Haas, Hugo, 64, 77, 154
Hakim, Robert, 156
Halffter, Rudolfo, 155

Hamlet (Shakespeare), 75
Hammond, Paul, 95
Hank, 156
Hansen, Harry, 14
Hardwicke, Sir Cedric, 154
Harnly, Perkins, 6
Harnoncourt, René d', 8
Hartung, Philip T., 30, 35
Harvard Poetry Society, 1
Harvard University, Lewin's studies at, 1, 11
hasard objectif (objective chance), in *Pandora*, 83, 92–93. *See also* surrealism/surrealists
Hatfield, Hurd, 42, 45–46, 48, 115, 154
Hathaway, Henry, 22, 155
Hawkesworth, John, 154
Hawks, Howard, 18
Hays Office, 16, 31, 78, 79
Hearst, William Randolph, 19
Hecht, Ben, 156
Heine, Heinrich, 83
Hepburn, Katherine, 45
Herzberg, Max J., 3
"Highbrow, Lowbrow, Middlebrow" (Lynes), 12
High Noon, 79
Hildyard, Jack, 155
Hitchcock, Alfred, 57
Hitler, Adolf, 61
Hoffmann, E. T. A., "The Sandman," 48
Hofstadter, Richard, *Anti-Intellectualism in American Life*, 15
Holbein, Hans, 87, 89
Hollywood: anti-intellectualism in, 15, 18–19; blacklist, 103; censorship, 16–17, 32; conventions, 15, 29, 51, 52; European émigrés in, 14; industrial changes, 1950s, 103; Motion Picture Production Code, 17, 65
Homer, 119
"Hommage à Albert Lewin" (Cinématheque Française), 8
homoeroticism, 17, 45–48, 106, 107
Hopewell-Ash, Tim, 154
Hour of the Wolf, 79
House of Representatives. *See* U.S. House of Representatives
Howard, Tom, 154
human sacrifice: illustrations by Carlos Mérida, 112–13; as theme in *The Living Idol*, 103, 112–13
Hunter, Kenneth, 154
Hunter College, 1
Huston, John, 7, 156
Huysmans, Joris-Karl, 70, 83

Ibsen, Henrik, *Peer Gynt*, 7, 20, 103, 156
Indonesian music and dance, 53
Ingram, Rex, 2
Ingres, Jean-Auguste-Dominique, *Portrait of M. Bertin*, 77

Janis, Harriet, 72

Janis, Sidney, 6, 65, 72
Jennings, Talbot, 155
Jensen, Wilhelm, *Gradiva: A Pompeiian Fancy*, 111
Jewish Tribune, The, 1, 11; "Playthings" column, 1
Johnson, Richard, 154
Joseph, Albrecht, 154
Joyce, James, 96, 119, 126; *Ulysses*, 125
Juarez, 29

Kafka, Franz, *The Castle*, 119
Kaper, Bronislau, 154
Kaufman, Joseph, 154
Keaton, Buster, 18, 119–20
Keats, John, "La Belle Dame Sans Merci," 83
Kellino, Pamela, 154
Kemp, Philip, 103
Kemplen, Ralph, 154
Khayyám, Omar, 70
Kiss, The, 2, 153
Kittredge, George L., 1
Knight, Arthur, 19
Knights of the Round Table, 4–5, 55, 155. *See also* Arthurian themes, locations
Knopff, Ferdinand, 68
Kozloff, Sarah, 29
Kramer, Stanley, 154
Krauss, Rosalind, 95
Kress, Harold F., 154
Kyrou, Ado, 21

Lacan, Jacques, 49
Ladies of Leisure, 153
Lady Eve, The, 155
Lal, Gobind Behari, 3
Lamont, Molly, 28, 154
Landfall, 5, 155
Langlois, Henri, 9, 104
Lansbury, Angela, 15, 42, 63, 64, 69, 154
Last Laugh, The, 22
Laurie, John, 154
Lautréamont, comte de (Isidore Ducasse), *Les Chants de Maldoror*, 124
Lawford, Peter, 42, 154
Lawson, John Howard, 117
Legion of Decency, 32
Lejeune, C. A., 22
Leonardo da Vinci, 34
LeRoy, Mervyn, 156
Lewin, Albert: art collection, 4, 6, 8, 9, 15, 22, 87, 114, 118; biography, 1–9; "Botticelli in Hollywood," 38; filmography, 153–57; "Golden Statue, The," 1; and perversity, 15, 29, 126; "Playthings," 1; "R.I.P.: Obituary for a Dead Art," 22; and style, 15–17, 51; unrealized film projects, 20, 89, 103–4, 155–57. *See also Living Idol, The*; *Moon and Sixpence, The*; *Pandora and the Flying Dutchman*; *Picture of Dorian Gray, The*; *Private Affairs of Bel Ami, The*; *Saadia*
Lewin, Marcus (father), 1–2
Lewin, Mildrid, née Mindlin (wife), 1, 4–9

Lewin, Sarah (sister), 1
Lewin, William (brother), 1–2, 8; "Photoplay Appreciation in American High Schools," 3; as pioneer of audiovisual pedagogy, 2, 3
Lewin, Yetta, née Mindlin (mother), 1, 8
Lewton, Val, 14
Leyden, Karin van, 7
Lin Yutang, 3
Little Journey, A, 153
Little Theater Films, 2
Living Idol, The, 89, 101–4, 110–15; credits, 155; delusion in, 111–112; as failure, 114–15; human sacrifice as theme of, 103, 112–13; and Jensen's *Gradiva,* 111; Mérida's watercolors for, 112–13; Mexico as setting for, 8, 103; plot summary, 110; reincarnation as theme of, 103; slide lecture featured in, 112–13
Livingston, Jane, 85
location shooting, 103
Loew, David L., 5, 6, 11, 15, 27, 154, 155
Loew-Lewin Productions, 5, 6, 11, 27, 66, 103, 154, 155, 156
Lola Montès, 17
London, 7, 8; blitz, 6; Festival of the Development of Cinema in the U.S., (1967), 9
Long Remember, 155
Loos, Anita, 2, 3
Loos, Mary Anita, 7
Lowry, Morton, 122, 154
Lubitsch, Ernst, 2
Luini, Bernadino, *Bath of the Nymphs,* 34–35
Lunt, Alfred, 2
Lynes, Russell, 12
Lys, Lya, 21

Macbeth (Shakespeare), 75
MacDonald, Dwight, 19
MacMurray, Fred, 29
Madame Curie, 6, 156
Mädchen in Uniform, 22–23
Mademoiselle de Maupin, 156
magical thinking, 50
Magritte, René, 57
Maldoror (Lautréamont), 124
Malory, Sir Thomas, *Morte d'Arthur,* 54
Man Ray, 57, 115, 124; *Explosante-fixe (Fixed-explosive),* 91; friendship with Lewin, 5, 6, 7, 22, 85, 118; *Head,* 94; influence on Lewin's films, 85–95; *Lovers, or Observatory Time, The,* 95; *Net, The,* 93; paintings of Ava Gardner for *Pandora,* 86–89; photograph of Ava Gardner in *Pandora,* 86–89; *Stream of milk pouring endlessly …, A,* 92; Untitled (Lee Miller), 93
Man Ray, Juliet, 6, 7
Manet, Edouard, 17, 126; *Bar at the Folies-Bergère, The,* 69; *Déjouner sur l'herbe, Le,* 125
Mankiewicz, Joseph, 85
Mann, Klaus, 75
Manon Lescaut, 155

March, Fredric, 155
"Marionette, The" (Lewin), 120
Marlowe, Anthony, 154
Marshall, Herbert, 28, 154
marvelous, in *Pandora,* 83, 90. *See also* Breton, André; surrealism and surrealists
Marx, Rudolph and Agnes, 2, 5
Mason, James, 82, 83, 85, 115, 154
Masterson, Reverend Patrick, 32
Mating Call, The, 155–56
Maugham, W. Somerset, 11, 19, 27, 29–30, 32, 33, 34, 41, 154
Maupassant, Guy de, 17, 41, 67; *Bel-Ami,* 6, 17, 63, 65, 72, 78, 154
Mayan art and culture, in *Living Idol,* 103, 110–11
Mayer, Louis B., 2
Mayne, Judith, 24
McVay, Douglas, 67, 69–70, 77
Medina, Henrique, 60, 154
Mediterranean, as setting for *Pandora,* 84, 95. *See also* Spain
Meerson, Mary, 2, 104
Meinhold, Wilhelm, *Sidonia the Sorceress,* 49–50
Melnitz, Curtis, 2
Meniñas, Las (Velázquez), 44
Mépris, Le. See *Contempt*
Meredith, Burgess, 156
Mérida, Carlos, 112–13, 155
Metro-Goldwyn-Mayer (MGM), 19, 154, 155, 156; Lewin's association with, 2–3, 6–8, 11, 15, 41, 89, 103, 106–7, 115; merger, 2
Metro Pictures, 2, 11
Metty, Russell, 69, 115, 154
Mexico, as location for *Living Idol,* 8, 103, 110–11, 119
Milhaud, Darius, 6, 115, 124, 154
Miller, Dorothy, 8
Miller, Lee, 7, 93
Milne, Tom, 17, 21
Minnelli, Vincente, 70
Miranda, Isa, 155
mirror stage, 49
misogyny, 31, 72–74
Miss Julie, 17
Missouri, University of, 1, 11
Montevecchi, Liliane, 89, 110–11, 155
Moon and Sixpence, The, 6, 11, 19, 27–37, 119; antinaturalism of, 29; censorship problems of, 32; compared to *Citizen Kane,* 19; credits, 154; critical response to, 30; depravity as theme of, 32; Lewin's choice of for directorial debut, 15–16, 29; misogyny in, 31; nostalgia as theme of, 19, 32–34, 37–38, 104; plot summary, 28; primitivism as theme of, 34, 38; problems of adaptation, 27; representation of sexes in, 31–32; similarities to *Picture of Dorian Gray* and *Private Affairs of Bel Ami,* 63, 115; use of art in, 33–36, 89, 104; use of color insert in, 34–36; use of sepia tone in, 33–34; voice-over narration in, 19, 27–29

Moreau, Gustave, 68, 83
Morocco (French), as location for *Saadia,* 7, 102, 107
mortality and vision, as theme in *Dorian Gray,* 58–59
Morte d'Arthur (Malory), 54
Motion Picture Production Code, 17, 43, 65, 122. *See also* Hays Office; censorship
Motion Picture Relief Fund, 9
Mrosovsky, Kitty, 69, 70
Museum of Modern Art, 8, 65
Mutiny on the Bounty, 3, 11, 153
Mystery and Melancholy of a Street (de Chirico), 119, 121

Naked King, A. See Roi nu, Un
Naked Maja, The, 8, 89, 104, 156
Native American culture, 103
Nazis, Nazism, National Socialism, 61; critique of modern art, 12, 61; Lewin's efforts to combat, 5; refugees of, 5
Neutra, Richard, 4–5, 8
New Wave, 21, 25. *See also individual directors*
New York University, 1, 3, 9, 11
New Yorker, 14
Newark, New Jersey, 1
Night Music, 6, 155–56
Niven, David, 72
Noriega, Eduardo, 110, 155
Norris, Charles, *Bread,* 2
Northwest Passage, 155
nostalgia, as theme in Lewin's films, 19, 32–34, 37–38, 104, 120
Novalis, 21

O'Brien, Catherine, 98
occult, 103. *See also* sorcery; supernaturalism
Odets, Clifford, 4; *Night Music,* 6, 155–56
Olympia. *See* Hoffmann, E. T. A.
One Touch of Venus, 85
Ophuls, Max, 17
orientalism, in Lewin's films, 52–53
Othello (Shakespeare), as source for *Pandora,* 86
Owen, Reginald, 154

Paalen, Wolfgang, 8
paintings, use in Lewin's films. *See* art/art objects
Pandora (of myth), 83, 88
Pandora and the Flying Dutchman, 6, 7, 20–24, 81–99, 101, 104; as "camp," 22, 85; credits, 154; critical response to, 21–24, 83; extravagent use of costume, color, and spectacle in, 83–84; and French New Wave, 21; Gardner, Ava, as essence of, 83, 89; and Lewin's black-and-white films, 81–83, 89–90; and Lewin's color films, 115; literary antecedents and sources, 83; literary qualities of script, 21, 84; love as theme of, 89–95; Man Ray's influence on and involvement in, 85–95, 124; mysticism and, 81, 93; objectivity vs. subjectivity in, 98–99; and other Ava Gardner vehicles, 85; and pastiche, 84, 97; plot summary, 82; representation of femininity in, 83, 115; romanticism and, 83, 99; setting, 83; and surrealism, 21–23, 83–97, 101, 106; use of antiquities in, 97; use of paintings and photographs in, 86–89, 105; use of Technicolor in, 83, 84
Panofsky, Erwin, 19
Paramount Decree, Supreme Court antitrust decision, 103
Paramount Pictures, 103, 155; Lewin's association with, 3–5, 120
Paris, 4, 8; Lewin's associates in, 2, 7; as setting for Lewin films, 28, 64, 103. *See also* France
Parish, Maxfield, 13
Parke-Bernet Galleries, 9
Partisan Review, 12
"Pat Hobby and Orson Welles" (Fitzgerald), 18
Patrick, Nigel, 82, 154
Peck, Gregory, 45, 156
Peer Gynt, 7, 20, 103, 156
Penrose, Roland, 7, 95
perversity, 15, 29, 126
Peter Ibbetson, 22–23
Peters, Hans, 154
Petit Guignol, and *Private Affairs of Bel Ami,* 69, 77, 79. *See also* Punch and Judy
Peza, Armando Valdes, 155
"Photoplay Appreciation in American High Schools," 3
Photoplay Studies, 3
phrenology, 12
Picture of Dorian Gray, The, 6, 9, 11, 24, 29, 31, 41–61, 91, 104, 119; Albright's painting for, 60, 63–65; Arthurian references in, 54–56; casting of, 45–46; censorship issues and, 17, 43, 45; and classical Hollywood cinema, 24, 51; credits, 154; critical responses to, 12–14, 24, 43; double as theme of, 49–50; equation of visuality and death in, 58–59; female desire as represented in, 45, 53, 58; and film noir, 45; framing as visual trope of, 51; Hatfield's performance in, 45–46, 48, 106; homoeroticism and homosexuality in, 17, 45–48, 77, 125; literary antecedents of, 70; Medina's painting for, 60; mise-en-scène of, 51, 60; as morality tale, 61, 90; narcissism as theme of, 45–46, 48, 59, 77; orientalism in, 52–53; plot summary, 42; portraits in, 60; production difficulties of, 15, 53; scene at Blue Gate Field as film-within-film, 121–25; spectacle in, 58; specularity of, 46–51; supernaturalism in, 55–56, 104; surrealism in relation to, 57–58, 60–61; symbolism in, 47, 52, 54; use of art in, 47, 51–54, 56, 59–60, 97, 104; use of music in, 121, 124; visuality as theme of, 43, 50–51, 57–61; and Wilde's novel, 43–44, 49–50, 52–53, 55, 56, 60, 65, 122; and World War II, 61
Pillina, La, 91, 154
Pippin, Horace, 65, 68

Pirandello, Luigi, 120
Playhouse, The, 119–20
Poe, Edgar Allan, "The Oval Portrait," 38
Pompeii: antiquities recalled in *Pandora,* 97; as setting for Wilhelm Jensen's *Gradiva,* 111
Poncin, Marcel, 106, 154
portraiture, use in film, 60
Powell, Michael, 17
Praz, Mario, 70
pretention/pretentiousness, as criticism of Lewin's films, 14, 17, 21, 38, 41
Primavera (Botticelli), 34, 37–38, 119
primitive art/primitivism, 34, 38, 105, 111–12, 118–19
Private Affairs of Bel Ami, The, 6, 63–79, 119; censorship issues and, 17, 65, 78–79; competition for painting to appear in, 6, 65–68; credits, 154; critical response to, 17, 63; echoes of *Moon and Sixpence* and *Picture of Dorian Gray,* 63, 70, 74–76, 115; Ernst's painting for, 63, 67–72, 77; existentialism and, 124; feminism and, 75–79; fetishism in, 76; and Flaubert's *Temptation of Saint Anthony,* 68–71; literary antecedents of, 70; masculinity as represented in, 77; and Maupassant's *Bel-Ami,* 63, 65, 67, 72, 78; Milhaud's score for, 115, 124, 154; and Minnelli's and Renoir's musicals, 70; mise-en-scène of, 66–68; misogyny in, 72–74; and nineteenth-century French painting, 67–70; plot summary, 64; psychological use of props and space in, 66–68, 74, 76; representation of female desire in, 72–73, 75–79; Sanders as protagonist of, 31, 64, 72, 74; scenes at Notre Dame and Forestier's deathbed as films-within-film, 121–25; *Temptation of Saint Anthony* as theme in, 65, 70, 104; use of dreams in, 77–78; use of painting in, 63, 65–72, 77, 104; use of real time in, 79
propaganda: during World War II, 60; *So Ends Our Night* investigated as, 5–6
psychoanalytic theory, 72; as illustrated in Lewin's films, 47–49. *See also* Freud, Sigmund; Lacan, Jacques
Punch and Judy, as motif in *Private Affairs of Bel Ami,* 67, 69, 77
puppets, in Lewin's films, 69, 77, 79, 120. *See also* dolls; Petit Guignol; Punch and Judy; voodoo
Pygmalion and Galatea (legend), 38, 48, 85

Quality Street, 2, 153
Quo Vadis, 7, 156

Rahon, Alice, 8
Raine, Patricia, 154
Rasch, Albertina, 7
Rattner, Abraham, 65, 68
Rawsthorne, Alan, 115, 154
Ray, Man and Juliet. *See also* Man Ray; Man Ray, Juliet
realism, 41–43, 120

reception, of Lewin's films, 11–25. *See also* individual titles
Redelings, Lowell E., 74
Red-Headed Woman, 3, 153
Redon, Odilon, 68
Red Pony, The, 155
Red Shoes, The, 17
Reed, Donna, 42, 154
reincarnation, 94, 103, 115
Remarque, Erich Maria, 5, 154
Renaissance; art and imagery, 34–38, 47–48
Renoir, Auguste, 70
Renoir, Dido, 7
Renoir, Jean, 2, 5, 6, 7, 8, 25, 70, 156
Reznikoff, Charles, 1, 4, 8, 9, 16, 61
Richter, Hans, 124
Rieff, Philip, 118
"R.I.P.: Obituary for a Dead Art" (Lewin), 22
Ritchie, Andrew, 8
Rivette, Jacques, 21
RKO, 5
Roaring Twenties, The, 29
Robbins, Jerome, 8
Robertson-Justice, James, 110–11, 113–14, 155
Robinson, Edward G., 29
Robson, Mark, 14
Rodenbach, Georges, *Bruges la Morte,* 157
Rohmer, Eric, 21
Roi Nu, Un (*A Naked King*), 7, 8, 103, 156
Roland, 119
Roman Catholicism, and censorship. *See* Legion of Decency
Roman d'un tricheur, Le (*The Story of a Cheat*), 19
Romulus Films, 154
Rops, Félicien, 72
Rotha, Wanda, 102, 106, 107, 154
Rubáiyát of Omar Khayyám, The, 70
Rushdie, Salman, *The Satanic Verses,* 125

Saadia, 7, 8, 89, 101–9, 111, 114–15, 156; allusions to Lewin's previous films in, 107; authenticity of detail in, 107; credits, 154; editing of, 106–7; and *Living Idol* and *Unaltered Cat,* 101, 104, 115; magical thinking and, 107–8; performances in, 89, 106; plot summary, 102; primitivism and, 105; rationalism vs. superstition as theme of, 106; as reflection of changes in Hollywood production and Lewin's interests, 103; sorcery/voodoo in, 106; supernaturalism in, 106, 115; use of art in, 107–8
Sade, Marquis de, 124
Saemundsson, Nina, 33, 154
Saint-Exupéry, Antoine de, *Wind, Sand, and Stars,* 156
Sales, Richard, 7
Sanders, George, 15, 28, 30, 31, 42, 63, 64, 65, 72, 74–75, 89, 115, 154
Sandman, The (Hoffmann), 48
Santa Monica, 4, 5
Sarris, Andrew, 14, 38

Satanic Verses, The (Rushdie), 125
Schary, Dore, 106–7
Schwalenberg, Henry Gustavus, 49
Scully, Frank, 3
sculpture, use in Lewin's films. *See also* art/art objects
Search, The, 45
Seastrom, Victor, 2
Seiter, William, 85
Seitz, John F., 154
sepia tone, 33–34
Seventh Seal, The, 17
sexual difference, as theme in Lewin's films, 31–32, 76–77, 124–25
Shakespeare, William, 119; Lewin on *Hamlet* and *Macbeth,* 75; *Othello* as source for *Pandora,* 86
Shute, Nevil, *Landfall,* 5, 155
Sidonia the Sorceress (Meinhold), 49–50
silent cinema, 19–20, 22–24, 120
Silva, Jose, 155
Silverstein, Maurice, 8
Sim, Sheila, 154
Simon, Michel, 102, 106, 154
Sjöberg, Alf, 17
Sjöström (Seastrom), Victor, 2
Smilin' Through, 2, 153
Soby, James Thrall, 8
Society of the New York Hospital, 9
Socrates, 156
So Ends Our Night, 5, 154
Solano, Solita, 2
Solomon-Godeau, Abigail, 34, 38
Sontag, Susan, 125–26
Sophocles, *Oedipus Tyrannos,* Lewin on, 75
sorcery, as theme in *Saadia,* 106. *See also* supernaturalism; voodoo
Southerner, The, 156
Spain, 7, 8; Costa Brava as location for *Pandora,* 7, 21, 83–86
Spawn of the North, 4, 153
Spellbound, 57
Spencer, Stanley, 65, 67
"Sphinx, The" (Wilde), 70
Spring (Botticelli), 34, 37–38, 119
Spring Fever, 153
Stein, Gertrude, 119
Steinbeck, John, *The Red Pony,* 155
Stevenson, Robert Louis, *Dr. Jekyll and Mr. Hyde,* 49
Story of a Cheat, The. See also Roman d'un tricheur
Stothart, Herbert, 2, 7, 115, 154
Stothart, Mary, 2, 7
Stradling, Harry, 115, 154
Stuart Galleries (Boston), 66
Sturges, Preston, 5, 155
style/stylization, 17, 126; as concerns of Lewin's work, 15–16, 51
supernaturalism, 55–56, 103, 115. *See also* occult; sorcery; voodoo
surrealism/surrealists, 37, 118, 120; and *Dorian Gray,* 57–58, 61; and *Pandora,* 21–23, 83–97.
See also individual artists and films; Breton, André
Swinburne, Algernon Charles, 70, 83
Sylos, F. Paul, 154
symbolism, 33, 47, 52, 54, 120
Syrkin, Marie, 8

Tahiti, as setting for *Moon and Sixpence,* 28, 31–36
Tanning, Dorothea, 6, 7, 65, 67, 124
Tavernier, Bertrand, 125–26
Taylor, John Russell, 14, 120
Tchelitchew, Pavel, 6
Technicolor, use in Lewin's films, 35, 72, 83, 84
Tedrow, Irene, 154
television, influence on U.S. film industry, 103, 107
Temptation of Saint Anthony, The, 6, 63, 65–72. *See also Bel-Ami* Competition; Ernst, Max
Tentation de Saint Antoine, Le (Flaubert), 68–71, 125
Tessier, Max, 41
Thalberg, Irving, 2, 3, 11, 14, 20, 115
Thatcher, Heather, 154
Third Reich. *See also* Hitler, Adolf; Nazis, Nazism, National Socialism; World War II
Thomas, Dylan, 7
Thorpe, Richard, 155
Tin Hats, 153
Tiomkin, Dmitri, 7, 154
Toronto, retrospective tribute to Lewin, 9
Toulouse-Lautrec, Henri de, 69–70
Tourneur, Jacques, 45, 101
Tourneur, Maurice, 2
travesty, and Lewin's films, 38, 85
Tristan and Iseult, 37, 54–56. *See also* Béroul *Tristan et Yseut*
Trosa, Sylvie, 24, 94
True Confession, 4, 153
Truffaut, François, 9, 21
Tully, Jim, 3
Two Bad Hats, 155
Tyler, Parker, 45–46, 48, 56

Ulysses (of myth), 83
Ulysses (Joyce), 125
Unaltered Cat, The (Lewin), 9, 101–4, 115, 124
United Artists, 6
Universal Pictures, 5
University of California, Los Angeles (UCLA), 8
U.S. House of Representatives: Committee on Un-American Activities (HUAC), 103; panel investigating propaganda, 5–6

Valdiosera, Ramon, 155
Vallier, Helene, 154
Van Dyke, W. S., 2
Van Enger, Richard L., 154
Varo, Remedios, 8, 87
Velázquez, Diego, *Las Meniñas* (*Ladies in Waiting*), 44

Verdugo, Elena, 28, 31, 154
Verrocchio, Andrea del, 47
Vidor, King, 2, 155
Villiers de l'Isle-Adam, *L'Eve future* (*The Future Eve*), 48
Villon, François, *Ballade des dames du temps jadis*, 37, 119
Vinaver, Eugène, 55
voice-over narration, 19, 27–29
voodoo, as theme in *Saadia*, 106, 115. *See also* sorcery; supernaturalism

Walerstein, Gregorio, 155
Wales: Arthurian locations in, 4, 155; as location for *Pandora*, 7
Walton, Douglas, 42, 154
Warrender, Harold, 82, 83, 154
Webster, Ferris, 154
Welles, Orson, 18–19
Wescher, Paul, 2
West, Mae, 8
Western Electric Company, Educational Sound Film Unit, 2
What Every Woman Knows, 153
Wilde, Cornel, 102, 105, 154
Wilde, Lady (Speranza), 49–50
Wilde, Oscar, 41–44, 83; "Ballad of Reading Gaol, The," 122; *Picture of Dorian Gray, The*, 12, 41–44, 49–50, 52–53, 55, 56, 65, 154; "Sphinx, The," 70
Wilder, Billy, 29
Wiles, Gordon, 63, 69, 81, 115, 154
William, Warren, 64, 73, 154
Willis, Edwin B., 154
Wilson, Marie, 64, 154
Wind, Sand, and Stars, 156
Wizard of Oz, The, 34
World War II, 5, 61; attack on Pearl Harbor, 6; British war effort, 5; British War Office, 45; German Occupations, 5; refugees of European war, 5, 22; U.S. entry into, 6. *See also* Nazis, Nazism, National Socialism
Wuthering Heights, 29

"You're Driving Me Crazy," 97
Ytuarte, Augustin, 155

Zaza, 4, 153, 155
Zinnemann, Fred, 45, 79
Zsissley (Malvin Albright), 6

THE AUTHOR

Susan Felleman is an art and film historian who has taught at a number of colleges, including Hampshire College and the School of Visual Arts. Among her publications are articles in *Camera Obscura, Iris,* and *Film History.*

THE EDITOR

Frank E. Beaver was born in Cleveland, North Carolina, in 1938 and received his B.A. and M.A. at the University of North Carolina, Chapel Hill, and his Ph.D. at the University of Michigan, where he chairs the department of communication. He is the author of *Oliver Stone* (also in this series), Twayne's *Dictionary of Film Terms,* and three books on the art and history of the motion picture. For 20 years he has served as media commentator for National Public Radio stations WUOM-WVGR-WFUM.

OHIO UNIVERSITY LIBRARY

Please return this book as soon as you
finished with it. In order to avoid a fine
be returned by the latest date sta
oks are subject to rec
ely if ne